Trade Association
Strategy
and Management

by **Mark Boléat**

Published by   Association of British Insurers
                      51 Gresham Street
                      London
                      EC2V 7HQ

                      Tel: 0171-600 3333

Designed and Produced by Delco Creative Services Ltd, Rochester, Kent ME2 4HU.
                          Tel: 01634-297444 Fax: 01634-297333.

ISBN 0 9525762 4 4

i

ANALYTICAL TABLE OF CONTENTS

SECTION B - THE FUNCTIONS OF TRADE ASSOCIATIONS

SECTION C - THE BUSINESS OF TRADE ASSOCIATIONS

Trade associations play an important part in the formulation and implementation of public policy in the United Kingdom. They have grown substantially in importance and influence over the last few years. As a group of institutions, however, they remain somewhat mysterious including to many of their members and to some of the staff who work in them. There are no authoritative studies of trade associations, and it is difficult to find even basic information on the number of associations, their size and the way that they operate.

This book seeks to provide a brief, but comprehensive, text on all aspects of trade association work. It is in three parts covering, respectively, the nature, functions and business of trade associations. The book is designed to be of interest to those working in trade associations and those working with them.

The book is based largely on my experience of over twenty years in working for three trade associations in the United Kingdom, the Building Societies Association, the Council of Mortgage Lenders and the Association of British Insurers, and also as chief executive of two international associations, the European Federation of Building Societies and the International Union of Housing Finance Institutions. My knowledge of trade associations and how they work has benefitted greatly from the many people with whom I have worked in those organisations. The book also draws heavily on published annual reports of trade associations and other information, some published and some unpublished, which has been made available to me by colleagues in trade associations.

I am grateful to a number of people for commenting on an earlier draft of this book and for help in other ways. They include my colleagues at the ABI: Tony Baker, Brian Hudson, Richard Regan, David Leighton, John Parker, Paul Smee and Jenny Frost; my former colleagues at the Building Societies Association: Adrian Coles, Ronald Armstrong, Chris French, Peter Williams and Michael Coogan; Harald Kraus, Director of Bipar; Mike Hudson, Senior Partner of the Compass Partnership; Tim May and John McHugh of Manchester Metropolitan University; Tom Machin, Director General of the British Printing Industries Federation; and Leslie Rocker, Secretary of the Society of Association Executives.

Finally I am grateful to my wife, Elizabeth, with whom this book has been a joint venture. She has acted as research assistant, computer operator and in some respects co-author.

Mark Boléat

February 1996

CHAPTER 1

The Role of Trade Associations

Trade associations are established by a number of organisations, operating in the same market and often in competition with each other, to represent them and provide them with services. They exist because they can provide these services to their members more efficiently than the members can provide them individually. The two basic functions of trade associations are representation and the provision of information to members. Some trade associations are involved in other activities including collective bargaining and seeking to influence the market, in particular by regulation.

THE NATURE OF TRADE ASSOCIATIONS

Trade associations have their own distinct characteristics which differentiate them from industrial and commercial organisations including those which they represent. They cannot exist in a vacuum but rather their role, size and importance depend crucially on the sector which they represent and government policy towards that sector.

A trade association is set up by a number of organisations to provide representative and other services to them. The members of the association provide the governing body and finance. They are primarily responsible for the policy and general strategic direction of the trade association, although in the larger associations full time staff are responsible for implementing policy and to a large extent also for developing it. They are not profit-seeking organisations, although increasingly they are expected to be run on businesslike lines and to be subject to the same financial disciplines as organisations with more commercial objectives.

Trade associations cannot plan their activities with great precision. They are dependent to a large extent on the actions of others including what their members want and are prepared to finance and developments in their particular sector of the economy which call for collective action.

THE NEED FOR TRADE ASSOCIATIONS

Trade associations exist because the members believe that the benefits they gain from membership exceed the costs. For this to happen trade associations must be able either to take advantage of economies of scale, or through their intrinsic nature to be able to do some things better than their members individually or other institutions.

Many of their services to members could be provided by others or indeed by the members themselves. Indeed, in some trade associations there are members who will argue that it

1

should cease to exist and who, in some cases, may take positive action to seek to bring about the demise of the association.

A primary rationale of trade associations is that they are better able to represent the interests of an industry than are individual companies in that industry. Any industrial or commercial company arguing for a particular policy measure is likely to be seen as seeking a competitive advantage for itself as against other organisations in the same sector. If one organisation is making representations that protect its interests others will do so also, and as a result there may be a confused message from the industry. There will be issues where there is common ground between all organisations in a sector or where the organisations are prepared to sacrifice some of their own interests in exchange for a package of measures which on balance will benefit them. The trade association can exercise the representative function more effectively than its constituent members precisely because it does not have a direct commercial interest. Trade associations can also become expert at exercising the representative function and are therefore able to take advantage of economies of scale by providing the same service to a large number of organisations.

More generally, trade associations exploit economies of scale for the benefit of their members. If there is, for example, an Act of Parliament or a court case which has a material effect on members then it makes sense for one expert lawyer to analyze the effect and advise all members than for this to be done in perhaps hundreds of different companies. Similarly, most companies want detailed industry statistics but are unwilling to let any one member compile these because it would have access to information about its competitors. Again, trade associations fulfil this function.

In the case of either legal advice or statistical analysis it may be argued that these functions can be provided by completely independent organisations, for example, solicitors, management consultants or companies that specialise in inter-firm comparisons. This is undoubtedly true but outside organisations suffer the disadvantage that they do not have the same access to either government or experts within the industry. Having said this, trade associations do not enjoy a uniquely protected position. If they fail to operate effectively in representing their members or in providing them with information or in giving them statistical services then other institutions will compete with them. A trade association may have a distinct advantage over such competitors but it is not an overwhelming one if it does not operate efficiently.

REPRESENTATION

The point has already been made that representation is the prime function of trade associations and that in exercising the representative function associations are able to use economies of scale on behalf on their members. As importantly, a single voice on behalf of an industry is more likely to be heard and to be influential than a number of conflicting voices. This is particularly true as far as government is concerned.

The question then arises as to the issues on which trade associations represent their members. The range is infinite. Typically, trade associations will represent the interests of all of their members, that is they will be seeking perhaps to influence public policy or the media on a particular issue which is relevant to every single member. However, there will also be issues where a trade association will wish to represent the interests of only some of its members with other members being disinterested. Indeed, there will be cases where trade associations will represent the views of a single member where it has special interests and where these do not conflict with the membership generally. Some examples can usefully illustrate this point. The Association of British Insurers might, for example, represents the interests of all of its members, that is insurance companies authorised do business in the UK, in seeking to reduce the amount of information they have to provide to the prudential supervisor, the Department of Trade and Industry. The Association might then wish to represent the interests of a dozen or so of its members which provide creditor insurance, a business in which other members are not interested. Finally, perhaps a single company might wish to begin business in, say, Chile and in so doing faces obstacles from the Chilean authorities which the trade association can help to overcome.

The range of issues on which members' interests will be represented is very wide but is likely to concentrate on legislation, regulation, taxation and issues in which there is significant public policy interest.

The target audience for the representative function is also wide. For most large trade associations, the government is the most important target. Government can be defined widely here to include ministers, civil servants and also, as far as the UK is concerned, the European Commission. Related to government are specific regulatory bodies that are not part of the government although they are set up by statute and are ultimately responsible to a government department. Specific regulatory bodies include the Securities and Investments Board and the Personal Investment Authority for investment firms, the Building Societies Commission for building societies, the Housing Corporation for housing associations and the General Medical Council for doctors. For many industries there is no specific regulatory body, in which case the burden of representative work is reduced. However, there are also general regulatory bodies the activities of which can affect all industrial sectors. They include the Office of Fair Trading, the Advertising Standards Authority and, at local level, local authorities and trading standards officers.

Members of Parliament are a second target for representative work. They are important both because they are in a powerful position to influence the government of the day and also because in their own right they are significant opinion formers.

The media are the other most influential opinion formers. Almost all trade associations will have as one of their prime functions handling the media. In the case of those industries which are of national importance, in particular the large financial industries, banking and insurance, then representative work with the press will concentrate on the national press, television and radio. For many other industries the trade press and local radio might be more important.

Finally, some trade associations see themselves as having a role in communicating directly with the public or perhaps indirectly through advertising.

The broad objective of the whole of the representative function is to help create the right environment which enables member companies to conduct their business in a satisfactory way. A good public image is always helpful directly and also because is makes it more likely that there will be a favourable government response towards any representations in respect of regulation and legislation.

The representative function is discussed in detail in Chapters 7,8 and 9.

SERVICES

Representation can be seen as one of the services that trade associations provide to their members. It is an unusual service in that it is intangible. Indeed, often the best representative work is done in private and is unknown to the members. Members may well appreciate more concrete services which the trade association is able to give.

A number of these services will derive from the representative function. Where, for example, a trade association is involved in putting forward to government or to regulators views about new legislation or new regulations then the association is in a good position to inform its members about the final form of the legislation or regulations, to advise what they have to do in order to comply and so on. The monitoring that trade associations have to do can also be used to provide members with information relevant to their business. For example, for those industries where tax is important, the trade association will need constantly to monitor new legislation and proposals for legislation. In addition to making representations where appropriate the trade association can also simply provide information to members and assist interpretation thereby avoiding the need for this work to be done by each member individually.

Many trade associations provide information that goes beyond that deriving from their representational work. They may, for example, undertake economic analyses relevant to the industry and pass this on to their members. They may monitor market developments in Britain and other relevant countries and provide this information to their members.

The provision of statistics is an important function for many trade associations. Almost all companies want industry statistics to enable them to assess how they are doing in relation to the competition and also to give an indication of industry trends. A trade association is seen as a neutral body which can collate statistics, preserving confidentiality in respect of individual members, while providing an efficient service in respect of aggregate statistics to the members. The statistics can often be combined with analysis based on the expertise which the trade association has in the respective industry. Aggregate statistics can also form an important part of representative work and in areas where there is public interest provide a regular opportunity for press comment.

There are a range of other services which some trade associations provide. For example, they may negotiate arrangements with other trade associations or organisations on behalf of their members. Some may provide commercial services such as bulk buying of relevant equipment or services such as specialist legal advice. Some may even offer a management consultancy service to their members. Many will run seminars and conferences aimed primarily at their members but perhaps also a wider audience. Sometimes these services will be run on a commercial basis and indeed may aim to make a profit, while others will be provided as part of the overall service which the association seeks to give to its members.

EMPLOYMENT SERVICES

Many large trade associations are also employers' associations. Collective bargaining is generally a core function for an employers association. It is part of the representative function whereby the interests of members collectively are represented to another organisation, in this case a trade union or trades unions. Some trade associations started as employers' organisations and their principal function may well remain that of collective bargaining. In this case there will also be an extensive service in providing information to members not only about the results of collective bargaining but also about, for example, pay and conditions in the industry and other relevant industries and also information on employment law, health and safety legislation and so on.

Some trade associations which started essentially as employers' organisations subsequently developed much wider functions and have become all-purpose trade associations. In some cases the original collective bargaining role has been dropped with other employment services remaining. Most trade associations have no collective bargaining role and some would see this as being an obstacle to performing their basic representative function. There has generally been a radical change in collective bargaining over the last twenty years away from negotiating industry-wide agreements where trade associations obviously have a role towards bargaining at the local company or even plant level.

A recent development in trade associations is the growth of a training function. This function can be undertaken by employers' associations or by associations which traditionally have not provided employment services.

INFLUENCING THE MARKET

Few trade associations now have the objective of influencing the market. Indeed, to attempt to do so may well be illegal. However many trade associations were founded with the objective of regulating competition between their members. The objective may have been laudable, that is to provide a higher standard of service or to protect the public against unscrupulous organisations, although often the real objective or the objective which finally emerged was that of restricting supply and regulating the market with a view to increasing profits. For example, a principal function of the Building Societies Association for many years was that of recommending interest rates to its members, something which the Association regarded as a public service to hold the mortgage rate down and introduce more stability into the market, but which was generally perceived elsewhere as being a cartel which enabled the margin between savings and lending rates to be held at a wider level than would otherwise have been possible. Restrictive trade practices legislation has greatly decreased the scope for trade associations to act on behalf of their members to influence the market.

PROMOTING THE INDUSTRY

Most trade associations would say that one of their functions was to promote the products of the sector they represent. Some go no further than doing so through the representative role and seek to have no relationship at all with the public. Some associations, however, are more actively geared to promoting the products of their members with the public. They may run direct advertising campaigns, other marketing campaigns, offer freephone telephone lines and so on. In order for this service to be provided there has to be a substantial degree of cohesion between the members. In many sectors most larger members of a trade associations would not favour such a campaign as they would see it as benefiting their smaller rivals at their expense.

CHAPTER 2

Types of Trade Association and other Industry Bodies

Trade associations can range from those representing a subset of institutions in a particular industrial sector to those that represent the whole of a country's industry, nationally or internationally. Related to trade associations are professional bodies and chambers of commerce. A large company may be a member of many trade associations with its staff being involved in one or more professional bodies and the company also having membership of a number of chambers of commerce.

THE INDUSTRY ASSOCIATION

Most of the large trade associations represent definable industrial sectors. A good example is the Building Societies Association which has in its membership every single active building society but no other institutions. Building societies operate under special legislation and have their own regulator and accordingly a strong industry association is essential. Other prominent associations in this category include the Chemical Industries Association, the Society of Motor Manufacturers and Traders, the Paper Federation, the British Printing Industries Federation and the Electricity Association.

THE MULTI-INDUSTRY ASSOCIATION

A slight variation on the industry association is the multi-industry association where more than one identifiable industry can be identified. The Association of British Insurers can be counted as one such association. Although insurance might be regarded as a single industry, credit insurers and life insurers, for example, operate in quite different markets. Similarly, the British Bankers Association can be regarded as a multi-industry association representing institutions as diverse as the major clearing banks, the investment banks and foreign banks based in London. Some trade associations have deliberately expanded from being single industry associations to being multi-industry associations. For example, the Unit Trust Association has changed its name to the Association of Unit Trusts and Investment Funds as part of a policy of attracting a wider range of membership.

THE SPECIALISED ASSOCIATION

Specialised associations can exist within industry associations and may for example comprise particular sizes of organisation or companies in a particular region. For example, the Building Societies Association has three regional associations, all of its members belonging to one of those associations. Regional associations employ no staff but provide a forum in which members can get together to discuss industry issues without having to travel long distances, and also they provide some other basic services, in particular an annual conference. In the insurance industry the Associated Scottish Life Offices is a good example. There is a strong life insurance industry in Scotland, most of the companies having a mutual nature and operating predominantly through independent financial advisers. The fact that they are also located together gives them a commonality of interest. They are all members of the Association of British Insurers but also meet separately to discuss industry issues.

Specialised associations can also exist outside an industry association with members being either inside or out of the industry association. For example, some insurance companies belong to the Linked Life Insurance Group which seeks to represent their special interests. To some extent these specialised associations may act as a pressure group within or on the industry association. A specialised association is likely to develop wherever companies feel that their interests are being ignored or subsumed in the industry association.

THE COMPANY ASSOCIATION

There are some trade associations which do not represent a particular industry or industries but rather represent a particular type of company. For example, Scottish Financial Enterprise is a trade association representing companies located in Scotland. The Co-operative Union represents co-operative organisation of a wide variety of types. In a number of towns and cities trade associations have developed representing the companies based in those particular areas. The binding force in respect of company associations invariably is a commonality of interest in respect of location or structure.

THE FEDERAL ASSOCIATION

The federal association comprises a number of separate trade associations grouped together under an umbrella organisation. The umbrella organisation generally provides central services and may also provide the full range of services to the members of the individual constituent parts. A good example of the federal association is the Food and Drink Federation which has a membership of over thirty separate associations, the largest being the Biscuit, Cake, Chocolate and Confectionery Alliance, the British Meat Manufacturers Association, the National Association of British and Irish Millers, the Sugar Bureau, the Snack, Nut and Crisp Manufacturers Association and the UK Association of Frozen Food Producers. In addition the Federation provides secretariat services to 32 sector trade associations and two European associations. A second good example is the Building Employers Confederation which has within it six sectors, the National Contractors Group, the Building Contractors Federation, the

National Committee for Smaller Builders, the Housebuilders Federation, the British
Woodworking Federation and the Federation of Building Specialist Contractors.

THE NATIONAL ASSOCIATION

In the UK the national association is the Confederation of British Industry. It has a
widespread representation comprising almost all sectors of industry and commerce, and is
universally recognised as being the national representative body for British business. Its
representation is stronger in some areas, eg manufacturing, than in others, eg financial
services. Similar associations exist is most other countries. The CBI however is not without
challenge and on particular issues it is in competition to some extent with the Institute of
Directors, the British Chambers of Commerce and the Engineering Employers Federation.

THE EUROPEAN ASSOCIATION

Europeanwide associations exist now for almost all sectors of industry and commerce as a
direct response to the European Union. At a very early stage the European Commission made
it clear that it preferred to deal with and would give more weight to Europeanwide trade
bodies rather than those representing a particular country. Most European trade associations
are based in Brussels and comprise the national trade bodies although some also have
individual membership of companies. The European trade bodies represent their members'
interests to the European Commission and the European Parliament and also provide a forum
in which members can get together to exchange information about industry trends.

THE INTERNATIONAL ASSOCIATION

In many industries international associations have been established. In some sectors of
industry and commerce which are international by nature, for example transport, the
international association may be very important. In most sectors, however, they do not
generally have a representative function simply because there is no international regulatory
organisation; rather their main purpose is to provide for an exchange of information between
the members. Typically they issue regular newsletters, commission research and hold
international conferences.

PROFESSIONAL BODIES

Professional bodies are not trade associations but it is necessary to comment on them briefly
in this chapter because the work of some of them overlaps with that of trade associations.
Also, they may be in competition with trade associations. While trade associations represent

companies, professional bodies represent individuals. In some cases the nature of industry is such that the professional body is also the trade body. This is true in respect of the professions where people operate on their own account and where the professional body may have a training, disciplinary and regulatory function. Doctors, for example, are represented by the British Medical Association. Solicitors and accountants have to pass the examinations of and are regulated by their professional bodies. At the other extreme there are industries where there is a fairly sharp division between the trade association and the professional body with the two organisations perhaps working closely together although not overlapping or competing to a significant extent. The professional body has only a limited representative function on behalf of the industry. For example, staff who work for insurance companies may well be members of the Chartered Insurance Institute while the insurance companies themselves are members of the Association of British Insurers. Similarly, the professional body for staff of banks and building societies is the Chartered Institute of Bankers while the trade bodies are the British Bankers' Association and the Building Societies Association.

There are some industries where the professional body adopts some of the functions of the trade body by seeking to represent its members. For example, in the social rented housing market there are a number of different representative organisations most of which are organisations of local authorities but also, for example, the National Federation of Housing Associations. The staff who work for the landlords have as their professional body a single organisation, the Chartered Institute of Housing. The main area of concern of the Institute is housing management but the Institute has sought to go wider and comments on matters of broad housing policy, and also it runs a major annual conference. This is an example of where the professional body has to some extent captured trade association business because of the diversity of trade associations.

Chambers of Commerce

Chambers of commerce are similar to trade associations in that they are bodies established to represent the interests of a variety of industrial and commercial organisations. They are, however, fundamentally different in that their membership is geographically rather than industrially based. Chambers of commerce exist in most major towns and provide a forum where local businesses can get together to discuss matters of common interest and to undertake joint promotional work.

There are 90 chambers of commerce currently belonging to the umbrella body, the British Chambers of Commerce. They have a total membership of 88,446 companies. Of the membership, 29% are in manufacturing, 9% are in the retail industry with the remaining 62% being other companies. Small firms provide most of the membership; only 5% of the members have more than 200 employees and a further 26% have between 20 and 200 employees. 69% of members have under 20 employees. The annual income of chambers of commerce is estimated at £86 million, and they employ some 2,300 full time staff.

The chambers of commerce have recently been restructuring following the establishment of a development strategy in October 1990. The core functions of each chamber have been agreed to cover representation, international trade, education and training and information.

A research study undertaken by Professor Robert Bennett of the London School of Economics suggested that each chamber needed to have a staffing infrastructure of approximately 34 full time equivalents and to support this a membership of at least 1,000 businesses initially, growing to 2,000-3,000, was needed. On this basis there would be scope for a network of slightly over 50 chambers in the UK as a whole. About 30 chambers are currently considered to meet the required standards. Subsequently there have been a number of mergers between chambers.

As noted, the umbrella body for chambers of commerce is British Chambers of Commerce. This co-ordinates business opinion as represented through member chambers and articulates those views to government. It provides a means by which chambers can develop a common strategy, set common goals and implement priorities. It co-ordinates activities between chambers. It has instituted a system of approved and accredited chambers.

OVERLAPPING TRADE ASSOCIATIONS

An increasing trend in industry and commerce has been for the barriers between markets and industries to break down. This has occurred for a number of reasons including technological developments and deregulation. This means that companies may find themselves belonging to a number of different trade associations as they expand their business by moving into related markets, either directly or through a subsidiary. The Association of British Insurers recently calculated that of its largest 60 members, 28 belonged to the Association of Unit Trusts and Investment Funds, 22 belonged to the Council of Mortgage Lenders, 22 belonged to the Institutional Fund Managers Association, 20 belonged to the Personal Equity Plan Managers Association and nine belonged to the British Bankers' Association. Such a situation will inevitably cause tensions and pressures for mergers.

The Manchester Metropolitan University, in a recent study, found that 24% of trade associations were affiliated to the CBI, 11% to a chamber of commerce, 51% to a European trade association and 40% to another trade association.

BIBLIOGRAPHY AND FURTHER READING

T C May, J McHugh and T Taylor, *UK Trade Associations in the 1990's: A Research Note* (Manchester: Manchester Metropolitan University, unpublished, 1995).

CHAPTER 3

Trade Associations in the United Kingdom

There are well over 1,000 trade associations in the United Kingdom, ranging from those representing small sectors of an industry and which employ no staff to large organisations with over one hundred staff representing major industrial sectors. An analysis of industrial sectors shows a wide variety of trade association structures ranging from single industry associations to federations to multiple federations. There are about 15 associations with subscription incomes over £3 million a year.

HISTORY

There is no detailed historical study of trade associations collectively, although there are many excellent studies of individual associations. The early history is usefully described in an American book on trade associations by Charles Mack. He notes that records of ancient civilisations in China, Japan, India, Egypt, Phoenicia and Rome contain references to trade groups of different kinds. Historians have found references in sixth century Italian cities to societies of bakers and soap makers, and in the twelfth century to organisations of clothiers, wool merchants, bankers, physicians, innkeepers and so on. Such societies eventually evolved into the medieval guilds. Mack says that the significance of the guilds to the rise of trade associations lies in two rounds of activity. First, the guilds sought to protect and advance the economic interests of their members in every way possible, including the regulation and restraint of competition. Secondly, like the guilds, trade associations have always been the interface between their members and government.

In his brief section on the development of associations in Britain, Mack says that British trade and business associations are among "the weakest among the industrialised countries". He notes that trade associations developed in the eighteenth and nineteenth centuries often on a local, narrowly specialised basis. Given the prevailing laissez faire philosophy, economic behaviour was largely unregulated and unprotected. Trade associations sought to moderate market competition but had no way to enforce restraint agreements.

The twentieth century history of trade associations is usefully covered in the *Report of the Commission of Inquiry into Industrial and Commercial Representation* (The Devlin Report), published in November 1972.

Like Charles Mack, the study noted that trade associations at national level began to emerge in the last quarter of the nineteenth century. In many cases their main purpose was to fix prices and quotas, an activity which was not illegal in Britain until the Restrictive Trade

Practices Act of 1956. Some associations were defensive in character while others sought to encourage rather than restrain trade. The Society of Motor Manufacturers and Traders was formed in 1902 to ensure that there was only one single motor show in the UK and to promote the use of motor vehicles. The Timber Trade Federation was established in 1892 so that importers of timber could negotiate more forcefully over inland freight charges.

In the First World War the government regretted the lack of representative bodies with which it could consult on such matters as the equipment of troops. In the Second World War the government made use of the trade association network, thereby strengthening them.

Wartime conditions also influenced the development of employers' organisations; thus industrywide pay settlements arose from the transfer to national level of decision-taking in a range of labour relations matters during the First World War. The role of many employers' organisations has subsequently changed from that of regulating wages and conditions to advising their members.

A major development was the Restrictive Trade Practices Act 1956 which outlawed price fixing. Trade associations had to justify their existence by more positive activities and providing services.

The Devlin Report estimated that in 1972 there were 860 associations with a further 800 associations affiliated to them. The report said that only 20% of all associations had annual incomes of £10,000 or more and full time executive staff. Over 300 associations were serviced by accountants or solicitors and about 50 were serviced by an executive in one of the member companies. The report went on to describe industries dominated by various types of organisation. The following were dominated by a single organisation: agriculture, engineering, automobiles, electrical engineering, shipping, ports, ship and boat building, chemicals, pharmaceuticals, plastics, printing, publishing, hotels and catering, rubber, timber, glass, ceramics, clay industries, paper and board, steel, leather and laundering. A smaller group of associations had a confederation structure: textiles, building materials, electronics and distributive trades. Industries where there were several effective associations were listed as construction, food and drink, newspapers and periodicals and non ferrous metals. Finally, industries in which representation was fragmented were listed as mechanical engineering, clothing, footwear, mining and fishing.

THE MAJOR INDUSTRIAL SECTORS

The Central Statistical Office produces a standard industrial classification of economic activities. This is used by the Department of Employment to publish statistics on employees in employment by sector. This is a useful basis for an analysis of trade associations by sector.

Table 3.1 shows for each of the major sectors the proportion of the working population in that sector and some of the major trade associations, together with their subscription income, where it is available, as recorded in their published accounts for years ending between 31 December 1993 and 30 December 1994.

Table 3.1 Trade Associations in the Major Industrial Sectors

Sector	Percentage of Working Population June 1994	Major Trade Associations	Subscription Income 1993 £m
Agriculture, forestry and fishing	1.18	National Farmers Union	14.0
Energy and water supply	1.47	UK Offshore Operators Association	2.0
		UK Petroleum Industry Association	
		Electricity Association	5.7
		Water Services Association	3.4
		Water Companies Association	1.0
Other minerals and ore extraction etc	1.37	Chemical Industries Association	4.4
		Association of the British Pharmaceutical Industry	5.0
Metal goods, engineering, vehicles	8.73	Engineering Employers Federation	2.1
		Metcom	
		BEAMA	
		Federation of the Electronics Industry	
		Society of Motor Manufacturers and Traders	3.1
		Society of British Aerospace Companies	
Other manufacturing	8.77	Food and Drink Federation	
		Dairy Industry Federation	1.6
		British Apparel and Textile Confederation	
		Timber Trade Federation	0.7
		Paper Federation	1.2

		Publishers Association	
		British Printing Industries Federation	3.3
		Newspaper Society	2.0
		Newspaper Publishers Association	
		British Plastics Federation	1.1
		British Rubber Manufacturers Association	0.7
Construction	3.66	Building Employers Confederation	5.6
		Federation of Civil Engineering Contractors	
		Federation of Master Builders	2.3
		Electrical Contractors Association	2.2
		Heating and Ventilating Contractors Association	1.3
Distribution, hotels, catering, repairs	21.83	British Retail Consortium	1.4
		National Federation of Retail Newsagents	4.3
		Association of British Travel Agents	2.9
		British Hospitality Association	0.9
		Retail Motor Industry Federation	3.2
		Vehicle Builders and Repairers Association	1.1
Transport and communications	5.79	Freight Transport Association	2.2
		Road Haulage Association	1.6
		Chamber of Shipping	1.9
Banking, finance, insurance, property services, business services	12.75	British Bankers Association	4.5
		Building Societies Association/Council of Mortgage Lenders	3.2
		Finance and Leasing Association	1.3
		Association of British Insurers	14.6
		Association of Unit Trusts and Investment Funds	1.7
		British Insurance and Investment Brokers Association	1.7
		National Association of Estate Agents	1.1
		National Federation of Housing Associations	2.4
		British Property Federation	0.5
Other services	33.10		

The selection of trade associations included in the table is to some extent arbitrary. Nevertheless the table usefully indicates the major associations and to some extent the pattern of representation. It is helpful to comment briefly on each of the major industrial sectors.

Agriculture now accounts for a relatively small proportion of the total labour force but is represented by one of the most powerful unions, the National Farmers Union, which represents both farmers and growers. (The Union operates only in England and Wales; there are separate organisations in Scotland and Northern Ireland.) In terms of size it is one of the three largest associations. It is different from other trade associations in that most of its members are individual farmers rather then corporate bodies.

The oil production industry is relatively new and has spawned a suitably large trade association in the form of the UK Offshore Operators Association. The onshore industry is represented by a different organisation, the UK Petroleum Industry Association.

The utilities are interesting, each having been denationalized and accordingly developed the need for representative services. The electricity companies have established a substantial trade association in the form of the Electricity Association, a successor body to the previous Electricity Council. The denationalized water companies have formed the Water Services Association which operates alongside and co-operates with the Water Companies Association which represents the companies which were already in private hands. The gas industry has no need for a trade association given that there is still a near monopoly supplier, British Gas, which performs its own representational work.

The chemicals industry is represented by one of the largest associations, the Chemical Industries Association, which acts as an employers' organisation as well as a trade association. It represents the whole of the chemical and allied industries sector and has 13 associations affiliated to it. Pharmaceuticals are represented separately by the Association of the British Pharmaceutical Industry.

Engineering presents a somewhat complex picture. The largest single trade body is the Engineering Employers Federation which comprises 15 autonomous organisations - 14 regional associations and the National Engineering Construction Employers Association. The entire EEF 'group' had total income from members of a little over £11 million in 1993. It is predominantly an employers' organisation but also has a representative function for the whole of manufacturing industry. Many members of the Engineering Employers Federation are also members of one or more of three other federations, the Mechanical and Metal Trades Confederation (Metcom), the Federation of British Electrotechnical and Allied Manufacturers Association (BEAMA) and the Federation of the Electronics Industry (FEI). BEAMA and

Metcom are currently considering a merger. Each of these organisations is itself a federation. Metcom has 34 associations in membership and BEAMA 18. Most of the major sectors within the metal goods, engineering and vehicles sector have their own trade bodies, the two largest of which are the Society of Motor Manufacturers and Traders and the Society of British Aerospace Companies.

The Food and Drink Federation represents the food and drink industry. Its members comprise a number of specialised associations. The dairy industry has separate representation, the Dairy Industry Federation.

The clothing and textile industry has recently changed its trade association structure. In 1992, the industry established the British Apparel and Textile Confederation, bringing together all the principal apparel and textile employer organisations and trade associations in the UK. It has three main component parts, the Apparel Knitting and Textiles Alliance, which exercises most of the trade association functions, the Textile Forum, which co-ordinates the interests of employers in the textile sector of the industry, and the British Knitting and Clothing Confederation.

The timber industry is represented by a straightforward industry association, the Timber Trade Federation.

The paper industry is represented by the Paper Federation, which recently changed its name from the British Paper and Board Industry Federation. It services 12 other associations all with a paper connection. The printing industry is represented by one of the largest associations, the British Printing Industries Federation. The publishing industry has three major associations. The Publishers Association is the representative body for the book publishing industry and for research journals and computerised publications. It covers everything except newspapers and magazines. The Newspaper Society represents the interests of Britain's regional and local press, the national press being represented by the Newspaper Publishers Association.

Plastics and rubber each have industry associations in the form of the British Plastics Federation and the British Rubber Manufacturers Association.

In the construction industry the major association is the Building Employers Confederation. This is an umbrella organisation covering six major groupings, the General Contractors Group, the National Contractors Group, the National Committee for Small Builders, the Housebuilders Federation, the Federation of Building Specialist Contractors and the British Woodworking Federation. The Confederation acts as both a trade body and an employers' association. The second major trade body in the construction area is the Federation of Civil Engineering Contractors. Many smaller builders are represented by a third association, the

Federation of Master Builders. A fourth major association in this field is the Electrical Contractors Association whose members undertake all types of electrical work. The largest of the specialist groupings within the construction sector is the Heating and Ventilation Contractors Association.

In distribution the major trade body is the British Retail Consortium which represents all forms of retailing through its company and trade association members. The largest specialist association within distribution is the National Federation of Retail Newsagents. A second large specialist association is the Association of British Travel Agents. The hotel and catering industry is represented by the British Hospitality Association. The motor industry has its own retail trade association, the Retail Motor Industry Federation, which itself is made up of eight separate specialist groups. Also in the motor area is the Vehicle Builders and Repairers Association.

The transport industry is now a major industry in its own right. There are two trade associations in the inland transport sector. The Freight Transport Association is the largest single association and represents the transport industry comprehensively in that its members operate or use freight transport for or in connection with their business. The Road Haulage Association is more narrowly focused representing companies that provide road haulage services. The shipping industry has its own trade association in the shape of the Chamber of Shipping. Interestingly, for the size of the sector, the air transport industry has a very small association in the form of the British Air Transport Association. This can largely be explained by the fact that regulation operates at the international level, and accordingly it is the international body, the International Air Transport Association, which is important. There are no strong associations in respect of telecommunications and postal services, recognising the near dominant positions of BT and the Royal Mail. However, this position is now changing as the telecommunications industry continues to fragment.

The banking and finance industry is well represented by a number of major associations. In the banking field the major association is the British Bankers Association which represents the whole banking sector including the retail banking groups, merchant and investment banks, discount houses, private banks and foreign banks. A specialist association linked to the BBA is the London Investment Bankers Association which represents the investment banking and securities industry. Although building societies are in much the same business as retail banks they are subject to their own special legislation and regulation and are represented by an industry trade body, the Building Societies Association. The conversion of the second largest building society to banking status and the growth of other institutions in the mortgage market led to the establishment in 1989 of the Council of Mortgage Lenders, which now represents the whole mortgage lending industry. It is run alongside the Building Societies Association, the two organisations sharing a single secretariat. Most of the largest banks and building societies are members of the Association for Payments Clearing Services. This is a forum for discussion and resolution of issues relating to money transmission. It also manages the principal UK payment clearing systems. The finance and leasing industry is represented by the Finance and Leasing

Association, most of the members of which are subsidiaries of banks or building societies.

The unit trust industry is represented by the Association of Unit Trusts and Investment Funds. This recently changed its name from the Unit Trust Association as part of a programme to expand its role and membership. In the insurance industry, the major association is the Association of British Insurers, formed by a merger of a number of industry associations in 1985. This represent insurance companies, the Lloyd's market having its own representative role although it works with the ABI on some issues. The insurance broking industry is represented by a number of associations, the largest of which is the British Insurance and Investment Brokers Association.

There is a specialised trade association for the estate agency business, the National Association of Estate Agents. However, many estate agents are also members of one of the professional bodies, in particular the Royal Institution of Chartered Surveyors and the Incorporated Society of Valuers and Auctioneers. These are among the professional bodies which also perform trade association functions.

In the real estate industry the major associations are the British Property Federation which represents commercial landlords, the National Federation of Housing Associations, which represents housing associations, and again the Royal Institution of Chartered Surveyors. In addition, the local authority associations undertake representative work, for example in respect of housing matters given that local authorities are very large landlords.

The legal and accountancy industries are represented by professional bodies which in addition perform trade association services. The largest of these bodies are the Law Society and the Institute of Chartered Accountants in England and Wales.

The other services sector of the economy now accounts for around a third of the working population but is not well represented by trade associations. This is partly because much of the other services sector is in the public sector and in monopoly supply conditions where trade associations are not needed. However, a major development in the public sector over the last few years has been the introduction of commercial disciplines, in particular through contracting out services and splitting the purchasing capacity from the providing capacity. This has spawned a number of new trade associations to represent either the providers or the purchasers. Good examples are the NHS Trust Federation and the Association of Direct Labour Organisations. There are also a number of specialist trade associations in this sector, for example the British Sports and Allied Industries Federation and the Producers Alliance for Cinema and Television.

THE TRADE ASSOCIATION INDUSTRY

There are no comprehensive figures on the whole of the trade association industry in the United Kingdom. The only substantial information is that available in the report of the Devlin Committee. In 1994, the Trade Association Research Unit of Manchester Metropolitan

University undertook an analysis of associations. The conclusions are summarised here. By studying directories of trade associations and professional bodies, 1,300 organisations were identified as likely trade associations and a questionnaire was sent to each association. The survey, carried out in February 1994, produced a total response rate of 45% and an effective response rate of 38%.

The survey showed a dramatic increase in the number of trade associations formed in the 1970s and 1980s. A third of the associations surveyed were formed in that period and the authors suggest that as Devlin identified some 2,500 likely trade associations, while their survey could find only 1,300, one could conclude that many of those formed in the 1970s and 1980s were the result of mergers. 13% of the associations had been involved in a merger in the previous five years.

The survey showed considerable variations in the size of associations in terms of membership. The largest 20% of associations had 485 or more corporate members and the largest 10% had 1,600 or more. At the other extreme, 30% of respondents had fewer than 45 corporate members on average with the smallest 10% having fewer than 15. The median was between 120 and 150.

Table 3.2 shows the analysis of the sample by subscription income.

Table 3.2 Trade Associations Annual Income

Income Band £	Percentage of Associations	Number of Associations
Under 3,250	4.0	52
3,250 - 65,000	30.2	393
65,000 - 325,000	30.7	399
325,000 - 450,000	6.8	88
450,000 - 650,000	7.8	101
650,000 - 1m	6.6	86
Over 1m	13.9	181
Total	100.0	1,300

Note: The figures on numbers of associations have been calculated by applying the percentages to the total estimated number of associations of 1,300. However, it cannot be certain that the sample was representative or that the total number of associations of 1,300 is correct.

A very rough calculation suggests a total income for the trade association industry of £580 million in 1994. Data from the Certification Officer for Trade Unions and Employers Associations suggests that subscription income is 47% of total income which would imply a total subscription income of about £270 million a year.

The study showed that 75% of associations employed some staff. Over 70% of associations employed less than ten staff and only 10% had 30 or more staff. These figures suggest total number of staff employed in the region of 9,000.

The table below lists the largest sectoral associations (that is, excluding the CBI) on the basis of 1993 subscription income. There are probably a few other associations, for which subscription income is not available, which come into this category.

Table 3.3 The Largest Associations

Association	Subscription Income 1993 £m
Association of British Insurers	14.6
National Farmers Union	14.0
Electricity Association	5.7
Building Employers Confederation	5.6
Association of the British Pharmaceutical Industry	5.0
British Bankers Association	4.5
Chemical Industries Association	4.4
National Federation of Retail Newsagents	4.3
Water Services Association	3.4
British Printing Industries Federation	3.3
Retail Motor Industry Federation	3.2
Building Societies Association/Council of Mortgage Lenders	3.2
Society of Motor Manufacturers and Traders	3.1

Source: Annual accounts and individual associations.

The table shows that the largest associations, the Association of British Insurers and the National Farmers Union, are more than twice the size of the next group of associations. There then follows associations representing major industrial sectors such as electricity, construction, banking, chemicals, the water industry, printing and the combined Building Societies Association and Council of Mortgage Lenders. The National Federation of Retail Newsagents stands out as a large association for a comparatively small industrial sector.

There is one other additional source of information on trade associations, that is the Annual Report of the Certification Officer for Trade Unions and Employers' Associations. This does not cover those trade associations which do not have an employers' association function (that is the majority of them) and does also include some organisations which would not in any circumstances be counted as a trade association, for example the Test and County Cricket Board. However, it is helpful to reproduce from the Annual Report of the Certification Officer a listing of employers' associations with total income in excess of £1.5 million in 1993.

Table 3.4 Employers' Associations with over £1.5 million Total Income in 1993

Association	Income from Members £000	Total Income £000	Total Funds at Year £000	Number of Members
Engineering Employers Federation	1,868	4,947	18,531	17
EEF West Midlands	1,224	4,468	2,811	1,133
National Engineering Construction Employers Association	1,456	1,783	963	292
EEF South	918	1,641	2,272	474
Engineering Employers Western Association	700	1,551	666	325
10 other Engineering Employers Associations	2,859	5,390	3,205	2,269
• National Farmers Union	18,488	35,481	32,133	107,209
Test and County Cricket Board	-	24,601	-	20
• Freight Transport Association Ltd	2,220	10,979	4,031	11,596
Electrical Contractors Association	2,027	9,738	21,549	1,958
Building Employers Confederation	5,582	9,037	5,585	5,638
Heating and Ventilating Contractors Association	1,351	8,588	5,543	1,118
British Printing Industries Federation	3,308	5,861	1,085	3,050
Retail Motor Industry Federation	3,156	5,139	1,505	12,405
• Chemical Industries Association Ltd	4,084	4,940	215	174
National Federation of Retail Newsagents	4,224	4,330	2,558	28,074
Newspaper Society	3,078	3,590	1,042	240
• Road Haulage Association Ltd	1,641	3,426	3,466	9,780
Federation of Master Builders	2,351	3,179	3,959	17,362
• British Jewellery and Giftware Federation Ltd	522	2,905	5,959	1,787
National Pharmaceutical Association	1,881	2,581	1,536	6,894
Federation of Civil Engineering Contractors	1,711	2,103	845	290
• BFM Ltd	335	1,906	1,028	264
Vehicle Builders and Repairers Association	1,816	1,902	839	3,194
• West End Theatre Managers Ltd	1,669	1,750	77	90
Paper Federation of Great Britain Ltd	1,202	1,677	1,265	59
Producers Alliance for Cinema and Television Ltd	342	1,616	254	1,267
Dairy Trade Federation Ltd	1,558	1,612	784	3,300
National Farmers Union of Scotland	1,206	1,595	881	13,502
Total for above Employers' Associations	72,777	168,316	124,587	233,781
Total for 90 other listed Employers' Associations	11,178	18,353	17,329	31,080
Total for 117 other unlisted Employers' Associations	10,213	14,955	8,852	13,274
Total for all Employers' Associations	64,168	201,624	150,768	278,135

• *Unlisted Employers' Association*

Bibliography and Further Reading

Annual Report of the Certification Officer 1994 (London: Certification Office for Trade Unions and Employers' Associations, 1995).

Report of the Commission of Inquiry into Industrial and Commercial Representation (the Devlin Report) (London: Confederation of British Industry and Association of British Chambers of Commerce, 1972).

T C May, J McHugh and T Taylor, *UK Trade Associations in the 1990's: A Research Note* (Manchester: Manchester Metropolitan University, unpublished, 1995).

Charles S Mack, *The Executive's Handbook of Trade and Business Associations* (New York: Quorum Books, 1991).

CHAPTER 4

The Confederation of British Industry

The Confederation of British Industry is the national trade body for industry and commerce in Britain. Bearing in mind its importance it is relatively small with subscription income lower than that of the largest industry associations. It is however very influential as it is seen to be the representative body for the whole of British industry. Its representative role is particularly important in respect of matters that cut across all industrial sectors, for example economic and industrial policy and policy at the European Union level.

HISTORY

The following summary of the history of the CBI is taken from the Devlin Report. The Association of British Chambers of Commerce had been formed in 1860 and until the First World War was the only national organisation that could speak for commerce and industry. Wartime pressures led to the establishment of three national organisations between 1915 and 1919 -

(a) The National Union of Manufacturers (renamed National Association of British Manufacturers (NABM) in 1961) was representative of manufacturing industries. It had trade associations as well as individual businesses in membership. In practice the individual members tended to be small.

(b) The Federation of British Industries (FBI) was set up in 1916 by 124 companies to provide a means of giving views to government of the leading manufacturing companies. By the end of its first year it had 350 companies in membership. It decided to admit trade associations into membership and by the end of its second year it had 62. During the 1930s the FBI attempted to adopt a fairly protectionist stance although after the Second World War it consistently advocated liberal trading policies.

(c) The National Confederation of British Employers Organisations (renamed the British Employers' Confederation (BEC) in 1939) was concerned only with the employers' organisation function. Its membership was made up solely of national associations of employers, mainly but not entirely those concerned with manufacturing industry. It was formed with the help of the FBI.

Various unsuccessful attempts had been made from the early 1930s to amalgamate the three organisations. In 1963 the three bodies appointed Sir Henry Benson and Sir Sam Brown to frame proposals to create a single national association. As a result of their report the

Confederation of British Industry (CBI) was formed in July 1965. At the time the FBI comprised 280 trade associations and more than 8,500 companies and subsidiaries, the BEC comprised 53 employer organisations and the NABM comprised 53 trade associations and over 5,000 companies. Nationalised industries and commercial organisations were admitted as "associate members". This associate status was abolished in 1969 when the present five membership categories were introduced.

The 1972 Devlin Report was itself influential in framing the development of the CBI. It suggested that it ought to derive its representative power primarily from its place at the head of a hierarchy of associations. While it recognised that there was mutual value in larger companies being in direct CBI membership it proposed that membership should no longer be available to smaller firms and that membership of a sectoral association should also be mandatory for all CBI members. The report proposed the establishment of a director-general's heads of sector council of about forty members. Finally it recommended a merger between the CBI and the Chambers of Commerce movement to eliminate a perceived overlap on local and regional development. The CBI rejected the concept of restricting direct smaller firm membership and did not see any value in creating formal links with the Chambers of Commerce sector. However, an advice centre on industrial and commercial representation was established and operated until the mid-1980s, and the heads of sector group of thirty members, covering the larger associations, was set up under the Director-General's chairmanship.

In May 1975 the CBI President commissioned an inquiry into the CBI's aims and organisation from a three man committee, Lord Plowden, Philip Allen and John Partridge. The Committee was set up partly because there was a belief in part of its membership that it was not dealing as effectively as it might with the problems facing British industry. The Committee made a number of recommendations about the structure of the CBI including that there should be a President's Committee. The Committee considered the question of sectoral representation. The Committee argued that there was a compelling need to achieve a more effective pattern of industrial sector representation in Britain. It noted that although many government policies impacted on industry as a whole there was likely to be increasing emphasis on deeper analysis and understanding of the position of individual sectors of industrial activity. The Committee concluded that the essential co-operation between the CBI and the main industrial sectors could not be secured until the organisations representing them had been brought into a closer relationship with the CBI's policy and planning than currently existed. The Committee recommended that the newly established President's Committee should consider this.

STRUCTURE

The CBI currently has more than 250,000 public and private companies in membership together with more than 200 trade associations, employers' organisations and commercial associations. Membership falls into one of five basic categories -

(a) Companies in productive or manufacturing industry.

(b) Companies in the financial, trading, service and advisory sectors.

(c) Employers' organisations and trade associations representing individual manufacturing industries.

(d) Commercial associations with members in finance and commerce, local trade associations and chambers of commerce.

(e) Nationalised industries and public corporations.

The supreme governing body of the CBI is a Council with over 400 members. Proposals must be approved by the Council before they can become official policy. The Council is headed by a President, who typically serves a two year term, and membership is made up of the Deputy President, the last six past presidents, the chairmen of all CBI standing committees, representatives of employer, trade and commercial organisations, the public sector, the 13 CBI regional councils and people drawn from member companies of all sizes and activity.

The 13 regional councils each have about 40 members and are served by regional offices staffed by CBI employees.

A President's Committee is made up of leading CBI figures including the chairmen of key standing committees and the Smaller Firms Council, and has as its role to advise the President on major policy issues and to keep the CBI's public position and overall strategy under constant review. There are standing committees covering companies, economic affairs, education and training, employment, energy, environment, Europe, health and safety, industrial relations and wages and conditions, minerals, overseas, rating and valuation, technology and innovation, taxation, tourism and transport.

Other major parts of the CBI structure are -

(a) The Director General's group of chief executives of major sectoral organisations which considers policy work undertaken by the CBI and issues of common interest to them.

(b) The Smaller Firms Council which monitors and influences all CBI policy recommendations to ensure that the views of firms with fewer than 200 employees are fully represented.

(c) The National Manufacturing Council which was established in 1992 in recognition of the fundamental role manufacturing has in underpinning a large sector of economic activity. Its objectives are to ensure that the UK manufacturing sector is able to compete with the world's best, to secure wider recognition of the importance of a strong manufacturing base, and to identify the specific actions which need to be taken by industry, government and the financial community to meet world class standards.

The standing committees put forward ideas, draft policy proposals and present them to the Council drawing on the views of regional councils, the Smaller Firms Council and, if necessary, specific membership sectors.

The CBI has an office in Brussels, established, before Britain joined the European Community, in 1971. It has six basic functions -

(a) To represent the CBI on the spot, keeping channels open by liaising with the various European bodies, the UK's permanent representation, and by presenting the views of British business to the European Union's institutions.

(b) To maintain close contact with UNICE, the Union of Industrial and Employers Confederations of Europe, which is the European industries' principal representative body in contact with the Union's institutions.

(c) To monitor developments in the Union and contribute to the CBI's policy work by providing early warning to CBI committees.

(d) To help and advise CBI members in their dealings with the Union.

(e) To liaise closely with CBI members in Belgium and all other British interests that are monitoring the Union's institutions.

(f) To support and advise the CBI's European Committee in co-ordinating CBI's policies on Union issues.

In 1995 the Management Board and the Director General of the CBI carried out a strategic review of what the organisation did and how it did it. Three reasons were given for undertaking the review -

(a) The CBI was under some financial pressure, largely because of the escalating cost of occupancy of its head office at Centre Point in London.

(b) It was thought that the time was right to reassess the appropriateness of the organisational structure for the changing demands that the CBI faced.

(c) It was thought necessary to review the way which members relate to the CBI. In a letter to members, the Director General of the CBI, Howard Davies, commented "Our perception is that while members generally have a high regard for the CBI's policy work (and survey evidence supports that) there is too little sense of "ownership" of the organisation, outside a relatively small group."

Among the consequences of the review was a 10% reduction in staff costs and a reorganisation of senior management. Two new committees were also established, a Management Committee taking over the responsibilities of the Finance and General Purposes Committee but with a more active role in providing management oversight of the organisation at member level, and a Membership Committee. At regional level it is intended to give more emphasis to regional issues and also to find better ways of involving experts in policy formulation through interest groups at regional level. The member communication system has been overhauled as a result of which members will receive a monthly package comprising CBI News, a new monthly economic bulletin, and brief summaries of any major policy papers the CBI has launched during the month.

The CBI employed 292 staff in 1994. The secretariat is headed by a Director General who is the public figure of the organisation rather than the President. In August 1995, as a result of the strategic review, there was a substantial reorganisation of the CBI's policy staff into four directorates -

(a) A Business Environment Directorate covering company and commercial law, public procurement, regional development, energy, transport, environment and health and safety.

(b) A Human Resources Directorate covering work on education and training with work on pay, employment conditions and employee relations.

(c) An Economics Directorate covering macro-economics, economic surveys, tax policy and international trade policy.

(d) A Manufacturing and International Markets Directorate which supports the activities of the National Manufacturing Council, the CBI's contribution to technology policy and its extensive work in overseas trade promotion.

These four directorates are complemented by two smaller groups: the European Affairs Group, which supports the Brussels Office and co-ordinates European policy in London, and the Smaller Firms Unit which supports the Smaller Firms Council.

FUNCTIONS

The CBI has the following mission statement: "The CBI's objective is to help create and sustain the conditions in which businesses in the UK can compete and prosper. It represents its members' views on all sectoral issues to the government and to other national and international administrations. In addition, it supplies advice, information and research to members on those issues and provides a forum for the exchange and encouragement of best practice." In its promotional literature the CBI says it offers the following services to members -

(a) Effective representation at all levels of government.

(b) A voice in Europe.

(c) A constructive working relationship with the Trades Union Congress.

(d) Professional information and advice on most issues affecting business.

(e) Regular monitoring and dissemination of economic and industrial trends, pay data and other vital market information.

(f) Conferences, seminars, fora, workshops and informal meetings.

(g) Frequent meetings with high level trade delegations and visiting heads of state to expand members' overseas business contacts.

Given its very wide membership, the CBI naturally concentrates on national rather than sectoral issues. The range of its work can usefully be described by drawing on the CBI's Six Monthly Review for the first half of 1995. The review states that in that period the CBI focused attention on five priority areas -

"**First**, our dialogue with the Treasury and the Bank on the economy. We have argued that inflationary pressures in industry were beginning to ease, and that the recovery (which has scarcely begun in construction) was slowing in response to last year's interest rate rises, making further large increases unnecessary.

Second, the competitiveness debate, in Europe and domestically. In Europe we have made a major push to influence the new Commission, and the European Parliament. This work is bearing fruit. The Molitor report on deregulation, of which Sir Michael Angus was the UK signatory, was a significant breakthrough. And Jacques Santer's Competition Advisory Group (with David Simon from the UK) will be influential. Domestically, we spent a lot of time discussing the content of the Competitiveness White Paper with the DTI. It came out reasonably well.

Third, we have tried to raise the temperature of the debate on the transport infrastructure, where we believe the Government has lost its way. Our paper Missing Links which contrasted our directionless state with the more strategic approaches adopted by the French, Dutch and German governments, was well received. But there is much more to do.

Fourth, we have been working to ensure that three important Bills moving through Parliament (on the Environment, Pensions and Disability Discrimination) were responsive to business needs. This is time-consuming, detailed work, but several significant improvements have resulted.

Fifth, our attention has begun to turn to the formulation of Labour policy. We have sought, with some success, to influence the debate within the Party on the minimum wage, the training levy, industrial policy and corporate taxation. That work will continue from now to the election."

More detail is then given under thirteen separate headings -

(a) Economic policy. The CBI puts views on the stance of monetary policy to the Chancellor and the Governor ahead of their monthly meetings. A CBI working group report on long term public spending issues was discussed with the Chief Secretary to the Treasury. Recommendations include shifts in spending priorities towards transport and education and away from social security. CBI opposition to a minimum wage has been reaffirmed and a new survey of property confidence and future requirements was launched.

(b) Tax policy. Issues handled included Finance Bill provisions on directors and officers' liability, a review of the fiscal legislative process, new guidelines on the taxation of cross border affiliated company transactions and regional seminars on the new assessment system for income tax.

(c) Europe. A paper, Shaping the Future: A Europe That Works, was published restating the British business commitment to Europe and encouraging the government to negotiate energetically from within the European Union. The CBI has been particularly active in the deregulation initiative.

(d) Trade policy. In response to a request from the CBI, the DTI established a government/industry trade policy forum. More than a dozen conferences or seminars focusing on the business prospects in various overseas markets were held. Overseas visits were made by the President and the Director General.

(e) Employment/social policy. Efforts concentrated on European issues as the European Commission develops its social action programme and major domestic legislation on pensions, disability and employment rights. Work also continued on tackling long term employment.

(f) Education and training. Areas covered included the national education and training targets, which resulted from a CBI initiative, national vocational qualifications, and careers education and guidance. In response to increased political interest in the idea of a training levy the CBI took steps to reaffirm its opposition to compulsion.

(g) Transport. In February, the CBI launched its report Missing Links: Settling National Transport Priorities arguing that there have been years of under-investment in transport.

(h) Competition policy and competition law. The CBI published proposals for the reform of Article 85 of the Treaty of Rome which requires notification of restrictive agreements to the European Commission. The CBI has been at the centre of opposition to a draft technology transfer block exemption regulation.

(i) Environment Bill. The CBI lobbied successfully to improve the Environment Bill and organised a series of road shows on waste policy.

(j) On energy policy, work was undertaken on nuclear privatisation, business representation on the Electricity Consumers Committees, European energy policy and climate change.

(k) On smaller firms, the CBI was successful in influencing a government White Paper on competitiveness.

(l) Manufacturing industry. The Competitiveness Forum, launched in 1995, continued to go from strength to strength. The CBI has also been active in the Technology Foresight Programme.

(m) CBI regions. Among the activities listed are seminars, the launch of quality awards, the launching of a Scottish business agenda, and seeking to change the image of the South West region.

FINANCE

The CBI has an annual expenditure of around £17 million. Its income and expenditure for 1994 is shown in the following table.

Table 4.1 CBI Income and Expenditure 1994

	£000
Income	
Members' subscriptions	11,206
Rents and licence fees	976
Commercial activities	4,091
Interest on short term deposits and gilts	629
Other income	161
Total	17,063
Expenditure	
Payroll	6,476
Travelling and subsistence	717
Other staff costs	432
Office expenses	1,419
Premises costs	4,284
Subscriptions to other organisations	515
Commercial activities	2,562
Legal and professional costs	152
Promotional activities and surveys	146
Depreciation	307
Miscellaneous	42
Total	17,052
Operating surplus	11
Taxation credit/charge	372
Surplus transferred to accumulated fund	383

The CBI's accumulated fund at the end of 1994 was £5,437,000.

THE CBI IN THE CONTEXT OF THE TRADE ASSOCIATION INDUSTRY GENERALLY

The CBI occupies a unique position in the whole trade association industry. It is not particularly distinguished by its size, bearing in mind its wide-ranging functions. It has a relatively small staff and small budget. Some of the largest industry trade associations have subscription incomes in excess of that of the CBI.

The CBI concentrates on macro issues, for example tax policy, the overall level of public expenditure as opposed to its division, employment policy, transport policy and European policy. It has a very wide range of membership which means that its ability to promote particular industrial sectors is limited. Precisely because the CBI concentrates on macro issues it is more subject than most trade associations to the "free riding" principle. Individual companies and sectors benefit from the activities of the CBI regardless of whether they pay the subscription. It is less easy for companies to see the benefit of joining the CBI than the more direct benefits of joining an industry association

Because the CBI is essentially a representative voice dealing with major government issues its success depends entirely on its relations with the government. If it is seen by the government as being a representative voice for British industry and commerce generally then it will be very influential. If it is not seen in this way then it can degenerate into a pressure group. At present, there is no doubt that the CBI is an influential body. Its pronouncements achieve substantial publicity in the media, its director-general is very much a public figure and there is a steady stream of high level meetings between government ministers and the CBI. More importantly, the views of the CBI are clearly taken fully into account by the government.

BIBLIOGRAPHY AND FURTHER READING

Report of the Commission of Inquiry into Industrial and Commercial Representation (the Devlin Report) (London: Confederation of British Industry and Association of British Chambers of Commerce, 1972).

Confederation of British Industry, *Annual Report for 1994* (London: Confederation of British Industry, 1995).

The Voice of British Business (London: Confederation of British Industry, undated).

Report of the Committee of Enquiry into the CBI's Aims and Organisation (London: Confederation of British Industry, 1975).

Six Monthly Review, January-June 1995 (London: Confederation of British Industry, 1995).

CHAPTER 5

Associations of Trade Associations

Trade associations can be regarded as a small industrial sector which therefore needs some of the services which trade associations and professional bodies provide. The CBI comes nearest to being the "associations' trade association" although in Britain there are few issues on which trade associations need a collective view. There is a small professional body, the Society of Association Executives, and various other formal and informal groupings of trade associations or their staff. The "industry" is not well served by publications.

THEORETICAL ISSUES

In Chapter 1 of this book it was stated: "Trade associations exist because the members believe that the benefits they gain from membership exceed the cost. For this to happen trade associations must be able either to take advantage of economies of scale, or through their intrinsic nature to be able to do some things better than their members individually or other institutions." Given this definition it is clear that there is little need for a trade association for trade associations. There are few issues that apply to a number of trade associations but which do not have application more generally. There are for example few tax issues that apply specifically to trade associations and there is no legislation governing trade associations. This is in contrast with the position in the USA, where the nature of the political system which depends on lobbying has spawned a huge trade association industry and also legislation governing the activities of associations.

In Britain perhaps the only issue in which trade associations as a sector have an interest is lobbying. Even here however, there is little regulation or legislation in Britain and also no great public concern. This has changed recently with attention being focused on the way MPs can be influenced. Interestingly, the public debate and criticism has concentrated not so much on trade associations, which are generally regarded as performing a useful function, but rather on the recipients of lobbying, that is MPs and to a lesser extent Ministers, and professional lobbying firms. In October 1994 the government established the Committee On Standards in Public Life (better known, after its chairman, as the Nolan Committee), the work of which will include the activities of trade associations.

Trade associations also have a common interest in the exchange of information and perhaps also training programmes. Trade associations are different from other organisations, requiring special skills among staff that are not generally found in other industrial and commercial organisations. Trade associations compete with each other for influence and staff and can

34

learn from each other. Not infrequently chief executives of large trade associations are appointed from among the ranks of chief executives of smaller associations.

Generally it can be concluded that the need for trade associations to get together, either as organisations or through their staff, is fairly limited. This reflects the nature of the political situation in Britain, in particular the absence or any legislation or regulation governing the activities of associations.

TRADE ASSOCIATION ORGANISATIONS

In Britain there is no formal trade association for trade associations. The CBI, where necessary, does provide a meeting place for trade association chief executives and can represent the whole sector, although the extent to which it does so is fairly limited. In this respect it is helpful to go back to the Report of the Commission of Inquiry into Industrial and Commercial Representation (the Devlin Report) published in November 1972. The Committee was strongly in favour of fewer and stronger industrial organisations. It did not believe that this could be achieved if the structure of the CBI remained as it was. The Committee observed that the CBI membership included 4,100 small businesses and about 30% of them were not members of a trade association or an employers' organisation. The Committee went on:

"If they join an association, it is unlikely that they will want to pay a subscription to the CBI as well. Nor do we think it desirable that they should. A sector organisation cannot satisfactorily represent an industry unless the great majority of companies in the industry not only belong to it but use it. It is only through constant interchange between the staff of an organisation and its members, the sort of interchange that comes from the giving and receiving of advice and information and the discussion of problems, that the director and office bearers of the organisation can make themselves truly representative of the industry and able to act confidently in the knowledge that they know what their members are thinking. If a member has a problem that needs the attention of the CBI, he should obtain it through his sector organisation. Otherwise the two way channel of representation is not kept open."

The Committee went on to consider whether all company membership from the CBI should be excluded. It said that it would be neater if membership of the top body was mixed. It discussed whether the CBI should be a federation of associations, noting that this was a logical structure and the one that was predominant in Europe. The Committee in fact concluded that companies should be able to have direct representation. However it still favoured the CBI being a federation of associations:

"We think that the CBI ought to derive its representative power primarily from its place at the head of a hierarchy of associations. We think it to be inconsistent with this that it should have to rely for as much as 80% of its income from individual companies. We advise a practicable compromise which we believe would be an improvement on the general continental principle of excluding company membership altogether. The compromise is that while, for the reasons given in the preceding paragraph, the large companies should continue to enjoy direct membership of the CBI, the total number of companies in direct membership should be progressively diminished with the ultimate objective that at least 50% of the CBI's annual income be provided by member associations."

The Committee went on to propose that there should be a reliable means of exchanging information between associations with this taking the form of regular meetings between the Director General of the CBI and the chiefs of the principal sectors.

In the event the Devlin Committee's report was not implemented and the CBI does not act as a representative body for trade associations generally. However, about 30 of the largest associations do belong to the committee which has meetings with the Director General. These used to be on a monthly basis but proved to be generally unsatisfactory as they had little influence on what went on in the CBI. The meetings are now quarterly and provide for an exchange of views about current issues that concern the associations and possibly the discussion of a specific policy item. The meeting also provides a useful meeting place for chief executives of trade associations and there is much informal liaison between them on matters of common interest. On issues that affect more than one industry, the CBI input to government is often more effective than a number of trade associations making slightly different representations in exactly the same way that a trade association input is better than a number of companies making similar but slightly different submissions. The CBI has a closer relationship with government on such generic issues than individual trade associations and the sensible association will on some matters use the CBI to promote its views.

Generally, the CBI can be said to have an important and effective role as the overall representative body for British business. While it has no formal role as the trade associations' trade association it does in some respects act informally in that capacity. For example, it now runs an annual trade association conference.

One particular function relevant to trade associations which the CBI undertakes is an annual survey of salary and benefits of trade associations and employers organisations. About 30 associations participate. The survey records for each association the salary of the chief executive and the number of staff and minimum and maximum salaries for four levels of management, the dates of the last and the next salary review and the number of staff employed.

A second grouping of chief executives is what is known as the Trade Executives Group. This has about 15 members, all of whom are chief executives of major trade associations or professional bodies. The group meets monthly over dinner, generally with a guest, the objective being to facilitate an informal discussion of an issue affecting all trade associations, for example the recent government deregulation initiative, the implementation of European legislation, government attitude to business and the government attitude to trade associations.

The professional association most relevant to trade associations in the Institute of Chartered Secretaries and Administrators (ICSA); many trade association executives have an ICSA qualification. Interestingly, however, because many trade associations are not companies there is little need for the typical company secretary functions to be performed. The ICSA has a trade and professional associations panel which currently has a membership of thirteen.

The panel recently considered its own role as part of an internal exercise by the Association and concluded the following -

> "(a) Our area of specialism is even more appropriate in the current business environment, particularly in regard to the relationship associations enjoy with government. In February [1995] at a well publicised conference the President of the Board of Trade reiterated his determination to deal with far fewer, albeit stronger, trade associations. Both Government and financial pressures are exercising similar pressures on professional institutes and the progress of the EU adds further to representational demands. To respond to this will require considerable transformation. In any period of change those involved need additional support and professional guidance which the Institute should, with and through the Panel, be in a position to provide to its members.

> (b) Although there are several important differences between trade associations and professional institutes there is much in common. We believe the Institute can best continue to support both groups of organisations by maintaining a single panel but recommend a change of name to the Trade Associations and Professional Institutions Panel.

The Panel aims to contribute towards achieving the Institute's mission by:

> Disseminating information to Group members via a newsletter, symposia etc.

> Offering a telephone "networking" facility sharing the expertise of members.

> Encouraging professionalism and "life-long learning" among members.

> Helping to improve the profile of the Institute by being able to respond to consultation documents on relevant topics from government in Whitehall and Brussels."

THE SOCIETY OF ASSOCIATION EXECUTIVES

The Society of Association Executives (SAE) is a specialist professional organisation for staff who work in trade associations. The Association has the following classes of member -

(a) A member is a person holding a senior executive appointment, secretarial, specialist or administrative in character, and/or having responsibility directly to the governing body of an organisation of which membership is mainly voluntary and whose activities are representative of or related to trade, industry, commerce or a profession.

(b) A fellow who is the chief or principal executive of an organisation as described above for not less than three years.

(c) An associate who is a member of the staff of a member or fellow of the Association.

(d) A retired member is one who has previously been a member.

(e) An honorary member is one who has rendered distinguished service to the Society or who has reached a position of eminence in public life.

(f) A business affiliate is a corporation, limited company, firm or business which supplies services or goods to organisation represented by the membership.

(g) An affinity association is an organisation not having a paid executive but is otherwise similar to a business affiliate.

The governing body of the Society is a council comprising the president, the immediate past president, a senior vice president, a junior vice president, the secretary, a treasurer, and no more than twelve other elected fellows or members. The Society has about 400 members representing 1,000 association, not all of which are trade associations, and 22 business affiliates. The Society publishes an annual handbook and list of members which includes advertisements from companies offering services to trade associations. It publishes a newsletter, Association, and deals with enquiries including giving legal advice. It arranges a series of educational seminars intended to help develop skills and effectiveness for association executives.

The Society is a relatively small organisation with an annual budget of £40,000. Its membership for the most part comprises executives in smaller trade associations although a number of the largest associations are now also represented.

The Association is based in Westbury Leigh in Wiltshire but holds almost all of its meetings in London.

THE EUROPEAN SOCIETY OF ASSOCIATION EXECUTIVES

At the European level is the European Society of Association Executives (ESAE), based in Zurich. The Society describes its objective as being "To promote the profession and the professional standing of managers of international and national associations, educate members and the public in all areas dealing with the development and improvement of associations or similar international organisations." The membership comprises full members, those who have passed the European Certificate in Association Management or are distinguished association executives invited into membership by the board, associate members who are other persons engaged in the profession of association management, and corporate members. The governing body of the Society is the General Assembly which comprises all full members. The business of the Society is administered by a board of directors of between four and eleven members. The titular head of the Society is the president.

The Society's promotional leaflet states that it was founded in 1980 "To bring together senior association managers in Europe, to enhance the status of their profession and to allow them to increase their skills by formal training and certification and by informal networking with their peers in other associations and countries." The Society lists its functions as being -

(a) To build a framework in which the job of association management acquires true professional status.

(b) To help association managers improve their skills.

(c) To network senior association executives so that they benefit from a sharing of knowledge and experience.

(d) To ensure that association management skills are widely used in associations and that association executives operate according to the highest professional standards.

(e) To emphasize nationally and internationally the important role that is and can be played by associations in a democratic society.

The Society lists as benefits of membership -

(a) Promoting the concept of association management as an integrated profession and enhancing the status of the profession.

(b) Administering a pan-European and international certification programme in association management resulting in the European Certificate in Association Management.

(c) Assisting members enhance and expand the skills required to be effective association managers by providing training seminars and round table discussions.

(d) Holding an annual conference giving a unique opportunity to meet and exchange ideas among association executives.

(e) Issuing periodic study papers on issues from an association management perspective.

(f) Linking senior executives throughout Europe partly through publishing a handbook of members and associates.

(g) Maintaining close links with societies of association executives worldwide.

The Association publishes a handbook for members, listing the members and including the statutes, details of training and certification programmes, and other relevant information.

The Association is a small organisation with just 90 individual members. The countries with the largest membership are Belgium, the Netherlands, Switzerland and the United Kingdom. There are nine corporate members, almost all of which provide conference facilities.

The Association's accounts for 1994 show subscription income of £23,500 with other income of a little over £3,000.

An interesting feature of the work of the Society is its promotion of the European Certificate in Association Management (ECAM). The ECAM process is in three parts: a personal data form listing educational qualifications, work experience, specific training, proficiency in languages, community involvement, and any articles published relevant to the association world; private study, and an examination dealing specifically with association work. Two annual training seminars are held in association management which although not specifically geared to the ECAM examination are particularly relevant to those studying.

THE AMERICAN SOCIETY OF ASSOCIATION EXECUTIVES

America has a very different political system to that of the UK. Legislation is made not by the government in the form of the administration but more by Congress in the form of the Senate and the House of Representatives. Intensive lobbying is a vital part of the American political process. This applies not only at national level but also in each of the 50 States.

Accordingly trade associations need to be larger than they do in the UK and there are many more of them.

There are over 100,000 associations of various types in the USA with 23,000 operating at national level. Over 500,000 people are employed by associations. Not surprisingly there is a strong professional body for association staff in the form of the American Society of Association Executives (ASAE). This factual description of the Association is taken from its promotional publication *The ASAE Advantage*.

The Society was founded in 1920 and now has over 21,000 members. It has the following main categories of membership -

(a) Regular membership, entitling a member to voting privileges, full membership benefits and eligibility to hold office.

(b) Section membership, entitling members to full membership benefits except for the right to vote and hold office. This gives access to one of the ten special interest sections.

(c) Associate membership, available to those who market to ASAE members, members of learned professions and others who are not full time association executives.

(d) Paying life membership, available to retired association executives who have been ASAE members for ten or more years.

(e) Non-paying life membership, which gives entitlement to a listing in the ASAE's membership directory and to discounts on certain publications.

The ASAE lists its primary responsibilities as being -

(a) To enhance the professionalism of association executives.

(b) To improve the performance of the organisations which employ ASAE members.

The Society operates on an annual budget of a little over $16 million (just over £10 million). It has reserves of $6,427,000 (about £4,300,000).

The Society is governed by bye-laws which set out the objectives, eligibility for membership, organisational structure, arrangements for collecting dues, meetings of members and voting, duties of officers, the board of directors, the executive committee, special and standing committees, the executive and staff, and finance.

Members pledge themselves to abide by a code of conduct which is set out in full below -

"As a member of the American Society of Association Executives, I pledge myself to:

- Maintain the highest standard of personal conduct.

- Promote and encourage the highest level of ethics within the industry or profession my association represents.

- Maintain loyalty to the association that employs me, and pursue its objectives in ways that are consistent with the public interest.

- Recognize and discharge my responsibility and that of my association to uphold all laws and regulations relating to my association's policies and activities.

- Strive for excellence in all aspects of management of my association.

- Use only legal and ethical means in all association activities.

- Serve all members of my association impartially, provide no special privilege to any individual member, and accept no personal compensation from a member except with the knowledge and consent of my association's governing board.

- Maintain the confidentiality of privileged information entrusted or known to me by virtue of my office.

- Refuse to engage in, or countenance, activities for personal gain at the expense of my association or its industry or profession.

- Always communicate association internal and external statements in a truthful and accurate manner.

- Cooperate in every reasonable and proper way with other association executives, and work with them in the advancement of the profession of association management.

- Use every opportunity to improve public understanding of the role of associations."

The Society lists member benefits in five categories.

The first category is information and resources. It operates Information Central which is described as the nation's leading information clearing house on association management. Information Central staff provide a wide range of information and have access to a large library. Among the major publications are a monthly magazine, *Association Management*, *Leadership*, a yearly magazine aimed at strengthening the partnership between association staff and elected leaders, and *Who's Who in Association Management*, a comprehensive directory of association executives and suppliers to the association community.

The second category of benefits is organisational resources. ASAE salaries administration, association evaluation and consulting services help identify problem areas within an association and establish objectives for improving performance. An executive search service is offered and a directory is maintain of current association job earnings. Other services include "legal first aid", assistance with basic accounting and tax questions, and relevant research conducted through the ASAE Foundation.

The third category of benefits is representation. The ASAE is the representative body for associations and is recognised as such by policy makers and the media. It helps to interpret laws and regulations and represents the industry before Congress, federal agencies, state governments and the media.

The fourth category of benefits is related to professional development. The opportunities for professional development include attending meetings and conferences and many specialist educational programmes and seminars. A qualification is offered in the form of a Certified Association Executive (CAE). The ASAE makes various awards for industry leaders in a way typical of American organisations.

Finally, membership of the Society offers insurance and money savings opportunities. There were fourteen insurance plans covering risks such as professional liability, property and casualty, group major medical, life, dental, disability, retirement, executive deferred compensation, savings and convention cancellation insurance. Discounts are available on a wide variety of goods and services and an executive travel service is offered giving up to 25% discount on accommodation in hotels and on car rentals. Other services cover investment and leasing.

The Society has ten specialist sections: chapter relations, communications, education, finance and administration, government relations, international, legal, marketing, meetings and expositions and membership. Most of these sections publish a bimonthly newsletter, have regular meetings and publish a networking and resource directory.

OTHER INTERNATIONAL ASSOCIATIONS

A world congress of association executives is held every other year with various national associations taking responsibility for the organisation. The congress covers both issues relevant to international associations and major issues facing national associations.

The ASAE's *Who's Who in Association Management and Buyers' Guide 1994* lists ten of its international affiliates -

Australian Society of Association Executives
Brazil Society of Association Executives
Canadian Society of Association Executives

Study Centre of Directors of Professional Associations (France)
Dominican Association of Executive Directors of Entrepreneurial Organisations
European Society of Association Executives
National Association of Executives of Business Association Chambers (Mexico)
New Zealand Society of Association Executives
Philippine Society of Association Executives
Society of Association Executives (United Kingdom)

PUBLICATIONS ON TRADE ASSOCIATIONS

The trade association sector in the UK is comparatively small and it is not well served by literature, certainly when compared with the USA. There is no substantive regular publication devoted to association management and the subject rarely merits mention in more wide ranging management journals such as *Management Today*. The Society of Association Executives publishes a short regular newsletter, *Association*, and a commercial publisher publishes a similar document, *Institute Forum*. *Association Quest* is a relatively new publication which covers association management, biased towards conventions. Public policy issues are of course well covered in journals such as *The Economist*. *Public Policy Review*, which is published eight times a year, does give specific coverage to the handling of public policy issues.

The major publisher of directories is CBD Research Limited. Its major annual publication is the *Directory of British Associations* which runs to over 600 pages. This lists associations, societies, institutes, chambers of commerce and similar organisations which have a voluntary membership. It gives concise but comprehensive information about each organisation including the type of organisation and its areas of interest. The company also publishes a series of other directories including the *Directory of European Industrial and Trade Associations* and *Pan-European Associations*.

Trade Associations Organisations and Publications

Society of Association Executives
Courtleigh
Westbury Leigh
Wiltshire BA13 3TA
Publisher of:
    Handbook and List of Members
    Association

European Society of Association Executives
Weinbergstrasse 31
CH 8006
Zurich
Switzerland

American Society of Association Executives
1575 Eye Street, NW
Washington
DC 20005-1168
USA
Publisher of:
    Association Management (monthly)
    International News (bi-monthly)
    The ASAE CEO Center Letter (quarterly)
    Who's Who in Association Management and Buyers' Guide (annual)
    Association Fact Book 1993
    Principles of Association Management, 1988
    Assess Your Strengths and Weaknesses, 1988
    Starter Kit for Societies of Association Executives Forming
        Outside the United States (1993/94)

Public Policy Review
17 Ashlake Road
London SW16 2BB

Institute Forum
The Chameleon Press Ltd
5-25 Burr Road
London SW18 4SG

Association Quest
58-60 Rivington Street
London EC2A 3AY

CBD Research Ltd
15 Wickham Road
Beckenham
Kent BR3 2JS
Publisher of:
    Directory of British Associations
    Directory of European Industrial and Trade Associations
    Pan-European Associations

CHAPTER 6

International Trade Associations

International trade associations exist for most major industrial sectors. With a few exceptions, in particular those concerned with activities that cross national boundaries, such as transport and travel, they do not have a representative function in the same way as national associations. The primary objective of most of them is to facilitate an exchange of information and to promote contact at the international level. The organisation and operation of international trade associations is difficult because of different market structures, languages and interests of member countries.

THEORETICAL ISSUES

Companies in an industrial sector get together at the national level through trade associations because there are certain things which those trade associations can do that the companies either cannot do or can do only at substantially higher cost. This applies particularly to representation where a single voice for an industry is many times more effective than a multitude of voices. To a lesser extent it is true in respect of certain services such as the provision of information on legislation, regulation and taxation, and the provision of services such as statistics. The same principles apply at international level. In the case of some industries there may be a need for representative work to international bodies and this is best done through international rather than national associations. There is also a need for information to be shared between countries given the increasing globalisation of the economy with common trends applying in many industrial sectors. It is necessary to develop these points in more detail.

Almost all industrial sectors are subject to some legislation and regulation at the national level and therefore national trade associations are essential. This does not apply at the international level. In most sectors there are no legislative or regulatory bodies at the international level. This is true, for example, in respect of the utilities and retailing. The main area where there is international regulation is air and sea travel which by definition are activities that to a large extent are conducted across national borders. In the case of air travel it is essential that a single set of rules applies to international flights rather than different rules being applied by different countries. The case for sea travel is somewhat less strong although still powerful.

There are some industries where regulators or legislators get together on a basis which may range from totally unofficial to official, and where therefore some representative work may need to be done at the international level. This is true for banking where regulatory measures have been proposed through the Basle Committee of Banking Supervisors. Insurance and securities trading are other areas where there is an element of de facto international regulation.

Various official international bodies, in particular the United Nations, the Organisation for Economic Co-operation and Development and the World Bank, have no legislative or regulatory power but nevertheless are influential and may require representative work at the international level. The OECD for example conducts detailed international analyses of particular sectors which can be influential. The World Bank and United Nations are particularly important in respect of developing countries, and the policies they formulate may be of considerable importance to some industrial sectors, particularly those concerned with either aid to or trade with developing countries. The World Trade Organisation is relevant to some sectors although the British view is generally channelled through the European Union.

There are many industrial sectors where there are no international bodies of any relevance but still there is a justification in having an international trade association. It can facilitate the formal exchange of information, for example through journals and newsletters, and also informal exchanges by bringing people together, for example at conferences, thereby facilitating contact between trade associations in different countries. Given the globalisation of the economy it is generally the case that common trends apply in the same industrial sectors throughout the world. Recent examples include growing concern about the environment and the increasing influence of consumerism. Governments are quick to learn from what is going on in other countries assisted by a regular programme of official visits. A policy or a programme that is seen to work in one country might be used as a model in others. In seeking to rally support for a particular policy governments are often quick to point to the experience of other countries. The sensible trade association therefore needs to be equally aware of what is going on elsewhere, perhaps to add support for its own policy proposals, perhaps to add support to government proposals, and perhaps at times to counteract government proposals. A government might for example misrepresent what is happening in other countries or it might put forward proposals that have been tried in other countries and failed.

It might seem a relatively easy task to discover what is going on in a particular industrial sector in another country. In practice this is not always easy given an unfamiliarity with the country and possibly its language. However if there is a direct personal contact between trade association executives in two countries then this facilitates the free flow of information as often all that is required is a telephone call or a fax in order to elicit a precise account of what is going on. An effective trade association representing a major industrial sector certainly needs to have an international perspective and while this can be obtained without the assistance of an international trade association the latter can provide valuable assistance.

FUNCTIONS

There are five basic functions which international trade associations can have although it is important to note that there is strong inter-relationship between them. Most international associations do not engage in all five functions and indeed, as has already been mentioned, very few are concerned with regulation and representation.

The first function, confined to a few activities, is regulation. In areas such as international air travel and shipping, an international trade association may have a regulatory function in relation to certain contractual terms and standards. However, in the same way that it is difficult for a national trade association to act as a regulator so it is more difficult for an international association to do so because there will always be a temptation for some countries to ignore the agreed standards with little scope for action to be taken against them.

One of the best known regulatory international trade associations is in fact an inter-governmental organisation, OPEC, the Organisation of Petroleum Exporting Countries. This has sought to influence the price of oil by holding down supply but it has not been effective other than in the short term precisely because some countries have opted out of the arrangements.

In the transport field the International Air Transport Association, the International Chamber of Shipping and the International Shipping Federation are influential bodies in the regulation of air travel and shipping.

The second function is that of representation, in particular to international bodies such as the United Nations and its various agencies, the OECD, the World Bank and the World Trade Organisation. It will often be difficult for international trade associations to come to a common view in which case national trade associations will make their own points. There may however be areas where an entire industry does have a single view which can then accurately be represented to whichever international body is relevant. An international trade association can also help international bodies by providing objective information and being a central point of contract.

The third function is the commissioning of research projects which may be related to representative work or may simply cover areas where more than one country has an interest. This function uses economies of scale although on many issues there will be no unanimity of view as to precisely what research needs to be done or how it is to be commissioned.

While many international trade associations have no involvement in regulation, representation or research, the fourth function, the provision of information, is common to almost all of them. This is largely achieved through publications, for example a regular newsletter or journal. There may well be an annual report which might include country reports from various members. A directory of members will provide a useful reference work. An international trade association may also maintain a library and relevant bibliographies so that it can quickly point its members to relevant publications in different countries.

The final function is the arranging of seminars and conferences. Some of the major international associations have regular major bi-ennial or tri-ennial conferences while others have more modest affairs, perhaps on an annual basis. For many people the international conferences have been very attractive, almost as a sort of paid for holiday, although these conferences are now rather going out of fashion with shorter more businesslike conferences being more popular. Conferences not only enable issues to be discussed thereby meeting the information function but most importantly they bring people together, and contacts made during conferences can prove useful subsequently.

 MANAGEMENT

The management of international trade associations is fraught with difficulty. All of the problems identified in Chapter 13 relating to British trade associations apply but in addition there are several others.

There is an obvious language difficulty. While English may be recognised as the universal business language there will be a requirement for documents to be translated into other languages, and for simultaneous translation at meetings, partly to satisfy national feelings. There will be a particular difficulty in communicating with some countries where translation facilities are not easily available. Many trade associations have recently been actively seeking members from the countries of Central and Eastern Europe and the former Soviet Union, whose languages are not familiar to many. Here, however, English seems to have been recognised as the common language.

Meetings are difficult and costly to arrange, when, by definition, the governing body of the organisation will have representation from all parts of the world. The chairman and the chief executive may easily be separated by thousands of miles and several time zones. Conference calls are now the generally accepted method of dealing with the problem, but they cannot replace the importance of face-to-face contact which is essential in any organisation.

International associations may well face political problems. South Africa presented a problem for many associations when it was still a political outcast. South African companies and associations have been active participants in many trade associations and actively sought such participation as a method of keeping in touch with the rest of the world. While representatives from other African and some other countries may have been willing to turn a blind eye this could be done only if everything operated on a low key basis. Some associations faced moves to expel South Africa while for others the price of having South Africa as a continuing member was the loss of membership from other countries. To a lesser extent, China and Taiwan pose a similar problem. Chinese institutions have begun to join international trade associations but generally will not do so if a Taiwanese institution is a member. There are also, of course, some national rivalries. Countries may vie for representation on the governing body and for a turn of becoming president and may exert substantial pressure. National rivalries can get translated into the international field. Where one trade association belongs to the international body it may prevent other associations from that country joining and this can cause a serious split. No international trade association is free from these sort of difficulties. They require controlling and managing with a recognition that they will never have a wholly satisfactory position.

International trade associations face a particular problem in resolving the conflict between efficiency and democracy. Countries want to be involved in the governing bodies of the organisation, in some cases because the people concerned feel they will get added prestige in their domestic market. Countries that feel they are not adequately involved may decline to participate in activities or even withdraw. Many international associations have found that the best way of dealing with these conflicts is to have an official structure involving as many people as possible and a much smaller unofficial structure which runs the association.

A typical structure is for there to be a council with at least one representative of every country in membership and often with the larger countries having more members. International councils frequently have well over a hundred members. Typically the council will have one meeting a year perhaps combined with a conference but will do little of substance other than receive reports and confirm various appointments. Nevertheless, membership of the council is often eagerly sought because of the prestige it might bring, particularly in developing countries, and because of the opportunities for foreign travel. The council may elect a smaller executive committee, ideally numbering no more than ten. This will need to represent the major countries and a sample of smaller countries. A typical format might be for the committee to comprise the officers, representatives of the three or four countries paying the largest subscriptions, and then representatives from each region. Where there are regional associations, for example covering Latin America, the Caribbean or Africa, then they may nominate an individual to be on the executive committee.

The titular head of an international association is usually called the president, although sometimes the chairman. A two or three year term of office is typical although some associations have reduced this to one year. The role of the president of an international association is difficult to fill. By definition it requires extensive international travel and a very high time commitment. Someone actively running a business would find it difficult to do justice to the job. In some cases a non-executive chairman of a leading company who previously had been chairman of the national trade body can be an ideal candidate. Often, however, international associations find great difficulty in getting the right sort of person to be president, that is someone who can spare the time and who, at the same time, is very knowledgeable about the industry and will do a good job as ambassador for the association. It is not a question of selecting the best candidate but rather of selecting the right country or group of countries and then trying to find the right candidate. Some associations have succeeded well in this respect while others have failed.

In addition to the council and the executive committee most international associations have a variety of committees covering either particular subject areas or functions, such as research and publications. Again, it helps to have a wide ranging membership of such committees as this will involve as many people as possible in the organisation. It is not essential that everyone attends all the meetings.

The chief executive of an international association generally has the title of secretary-general. Most associations have very small staffs, often no more than two or three, and some are staffed from national trade associations. The chief executive's job can range from being simply an administrator to the effective leader of the organisation who would travel extensively and become an international figure in his or her own right with the president or chairman playing a lesser role. Except in the case of those international associations which have a significant regulatory or representational role the job of being the chief executive of an international trade association is not a major one. Sometimes the job can be filled well by somebody retiring from a national association and sometimes it can be combined with a wider role in a national body. Sadly, sometimes, the position has been used to offload people who are no longer effective in a national organisation.

FINANCES

The financial arrangements for international trade associations are similar to those for national associations albeit with a number of important complications. The major complication is that there is unlikely to be a comparable basis on which to base subscriptions. Turnover or assets may be appropriate at the national level but not at the international level given that industries have very different structures. Most international associations, therefore, opt for a simple scale with a maximum figure paid by the largest members and a minimum figure, and a small number of steps in between.

Significant discretion has to be allowed to the secretariat in deciding what subscriptions to levy and on some occasions also what subscriptions to accept where a different figure is offered from the amount specified. Some smaller countries may have difficulty in meeting even modest subscriptions, either because of their own limited resources or because of exchange controls. Many international associations adopt a fairly liberal attitude, regarding it as preferable to have a large number of countries represented even if some of them are not paying the full or even any subscription.

Managing the finances of an international organisation is difficult and expensive. Payments in foreign currencies will be expensive to convert and transactions may also be difficult to trace. Many associations will stipulate that subscriptions must be paid in a single currency, either that where the institution is based or American dollars. Where there are a number of

51

members in one country then often the trade association in that country will make arrangements to collect the subscriptions and pay a bulk sum to the international association.

The finances of international associations may well hide substantial input from the larger countries, in particular the country where the organisation is based. Office facilities may not be fully charged for, travel costs may be met by the local association and sometimes national associations will also meet a significant proportion of the costs of the president when he or she is from their particular country. This is in many ways an unsatisfactory arrangement but sometimes the only basis on which an international body can continue to function.

EVALUATION

Trade associations tend to view those associations to which they belong very critically and this applies to international trade associations. They are seen as being costly, not so much in terms of the subscription but rather the travel costs and the time spent in attending meetings which often achieve very little. They can also be frustrating because of internal politics and the need to satisfy a number of countries regardless of the strength of their case.

However, they do provide an opportunity for people to get together and help to ensure an adequate flow of information between national associations. While formal meetings on an annual basis may achieve little there is much discussion in the margin of meetings and at social functions, all of which helps to keep trade association executives in particular informed about what is going on in other countries.

Provided international associations remain small and do not absorb significant resources they are generally welcomed by the national associations. Where they try to become large organisations in their own right with research staff and so on then their role is more likely to be challenged on financial grounds.

The few major international associations which have regulatory and representational functions are in a similar position to national associations. They need to be adequately resourced with an appropriate committee and management structure so as to ensure that the interests of their members are adequately represented. As with a national association, a strong chief executive is essential.

One route which some sectors, for example the insurance brokers and the savings banks, have followed is to combine European and international associations. European associations have the staffing and expertise to run international associations and there is generally a significant overlap of membership. However such an arrangement may well not be acceptable to associations in other parts of the world, particularly where American organisations dominate the international association.

CHAPTER 7

The Representative Function - Government and Regulatory Agencies

Many trade associations, and most larger ones, have as their principal objective representing their industry's interests to the government and to regulatory and other agencies. This is a skilled and complex function which requires an understanding of the decision-taking process within government and how to influence it, and expertise in determining members' interests and satisfying them that the representative function is being performed effectively. Most representative work is best done privately and at official level.

SEGMENTING THE REPRESENTATIVE FUNCTION

The representative function can be divided into three broad categories but with a substantial overlap between them.

The first broad category involves representation to official bodies, that is government departments, government agencies, regulatory bodies set up by Act of Parliament, European Union institutions, and, where relevant, international organisations. These bodies have a major influence on the way many industries operate through legislation, regulation, supervision and policy formulation.

The second category of representative work is promoting a favourable public image for the industry. The media are an obvious target for this work but there are also a range of other opinion formers including politicians, academic bodies, pressure groups, consumer groups and indeed other trade associations. Some associations also seek to represent their industry directly to the public.

Finally, some trade associations have to represent the interests of their members in discussions with other trade associations or commercial organisations. A trade association may, for example, negotiate a standard scale of fees with another trade association or may seek to settle working arrangements with a private sector body.

This chapter concentrates solely on the representative function to government and official bodies. However, the strong inter-relationship between the three types of representative work must be recognised. The public image of an industry will influence the attitude of government and regulatory bodies towards that industry, and equally the attitude of government and regulatory bodies can affect the public image. If, for example, the Office of Fair Trading or a specific industry regulatory body vocally criticises an industry then that in itself will lead to bad publicity which will adversely affect the image of the industry. Similarly, if one industry through a trade association attacks another industry then that could influence the public image of both industries and possibly also the attitude of government and regulatory bodies.

The organisation of what might be called the "public affairs" or "external relations" function is considered in the next chapter together with the last two aspects of the representative function. This chapter makes only oblique reference to representation at the European level as this is covered more fully in Chapter 9.

THE IMPORTANCE OF GOVERNMENT AND REGULATORY AGENCIES

Government and regulatory agencies are vitally important to industries and more particularly to their representative bodies.

Many industries are directly affected by primary legislation. In practice government alone is responsible for the decision to introduce primary legislation and the content of that legislation. Most secondary legislation, and certainly all important secondary legislation, is also the responsibility of the government.

The government determines tax policy, the overall level of public expenditure and the size of individual public expenditure programmes. For some industries, for example those relating to defence and the farming and construction industries, public expenditure is crucial. Other industries are greatly influenced by changes in tax policy, and almost every industry has some interest in taxation. Major tax changes such as, for example, the imposition of Value Added Tax can cause a great deal of work for almost every company in the country. Some industrial sectors will, because of the nature of their business, have a particular interest.

While the government may be elected and while it may react to public opinion it also influences public opinion. If ministers are known to feel strongly about a particular subject they can make speeches, leak stories to the press and generally seek to influence the climate of opinion, perhaps to secure a particular policy outcome.

The government also determines key public policy issues even where no legislation or regulation is involved. Even foreign policy issues can have an importance for some industries, in particular defence related ones, and changes of policy in respect of social security benefits which do not require taxation can be important for insurance companies and other financial service institutions.

The government sees itself as being in support of industry and commerce, and the sponsorship role is now taken very seriously, particularly in the Department of Trade and Industry. For most manufacturing industries, the Department of Trade and Industry is the sponsoring department. Where industries have a particular connection with a different department, for example, agriculture with the Ministry of Agriculture, Fisheries and Food, banking with the Treasury, and construction with the Department of the Environment, then that department will fulfil a sponsoring role. Agencies may also have a sponsorship function as the Building Societies Commission does in the case of building societies. The sponsorship role is difficult to describe. A sponsoring department or agency should help to represent the interests of the institutions it is sponsoring in Whitehall. This does not mean lobbying like a trade association but rather ensuring that the industry's positions are properly understood in other government departments, inter-governmental committees and so on. To some extent trade associations can undertake this work but they cannot do it as well as insiders. The Bank of England is over the years perceived as having playing an important role in sponsoring the banking industry (even to the extent of being described as its trade body), and similarly the Ministry of Agriculture, Fisheries and Food has been effective in its sponsorship capacity for the agriculture industry.

The government generally accepts a sponsorship role in respect of British industry and commerce abroad. Ministers will use foreign visits to help to promote British exports, and are often now accompanied on such visits by representatives of industry and commerce. In some cases overseas aid might be linked to the purchase of particular British goods or services. British embassies are now more active in representing the interest of British companies, and the British government represents industry and commerce in multi-lateral trade negotiations, negotiations relevant to particular industries that are predominantly international (for example, airlines and shipping) and in the European Union.

Governmental and quasi-governmental agencies can often be as important to industrial sectors as government departments themselves. Many have considerable discretionary power and that power has tended to increase over the years. One can identify a number of agencies which are particularly relevant to industrial sectors -

(a) The Bank of England for the banking industry.

(b) The Building Societies Commission for the building society industry.

(c) The Securities and Investments Board and self-regulatory organisations for investment firms.

(d) The General Medical Council for the medical profession.

(e) The Drivers' Vehicle and Licensing Centre for the motor manufacturing and motor retailing industries.

(f) The Housing Corporation for the social housing industry (the Corporation provides grants to housing associations as well as being their regulator and sponsor).

There are also some regulatory and quasi-governmental organisations which are relevant to all sectors of industry and commerce. The Office of Fair Trading is perhaps the best example. This was set up under the Fair Trading Act 1976 with a specific responsibility to promote fair trading. The Office has considerable autonomy in deciding which practices it will investigate and seek to take action against. An OFT investigation leading to a Monopolies and Mergers Commission inquiry can cause a huge amount of work for an industry even if the end result is favourable. For example, the OFT reviewed the provision of valuation and surveying services to mortgage lenders and then decided to refer the matter to the Monopolies and Mergers Commission. The report of the Commission was not unfavourable to the mortgage lending industry but costs in excess of £500,000 had to be incurred in making representations. At local level, trading standards officers and local authorities generally have certain enforcement functions which are important to some industries, for example, catering and retailing generally. Industries look for consistent application of rules and will seek to discuss contentious issues with national representative bodies of local authorities or trading standards officers.

The relationship between regulatory bodies, quangos and government is complex, and there are considerable variations not only between different institutions and the relevant government department but also between a single industry and a government department over time. Generally, the responsibilities of regulatory and other agencies will be laid down in statute, but the provisions are broad brush and will give much discretion. There may be a statutory requirement to consult with the relevant minister. Even if there is not, generally regulatory agencies and quangos will seek to maintain a close relationship with officials and ministers. There is inevitably an element of tension in the relationship between agencies and the relevant government department. The agencies will want more freedom while the government department will be concerned that they do not depart from general government policy. Quangos and regulatory agencies can "go native", that is being captured by the industries that they are supposed to regulate, or alternatively an agency may be over-zealous in regulating to the detriment of other government policies. Generally, ministers and civil servants, certainly at senior level, are likely to take a wider view of certain matters than are single purpose agencies which may take a restrictive and legalistic view.

DECISION-TAKING IN GOVERNMENT

Those seeking to influence government need to understand the decision-taking process in government. The level of understanding on this subject is low, as a result of which much trade association activity tends to be wasted. To many people, government is synonymous with Parliament which means that if one wishes to secure a change in government policy then this is best done through Members of Parliament. In reality, MPs have little influence on the vast majority of government decisions. Furthermore, ministers generally become involved only when an issue is politically important, requires primary legislation or where there is no logical answer. The majority of policy issues are handled by officials and even where a matter is ultimately determined by ministers, because they are at the top of the department, they will normally accept the advice of their officials. It is very rarely that ministers will overrule the advice of their officials. Where there is no logical answer to an issue or where there are significant political implications then officials will properly put forward a range of options with the pros and cons of each, leaving it to ministers to decide.

This does not mean that officials have usurped the powers of ministers or that officials have their own agenda; rather it means that if public policy issues are examined professionally then regardless of who is doing the examining the same end result is probable. Civil servants are expert in the handling of public policy issues. They are likely to understand the wider implications, both politically and in other respects, of policy proposals put forward by trade associations or individual organisations. Their training and experience also enables them to judge whether particular policy proposals or administrative measures would run counter to other government policies and if so for that to be taken into account. A trade association might, for example, present a perfectly reasonable case to a government department for a particular policy measure to be taken which has no public expenditure implications. At first sight the government could be expected to support such a measure. However, a trade association might well not appreciate that in order for the measure to be brought into effect there will need to be some amendments to primary legislation, which is always difficult to achieve. Alternatively, perhaps what is being proposed is contrary to a recent ministerial statement or perhaps there will be implications for another industrial sector which need to be taken into account.

The civil service system in Britain is highly professional at undertaking public policy work. Appointments are not political as is the case in many countries and promotion is now on the basis of merit. The work which civil servants do gives them a thorough training in the handling of public policy issues, and this training is relevant not only to a wide range of government departments but also to regulatory agencies and international bodies. A key feature of the British civil service is that the handling of public policy issues depends very little on individuals. Key officials are moved frequently (perhaps too frequently), but it is rarely the case that the movement of one or two key officials will have a material effect on a policy outcome. The fairly frequent movement of officials ensures that they cannot be "captured" by trade associations, and also removes any grounds for arguing that it is the personal views of officials which are determining policy.

There is a clear distinction between the functions of officials and the functions of ministers. Officials are permanent appointments. It is their function to advise ministers on key issues, either which they have identified, which ministers have identified or which may have been put to the government department by an outside body, perhaps a trade association. An effective civil servant will identify public policy issues before they get into the public eye and perhaps even before a trade association can identify them. They will seek to avoid ministers facing problems but will wish to alert ministers to problems which might have political or other important repercussions.

Ministers are very different from civil servants. They are transient, the average tenure being no more than two years. Many ministers, unlike senior civil servants, have had virtually no training in the handling of public policy issues. Unlike senior civil servants, ministers are of varying quality, from extremely good to poor. For some positions there will be a limited range of potential ministers from whom to choose (for example, a Conservative Government will want most Scottish Office and Welsh Office ministers to be MPs representing Scottish and Welsh constituencies of whom there are few). Ministers are political and ambitious. Many are looking towards the next job as well as doing their present job effectively. They have to be more concerned with the short term than the long term because they can be ministers only if they are in office and ministers have to be seen "to be doing something" about the problems of the day. In practice, some ministers are very concerned about long term issues but often these have to take second place to the more immediate policy problems.

It is helpful to mention briefly at this stage the role of special advisers. They occupy a place in the decision- making system somewhere between that of ministers and civil servants. Special advisers are appointed directly by ministers, and when a minister loses office so does the special adviser. On appointment they are temporary civil servants and are paid for out of public funds. Their seniority depends on their previous experience and ranges from fairly junior (typically people in their twenties with limited experience in the party political organisations) to more senior people with substantial experience. Almost all cabinet ministers and many other ministers have special advisers.

The role of the special adviser depends largely on the personalities involved. A basic function is to draft speeches for political audiences as these cannot be done by the minister's private office. They also liaise with each other and some have a role in briefing the press. The best political advisers have a major role as a source of new ideas, keeping the minister in touch with political opinion and generally giving political advice to the minister. They can act as a very useful sieve for the many ideas that come to a minister from political as opposed to official sources.

On major political issues the Prime Minister's Policy Unit, based at 10 Downing Street, can be influential. The Unit comprises a group of special advisers. The head of the Unit is the Prime Minister's principal political adviser and chairs regular meetings of departmental special advisers.

The decision-taking process in government is not dissimilar from that in commercial organisations. A problem will be analysed, generally using in-house staff but occasionally consultants. Alternative courses of action will be considered with the pros and cons being carefully weighed. A careful analysis of any problem by reasonably intelligent people, given agreed objectives, will generally lead to the same result so policy analysis will often conclude with a recommendation. In examining an issue, civil servants will take account of government policy generally, in particular manifesto commitments and previous ministerial statements. They will also take into account the practicality of any changes that are being proposed. It is difficult to secure primary legislation and therefore alternative routes will always be exhaustively explored before primary legislation can be contemplated. They will take into account any spin off effects for other industries, Britain's international obligations and so on. They will also have to look at the likely press and public reaction to a proposal.

If this work is properly done then in the vast majority of cases there is a logical answer. In some cases officials can in practice implement the answer but often there will be a need for formal ministerial clearance. Ministers will need to be appropriately briefed, another area in which civil servants are expert. The brief should set out all of the key facts and issues so that the accusation can never later be made that the minister was badly advised. If the brief includes a clear recommendation then ministerial approval can be a mere formality.

However, there are many issues on which ministerial approval is not a formality. These will include, for example, issues where there is no logical answer but rather where a balance has to be struck or issues where the logical answer may not be politically acceptable either in Parliament or in the country more generally. The skilful politician is the one who takes the correct decisions on such issues. Tactics are important here. It is not simply a question of deciding what the right decision is and then implementing it. There may well be a need to prepare the ground for the decision which can be done for example by the publication of consultation documents or by careful leaking of information to journalists. Even on these issues, civil servants will be skilled and can help advise ministers on the best way of achieving a very difficult objective.

It is helpful to illustrate these points. Matthew Parris, writing in the *Investors' Chronicle* on 18 February 1994, usefully illustrated ministerial action where there was no logical answer but rather a need to respond to a public policy issue effectively created by the press -

> "A couple of years have passed since the passage of one of this government's sillier pieces of legislation: the Dangerous Dogs Act. It is clear now, though it wasn't to ministers at the time, that this was a case of press and public hysteria bouncing parliament into "doing something", when doing nothing was probably the sensible response.

And that was only the last in a long line of canine crises. Do you remember the Dobermann "hound from hell" scare? Can you recall the Alsatian "wolf dog" panic? How long is it since you thought about the Rottweiler "devil dog" emergency? Is the Pit Bull Terrier "designer dog" hysteria still fresh in your mind? Can you remember how the newspapers reported horror story after horror story? ....

At the height of the national Rottweiler emergency I employed two researchers for an article I was writing. Their instructions were clear. Posing as freelance journalists they telephoned scores of randomly selected British newspapers claiming they had a story about a Rottweiler biting a child. Would the news editor be interested in taking it? Where editors expressed interest they undertook to get back to the paper with the promised lead. They then repeated the exercise with a new (random) sample of papers; but this time they claimed that the dog was a Labrador cross.

The results were striking. Almost no editor at that time was interested in a Labrador bite. "It would have to be a really vicious attack" was one response. "It would have to be a small kid, preferably a baby, and the kid would have to be in hospital."

Not so, however, with the Rottweiler story. Even a nip, it seemed, was worth reporting; and it did not have to be a child - anybody would do; even another dog as victim. My researchers were given the impression that where a mongrel mutt needed to kill, a Rottweiler needed to do little more than snarl, and that would be news.

Amateurish though our approach was, it showed beyond doubt that at least one reason why the media at the time were full of stories about Rottweilers - rather than dogs in general - biting people was that Rottweiler stories were the only ones that editors wanted to buy. An impression was being given (perhaps you remember it) that some kind of collective madness, growing by the day, was gripping Britain's Rottweiler population. In reality the madness was gripping the journalists, not the dogs. It was quite possible that the incidence and nature of dog attacks in Britain was continuing as it always had, unchanged. The only thing of which there was a "wave" was media investigation into one particular type of attack."

The media pressure led the government to introduce legislation which became the Dangerous Dogs Act. It cost the Government little. It has led to lengthy court cases concerned with establishing the exact breed of a dog. There was little "lobbying" in this exercise. Rather, an issue struck a chord with the media and therefore with MPs. The Government had to act even though it knew the legislation was silly.

A useful example of Ministers using the diversionary tactic is given in Lord Lawson's book, *The View From Number 11*. He commented that following the abolition of relief for life assurance premiums in the 1985 Budget, it was not difficult to guess that the tax-free treatment of lump sum pension payments might come next. He went on -

> "There followed the most astonishing lobbying campaign of my entire political career, devoted both to the preservation of the lump sum relief and to pension fund privileges in general".

Lord Lawson describes the campaign, which included various trade bodies and MPs. Mr Lawson was eventually convinced that he should not proceed to tax the lump sum. He went on the describe how he took action -

> "However as time went by, having experienced the awesome power of the pension fund lobby, I became increasingly convinced that a Green Paper would in practice serve only to assist the various vested interests in preserving the status quo - in other words, that reform would be more likely to be achieved by a well directed side offensive with no prior warning. And this is what, in the event, I embarked on, starting the very next year.

The side offensive began with the imposition in 1986 of a statutory limit on the size of pension fund surpluses".

Lord Lawson then went on to describe how in the 1987 Budget he levelled the playing field in two further ways, by extending the tax reliefs enjoyed by occupational pension funds to personal pensions and, under cover of this, a number of measures to stop the abuse of the tax privileges accorded to pensions, including a limit of £150,000 on tax-free lump sums. Finally, in his last Budget, he introduced a limit on contributions to occupational pensions eligible for tax relief.

The Art of Representation

A good trade association therefore does not confine itself to gathering together the views of the members and representing them to government. There is no reason to think that members of a trade association are particularly expert in knowing which way the political wind is blowing, what the upcoming regulatory issues are, and so on. It is the function of the trade association to identify such matters, to ensure that its members are fully informed about the political and regulatory framework in which they are operating, and that the policy views coming forward are in tune with this and have not been developed in a vacuum. Many trade associations fall down at this hurdle. A credibility problem arises if a reputation for pursuing lost causes develops.

The good trade association executive will, therefore, have a delicate role to play in ensuring that the members do not have unrealistic expectations, and that what they put forward to government has some chance of achieving the desired objective. Anything that requires the expenditure of more government money goes to the back of the queue unless there are overwhelming political reasons.

Any industry seeking to influence public policy, is, broadly speaking, selling a product, that is, the particular policy line they want. Their client or customer is the government. It follows that the sales technique should be that employed by any responsible salesman. The first essential is to have a good case, well presented, that is likely to be acceptable to the person buying the product. One is not dealing here with ignorant customers who will buy anything, but rather with highly expert people. While clever packaging and aggressive sales techniques might work in selling a product to someone for whom it is inappropriate, not only do they not work but they are counter-productive when used against the government.

Having done the background work how does the good trade association go about getting its views accepted in government? Again, it is like any other business relationship. Much depends on personal contact. Insulting ministers and officials does not help in this respect. There are few worse approaches than saying publicly to the minister that it is not his fault, rather "he has been badly advised", especially as the advisers concerned are likely to be sitting next to him. This way both the minister and his advisers are antagonised, probably unnecessarily and unjustifiably. Over 90% of representational work by trade associations should be with civil servants not ministers. If civil servants accept the strength of a case then it has an excellent chance of making progress. If they do not accept it then it is a major job to persuade a minister to overturn the advice of officials.

Civil servants and regulators are keen to maintain a close working relationship with trade association executives. They will accept lunch invitations (simply as a means of informal talking, not in the form of elaborate entertainment) and they will be willing to have informal discussions on a wide range of issues. Confidentiality needs to be respected on both sides. The trade association executive must establish a good track record of honesty and integrity as well as credibility in presenting the case if civil servants are to promote it. Where these relationships are established effectively it is not unknown for officials and trade association staff to exchange draft letters to each other with a view to ironing out differences before matters need to go to ministerial level.

In some trade associations there is too much emphasis on formal representative work, that is making submissions, either because the industry is seeking to promote a policy line or in response to a consultative document, and on meetings. These are of course important. However, policy submissions and meetings are more likely to be successful if essential ground work has been done first. In the same way that the President of America and the President of Russia do not meet without officials having sorted out most of the issues, so trade association representatives should not meet ministers without officials having gone through the agenda and settled as many points as possible. Some trade associations adopt a practice of seeking a meeting after they have made policy representations. The best approach is to have the meeting at an earlier stage so that it can help influence the final policy submission. Civil servants and regulators are very happy to talk with key trade associations in advance of formal submissions being made on key issues.

Sometimes in trade associations there is a temptation to concentrate almost exclusively on ministers, on permanent secretaries and other top officials. In reality the bulk of the work is done by middle ranking officials. (In the unified grading system these are grade 5 (previously assistant secretaries) and grade 7 (previously senior principals). Grade 3 staff were previously under secretaries, grade 2 staff were deputy secretaries and grade 1 were permanent secretaries. The permanent secretary title is still used with other staff having more functional titles such as head of division or director. The recent changes make it difficult to ascertain the seniority of a civil servant from his title.) The good trade association will know and maintain regular contact with all assistant secretaries relevant to their operations, quite possibly in a number of government departments. Assistant secretaries can quickly become under secretaries, deputy secretaries and permanent secretaries. They may also be future candidates for posts in the commercial sector or government quangos where they may be influential in areas of relevance to the trade association. Good relationships created with young officials will therefore serve a trade association well over many years.

Contact is not a sufficient condition to having a good working relationship with civil servants. Rather, the contact is part of the route to establishing credibility, both for an individual trade association officer and the association as an institution. An endless succession of phone calls, letters and lunches will, in themselves, achieve nothing. The trade association has to convince civil servants that it knows its sector, effectively represents its members' interests, has the confidence of the sector, understands how government works and, to some extent, can "deliver" its sector. Once this reputation is established it will quickly spread through the Whitehall machinery.

It is important to maintain contact with ministers. Again, the good trade association identifies ministers years in advance. Those MPs taking a particular interest in the relevant field should be closely monitored, kept informed of what is going on, invited to regular briefings and so on. They do not forget this when they become ministers. These relationships should be managed carefully however, with great emphasis on timely, accurate and credible briefings if they are to be sustained.

Lunching ministers is a useful part of the work of the larger trade associations. Most trade associations do this well, but a number manage to score own goals. Officials soon know which trade association lunches are worth going to, and a two line letter is often sufficient to secure acceptance by a minister. They also know which trade association lunches are not worth going to, that is typically those where a press release is issued in advance, or after, the minister is berated by opinionated people on complex issues, having been given no notice of the issues they will raise, and everybody goes away unhappy. The ideal lunch is strictly informal, with no reporting by either side (other than that the lunch has taken place), and the minister should leave in a good humour, having enjoyed his meal and having the feeling that he or she is dealing with reasonable people who had a couple of legitimate points to make. Discussion should concentrate on general issues. It is no use raising complex technical points at such lunches, unless this has been agreed in advance with officials. If such an issue is raised then it should be done so briefly, and followed up with a letter. At any meeting with a minister it is important to know the minister's personal views on the key issues being discussed. There is little point, for example, in arguing at length about a peripheral point on which the minister has strong views. Those views are not going to be changed by a good lunch. Where the minister's views differ from those of the trade association on a major point then it becomes a tactical matter; it may be wise to avoid raising the issue, at least at a social function.

It is also important to maintain close contact with relevant opposition representatives. The frontbench spokesmen, unlike government ministers, do not have a civil service to fall back on. They do have policy advisers and they also use a network of academics and others to help formulate policy proposals. It is necessary to use all of these channels and to offer whatever assistance one can to the opposition, including commenting in confidence on policy proposals. This should not be seen as conspiring against the government but rather giving opposition parties the information they need to produce sensible policy proposals. Once an illogical proposal has found its way into the manifesto then it is likely to be implemented, even if after the election it is accepted that it is inappropriate.

RESPONDING TO CONSULTATION AND POLICY DOCUMENTS

In exercising the representative function to government, trade associations have to participate in many consultation exercises. Generally, responses will be in writing although they can be supplemented and occasionally replaced by an oral response.

In responding to any consultation exercise an association should have four very broad objectives -

(a) To make a timely response. The time scale can vary from instant over the telephone to a period of years. There is certainly no point in making a response after an issue has been settled.

(b) To represent fairly the views of members, if necessary where there are conflicting views by indicating the range. Perhaps more properly it can be said that the objective is to represent the interests of the members and as far as possible to ensure that they coincide with their views. There is a feeling in some trade bodies that they have to give a single view even though this does not represent a significant proportion of their members. Where this is done then the members themselves will make their own views known and the result is invariable confusion on the part of those receiving the messages. It is better that a trade association states fully and frankly the full range of its members' views, indicating which particular groups of members hold what views.

(c) To provide good quality responses that address the issues being raised, written in a user-friendly way.

(d) To ensure that policy responses are consistent with each other and the general policy of the association. There is little point in making some hard hitting comments on a particular government proposal if it can be observed that the association has made precisely the opposite points at another time.

There are two basic types of consultation exercise with often both types being used for the same issue -

(a) Informal consultation which may be confidential between the secretariat of the trade association and a government department or agency. A department may, for example, conduct a pre-consultation exercise with the secretariat on a consultation paper before it is issued more generally so as to ensure that it is in as near final form as possible and does not raise unnecessary concerns and does not have obvious errors. There is also consultation on the telephone when instant responses are required. On informal consultations the secretariat may consult relevant practitioners.

(b) Formal consultation exercises where there is a published consultation document.

For formal exercises it is most sensible if a nominated member of the secretariat takes responsibility for each exercise. It is the job of the person concerned to ensure that the response meets the various objectives set out above. This does not simply mean sending the document to members and inviting their views, as if this method was used in many cases many trade associations would have no response at all and would have inconsistent or inaccurate responses on others. Rather, when the consultation document or a summary of it is being circulated the secretariat should, at the same time, indicate the main areas of interest to the members, the established policy of the association and issues on which comments would be particularly welcome. Individual members may well wish to make their own direct responses. There is nothing wrong in this although it is helpful if they are sent to the trade association and taken into account in its response. Provided the trade association's response is seen to represent the interests of all of the members and is of a high quality then it would always carry more weight than a response from a particular member of the association. If, however, the association fails to exercise its responsibilities effectively then it will be supplanted by individual members making their views known.

The secretariat should generally be able to draw up a response on its own initiative taking account of views of members. Ideally this is then circulated to the relevant committee or panel or occasionally to all of the members for comment before being finalised. Some associations have a ritual of the final response being formally approved by a committee or a board. This may be appropriate but should be unnecessary given a competent secretariat. The timescale for exercises is such that often it is not possible to put a final document before the governing body of an association.

Like any other document, the response to a consultation exercise should be as user-friendly as possible. It is helpful initially to indicate the interest of the trade association in the exercise. Although this may be obvious to a government department or regulatory agency the response is likely to be read by other people who will not immediately be aware of the particular interest that the association has in the exercise. Ideally the response should include a summary of the key points which can be used as a stand-alone document and can, for example, be included in a monthly newsletter to members. The key issues are best dealt with in a separate section so that the reader of the response is very clear what the main issues of concern are to the association. There are bound to be many comments on detailed points and these are best described as such.

Ideally, the response to a consultation exercise should be a stand-alone document which should not require the original consultation paper in order to be understood. While writing it predominantly for a civil service or regulatory audience it may also have a much wider audience and should be written accordingly. In addition to sending copies of the response to the relevant government department or agency it should be sent to any other relevant government department or agency, other relevant trade bodies and, if necessary, press released as well.For example, if the Association of British Insurers is responding to a Department of the Environment consultation exercise on environmental liability then it will want to send this document also to the Department of Trade and Industry as its sponsoring department, to the European Commission which has an interest in this area, to relevant MPs and MEPs, to the other trade associations with which it works, to Lloyd's of London, and to selected journalists.

Many consultation exercises are conducted rapidly, and it is a common complaint of trade associations that they do not have enough time to respond to government documents. There is little point in complaining. A balance has to be struck in meeting the various objectives set out earlier in this section. There is no point in producing a magnificent response carefully addressing all of the issues in a logical way and fully setting out the views of members if it is completed too late to have an impact on the decision taking process. Equally, there is no merit in making a quick response if this does not adequately reflect the interests of members. The overriding objective must be to represent the interests of members. This necessarily involves using a combination of the expertise of the secretariat in regulatory issues and representative work and the views and practical experience of members.

The Role of Members

What role, if any, do members have in this process? They do, of course, control the policy direction, but they also have a more direct role in the representative process. It is a weak trade association that believes that its members should leave everything to it. An industry body and its members must work closely together if they are to get the right results in terms of public policy. Sometimes, the actions of individual companies can be damaging to the whole industry's case. Government wants a single view, not half a dozen. If the industry is simultaneously making one case through its trade body, while its members are putting a different case directly through any number of means, then the industry's voice is greatly diminished, and the credibility of the trade body is undermined for the future.

In many industries it is the case that the way that they operate and their bottom line are likely to be as influenced by regulatory measures over the next few years as by anything they do or by market developments. Handling of public policy issues should therefore have a high priority. This is a two-way process. Somebody in a company should be responsible for identifying trends in public policy relevant to the company. To a large extent, companies can rely on their trade associations for this.

In many industries, the larger companies find it helpful to have an expert on public policy issues. This person might be the head of public affairs or he or she might have other responsibilities such as being company secretary or in charge of marketing. It is very important that where this work is done, it is done at a suitably high level and that there is an adequate quality check on public policy work to ensure that what is being said is sensible and in tune with the overall company views. What associations sometimes find is that policy views come from one particular quarter in a company. For example, if there is a consultative document on taxation, the views may come from the tax department which may be more interested in administrative matters than in minimising the tax burden on the company. On some policy issues, sometimes there can be more than one view coming from the same company with it being clear that there has been no proper consultation within the company. Companies need to be more sophisticated in how they handle public policy issues, and equally trade associations have to be more sophisticated in helping companies to do this by properly targeting requests for information and preparing suitable papers for consideration.

Companies should contribute to the formulation of industry views on public policy issues. Relevant policy documents, consultation documents and so on should be closely studied and a view given to the trade association and, ideally, directly as well, particularly if it does not conflict too much with the overall industry view. This work also pays useful dividends for companies, giving them an early warning of impending policy developments. Companies can play a more major role through direct involvement in the trade association's committees and panels. This is time consuming and therefore costly. On the other hand, it does give companies an early insight into the way public policy is developing, and perhaps that vital few months in which to change systems or policies before the companies that are a little slower catch up with what is going on.

BIBLIOGRAPHY AND FURTHER READING

Peter Hennessy, *Whitehall* (London: Martin Secker & Warburg, 1989).

Sarah Hogg and Jonathan Hill, *Too Close to Call* (London: Little, Brown and Company, 1995).

Gerald Kaufman, *How to be a Minister* (London: Sidgwick & Jackson, 1980).

Nigel Lawson, *The View from No.11* (London: The Bantam Press, 1992).

CHAPTER 8

The Representative Function - Influencing the Climate of Opinion

Trade associations need to represent the interests of their members to relevant opinion formers both because of the influence which opinion formers have on government and regulatory bodies and to try to secure a favourable business climate for their members. Who the relevant opinion formers are varies from industry to industry. Some associations also negotiate on behalf of their members with other trade associations and non-regulatory agencies, but this work has been declining in the face of regulatory action and growing competitive pressures.

THE IMPORTANCE OF OPINION FORMERS AND INFLUENCING THE CLIMATE OF OPINION

A favourable climate of opinion is helpful to the members of any trade association. People are more likely to buy goods and services from a sector which is seen to be "a good thing" rather than one which is constantly the target for public criticism. A good example is the way that building societies have benefited by trading on their image at the expense of banks. A favourable climate of opinion is also helpful for staff morale. People do not like working in an industry which is constantly subject to criticism, but do like working in an industry which is seen to be working for the public good. Perhaps more importantly, an adverse climate of opinion, whether justified or not, makes it more likely that there will be adverse regulatory and legislative measures.

Politicians respond to short term situations. If they see some advantage in taking action against an unpopular section of the community, however unjustified this might be, they will not hesitate to do so. The attitude of the Treasury towards bank lending to small businesses is a good example of this force at work. At a more mundane level is the example given in the previous chapter of the Dangerous Dogs Act. There was no justification for the Dangerous Dogs Act but dangerous dogs, and even dogs that were not dangerous, had a bad public image and as there was no substantive lobby in their favour penal legislation was implemented against them.

A favourable climate of opinion cannot be created in isolation. Almost every industrial sector is subject to some criticism. The view of many in the sector is that the critics do not understand and that a public relations campaign is needed to get over the message. Often, however, the critics do understand, and it is people in an industry, too close to events, who do not understand what is going on. An essential part of the work of a trade association is to ensure that the members are aware of the climate of opinion outside and to persuade the members that it is not all down to public relations. Rather, policies and practices must constantly be re-examined, preferably with the perspective of an outsider, and changes implemented where necessary.

The function of influencing the climate of opinion can be likened in military terms to an invasion. One does not invade by setting off in an armada and hoping that everything will be all right on the day. Rather, extensive intelligence work is needed to assess where the invasion should take place, careful training and preparation is needed for all of the personnel who will be involved, some behind the lines work may be needed in particular on the day or two before the invasion to break enemy communication lines, and some subterfuge may be needed, for example to persuade the enemy either that an invasion will not take place or that it will take place somewhere else. Without this groundwork any invasion is bound to fail. Similarly, without the groundwork of influencing the climate of opinion the more direct representative work of a trade body is likely to fail. Policy representations are more likely to be successful if they are made in circumstances where there is a generally favourable attitude towards the industrial sector. However good the representations might be they will be discounted to some extent if the sector or the trade association is unpopular.

AN OVERVIEW OF OPINION FORMERS

This section briefly summarises the key categories of opinion formers. How they can be influenced is dealt with in more detail subsequently for each of the sections.

The following categories of opinion formers can be identified -

(a)   Journalists. Journalists both report news and create their own news stories, often on issues which people within an industry would rather were not reported. Small industries generally need to be concerned only with the trade press unless there is some major event whereas bigger industries have to deal with the trade press and also the national media.

(b)   Opposition parties. Opposition parties are badly resourced compared with the government. On the one hand they are concerned with dealing with current political issues with often the government setting the agenda. However, they will also be preparing for power themselves. They may choose to raise particular issues which have implications for specific industrial sectors.

(c)   Politicians. MPs are part of the legislative process but as the previous chapter has suggested their role in influencing legislation is often comparatively small. They have a secondary role as opinion formers. Like the press they have power to develop issues of their own, and because of the contacts they have with other opinion formers their views on any issue are likely to be passed on to others.

(d)   Academics. Academics are concerned largely with influencing other academics but some have a major interest in public policy issues, and their independence can give them an important place in discussion of key issues. Some academics are also well plugged into the party political machinery.

(e)   Research bodies. Over recent years there has been a proliferation of bodies which exist purely to study and influence public policy. A few such bodies are aligned with particular parties or sections of parties or political philosophies. Other bodies are studiously non-political and seek influence through the quality of their research. These bodies are probably having an increasing influence on the development of public policy.

(f)   Consumer bodies. The Consumers Association (a private sector body), the National Consumer Council (a government funded body) and the National Association of Citizens Advice Bureaux (a private body with government funding) all have an important influence on the public policy debate. There are a number of smaller consumer bodies which are also important, particularly for certain sectors.

(g)   Pressure groups and trade associations. The rise of one-issue pressure groups has been a significant development in the political process in recent years. By concentrating on a single subject, generally ignoring wider implications, they are often able to have a big impact. Recently, for example, groups supporting animal welfare have been able to influence public policy, and also through direct action have been able to disrupt a lawful business. Other trade associations also come into the category of opinion formers particularly where there is an overlap of business between associations.

AN OVERVIEW OF INFLUENCING OPINION FORMERS

Influencing opinion formers is not dissimilar from influencing government. It is not a question of elaborate entertaining but rather of ensuring that one has a good case and putting it over well. Perhaps the essential difference between influencing government and influencing opinion formers is that there is more scope to be proactive with opinion formers. Much of the contact with government is on the government's agenda, and the government can, at the end of the day, decide what action it will or will not take. By contrast, opinion formers, taken together, have more wide ranging interests and may well be interested in considering and discussing ideas at an earlier stage than would the government.

Information is the key to influencing opinion formers. The same information can be used to influence a wide range of opinion formers and also government. A trade association should always have at its fingertips all of the relevant information about its members and the markets in which they operate. Accurate statistics, well presented and carefully analysed, are a vital part of the information for most industries. A trade association that can control the flow of statistics is in a strong position to influence the public debate. Statistics must also be readily accessible. An authoritative annual statistical publication and a regular quarterly bulletin with the same tables in the same place in each edition are valuable in ensuring that opinion formers in a wide range of areas have the key up-to-date information about the industry. It is also important that staff within the trade association know their way round statistics and other information and can quickly give enquirers the information that they are seeking and, more importantly, which the association wants them to have.

Information about the products of the members is also essential. Where products are directly bought by consumers then a range of consumer leaflets will not only be helpful for consumers themselves but also to those who advise them, to the press and to MPs. For associations representing sectors which are not directly selling to consumers then well presented authoritative literature about the products and their importance can be helpful.

Statistical publications are usefully supplemented by regular monthly or quarterly newsletters and are also by a healthy trade press, particularly where it is not trying to create controversy.

As with government, contact is also important. An effective trade association will know all relevant opinion formers whether they be university professors, MPs, journalists or leaders of various pressure groups. Regular contact over informal lunches can help keep the trade association up to date on what others are thinking and also help get the industry message over.

Ideally, a trade association will have a strategy for dealing with opinion formers. This will cover all of the various target groups mentioned above, identifying key people and institutions, describing the relevant publications which will be produced and also the programme for regular contacts with all opinion formers.

THE MEDIA

The media probably counts as the most important group of opinion formers, certainly for those associations concerned with major public policy issues and which are constantly in the public eye. However, it is wrong to view the media as a single group of institutions which need to be treated in the same way. The media can usefully be divided into the following categories -

(a)   National press - specialist correspondents. These are particularly important in areas where there is substantial advertising, for example financial services and motoring, as the amount of copy written about any section depends to a large extent on the amount of advertising. The specialists normally know their subjects well and will be partially dependent on the contacts which they have with the industry.

(b)   National press - news reporters and investigative journalists. There is a wholly separate category of journalists in the national press, that is those who do not cover particular subjects but rather who look for news. Some broadsheets even have their own dedicated teams of investigative journalists who might over a period of years pursue a wide range of issues which are not directly related with each other. Often, there is no ongoing contact with this group.

(c)   National TV and radio. To a limited extent the same subdivision can be made as for the press although it is less pronounced in radio and television because the amount of editorial time is not at all related to the volume of advertising. Radio and television journalists often have to work to much tighter timetables than their colleagues on the national newspapers.

(d)   Local press and radio. Local newspapers have been in existence for very many years and often are of little relevance to trade associations except those that represent an industry with a strong local interest. Local radio stations are a relatively new phenomenon. Local radio and TV are seldom likely to be critical of an industry and give a valuable opportunity for getting over the message through syndicated articles and interviews.

(e)   Trade press. The trade press varies considerably in quantity and quality. For some sectors there is only a very limited trade press, and it might effectively be under the control of the trade association or in any event be so closely tied to the fortunes of the industry that it will do little more than report news and educate. Other industries have a huge trade press, finance being probably the best example. Here journalists are able to be more critical, and in many respects are not dissimilar to their counterparts in the national press. Indeed, many aspire to move from the trade press to the national press.

Most trade associations of any size and which deal with matters which are of public interest have a press officer who will deal with all of these various categories, but they need handling in separate ways.

Particularly with journalists, having readily available information is of key importance. Journalists are not inclined to keep press releases or anything else which is sent to them, and even when they do they are seldom able to find them. Annual or quarterly publications which become accepted as the bible on a particular subject are therefore particularly helpful. Some trade associations produce extensive loose leaf folders for journalists which can be useful although they tend to have a limited life and attempts to keep them up to date are seldom successful, either because the trade association fails to do so or because journalists fail to put new information into the folder. Often, when they want information journalists will telephone a trade association. The good trade association will be able to respond instantly to requests for information from a journalist. If statistical information is required often this can be faxed while other information can be given over the telephone.

However, journalists do not just want information on key policy issues; they also want comment which has to be meaningful and which often can come only from the chief executive or another senior executive. A good press officer can probably deal with 80 or 90% of press queries and knows when to hand over to a more senior person when an attributable comment or background on a topical issue is needed.

Where a trade association is in the public eye then a key part of the work of the chief executive and other senior executives will be dealing with the press. They do not have the option of refusing to talk to the press. They have to be accessible, if necessary interrupting other meetings and work in order to give live radio or TV interviews or interviews which are to be recorded for subsequent broadcasting.

The secretariat must be given full authority to deal with the press. A stance of not being able to comment until members of a board or executive committee or even a public relations committee have been consulted is not acceptable. Sometimes trade association executives will get it wrong in talking with the press and will frequently be quoted out of context or even misquoted. Memories tend to be relatively short and unless a huge error has been made generally no damage is done. The good trade association will aim to ensure that 80 to 90% of the work which is does with the media is beneficial and that which does not seem to come out right at the time has to be set against the beneficial work which is done.

It is necessary to have a basis of trust with key journalists, and this can be achieved only with direct contact. Frequently this is done over lunch. Journalists used to be renowned for long and frequently alcoholic lunches. These are now very rare as the pressures on journalists have increased, including have to type their own stories, as they have on everyone else. Also, the dispersion of the press from Fleet Street makes contact more difficult. However, informal lunches and occasionally dinners still remain an important way of establishing contact and trust so that the journalist can trust the information he or she is receiving and the trade association can trust that it will not be misused.

Most information and quotes given to journalists can be used "on the record", but frequently a journalist can be helped by being given background information which should not be reported or "off the record" information which can be used but not attributed. On issues which are critical of an industry the trade association executives cannot be seen to be making critical comments about their own industry yet their own credibility is threatened if they attempt to pretend that everything is in order and that there are no problems. An "off the record" briefing can make what otherwise have been a very critical story less critical.

OPPOSITION PARTIES

Those trade associations which do not deal with major public policy issues need spend little time on opposition parties, and the opposition parties are likely to wish to spend little time with them. Where however big public policy issues are involved that are raised in Parliament and are the subject of political debate then it is essential that a trade association has a good working relationship with the principal opposition party and with other opposition parties. Where a trade association predominantly works in Scotland, Wales or Northern Ireland then it will wish to maintain a close relationship with the Scottish National Party, the Welsh National Party and the multitude of Northern Ireland parties.

In the short term the opposition can influence the course of legislation and raise issues at the political level. Many parliamentary bills are relatively uncontentious notwithstanding votes on political lines at some key stages of the debate. If the principal opposition party broadly supports legislation then its passage through Parliament will be easier and the government will be more inclined to bring forward legislation. It is not unknown for trade associations to be told that legislation will be forthcoming only if the industry is united behind it and if there will be not significant opposition. It is therefore important to keep the opposition fully briefed on any proposals that the trade association might have for legislation and on its views on the government's proposals. Obviously the trade association will endeavour to persuade the opposition party that what is happening is entirely in line with its own policies.

Opposition parties can be used to oppose legislation although this is seldom very effective and is a high risk strategy because of the damage which might be done to relations with the government. However, there will be some issues where the natural ally of the trade association will be the opposition parties, and through vigorous opposition in Parliament they can make it difficult for the government to implement its proposals. Trade unions traditionally have worked with Labour oppositions to oppose certain policies of the Conservative government often with some success. The defeat of the attempt to privatize the Royal Mail is a good example.

Opposition parties can also be used to raise issues to the political level. Questions can be raised in the House, Early Day Motions can be put down, issues can be put forward for an Adjournment Debate and the opposition may use its Supply Day time to raise an issue.

In addition to briefing the principal opposition party about current issues the party also has to be recognised as the government in exile, and throughout its period in opposition will be formulating proposals to implement when it comes into power. A trade association should be fully plugged into this process, seeking to ensure that the opposition fully understands its viewpoint and the effect of the policies it is proposing. Opposition parties are not well resourced and may be inclined to come up with policies which are superficially attractive and might make their appearance in an election manifesto but which would prove impossible to implement, or if they were implemented would cause major consequences for the members of a trade association which could severely damage their interests. The association therefore needs to ensure that opposition parties are fully aware of the consequences of what they are proposing. A useful tactic is to suggest that policies which are opposed will work against other policies of the party.

Maintaining contact with opposition parties is not easy because there is no formal structure. The major trade associations will be able to have meetings with opposition front bench spokesmen and MPs who show a particular interest in a subject. The party committees in the House of Commons are a valuable forum. Front bench spokesmen may have personal full time advisers and also will have a network of unpaid advisers including typically academics and journalists. It is sensible for a trade association to identify the key advisers to the leading opposition spokesman relevant to its field and to develop a relationship with them, ensuring that they are adequately briefed and have whatever information they require.

Confidential discussions with civil servants and ministers should not of course be reported to opposition spokesmen. Equally, where a trade association has offered to give technical help to an opposition spokesman it should not give details of this to the government of the day. At times a trade association will find itself working on proposals which are not in the best interests of its members but nevertheless it is sensible to do so in order to ensure that they are as least damaging as possible. The preparation of "anonymous" position papers which can be fed into the opposition's debate on policy issues is a useful tactic.

MEMBERS OF PARLIAMENT AND PEERS

The previous chapter covered the work of trade associations in dealing with government and the previous section dealt with opposition parties. It may perhaps seem paradoxical that MPs should in their own right be described as opinion formers; this needs some explanation.

MPs have a comparatively modest influence on most legislation. It is government which decides to introduce legislation and through the whipping system the government generally gets its way. Legislation is seldom amended significantly in its passage through Parliament except at the instigation of the government. However, it is fair to say that the situation has changed a little over the last few years largely as a consequence of the government having a small majority and also being seen to be weak. On issues where Conservative MPs have threatened rebellion the government has had to bow to their wishes. On some social issues, for example disability, Parliament has made the running and forced the government to introduce its own legislation. Most trade associations do not handle the sort of issues which lend themselves to parliamentary support against the wishes of the government. They can also seldom be instrumental in causing legislation to be brought forward although they can certainly be helpful to a government which is inclined to do this anyway. When legislation is going through Parliament MPs should be properly briefed about it and their assistance sought in amending it where appropriate, but generally it is more productive to work with the official government machinery through the civil service.

MPs are important to trade associations because most ministers are chosen from the ranks of MPs. Ministers are seldom chosen for their expertise in a particular subject, and therefore it is not easy for a trade association to identify years in advance which new MPs might be their minister in the years ahead. However, the sensible association will identify MPs who are likely to make rapid progress, something which can be done by following what is going on in Parliament, reading the quality press and journals such as *The Economist*. Where an MP who has developed a good working relationship with a trade association and respects that association becomes a minister in whatever field then it can be helpful to the trade association's interests in the long term.

Because of their status MPs are important to trade associations as opinion formers. They may not have a huge direct impact on legislation and most never occupy senior government positions. However, each MP has the potential to be a significant opinion former. They can raise issues in Parliament through asking parliamentary questions and putting down early day motions as well as contributing to debates. MPs can contribute to the public debate even by issuing press releases. More generally they spend much of their time talking with other opinion formers, in particular journalists, and they also have the access to ministers and the principal opposition spokesmen. If an MP chooses to pursue a particular issue vigorously then often he or she can have quite a major impact even if the issue concerned is relatively small.

For all these reasons trade associations need to influence MPs. The first stage of this process is to identify those MPs with an interest in their subject. This can be done by studying one of the biographical guides of MPs, by observing who asks parliamentary questions and participates in parliamentary debates and monitoring the press. Often MPs with a particular interest in a subject will directly approach the relevant trade association. Where a trade association is concerned with an issue which is geographically concentrated then local MPs can be expected to have an interest. Having identified relevant MPs they need to be supplied with regular briefing material. This should be short because MPs do not have the time to read everything that is sent to them. A short brief of one or two pages as a stand alone document, personalized as far as possible and giving contact numbers for further information, can be helpful. A learned 60-page academic study without a good summary is unlikely to make much impact.

Individual MPs can be invited to meetings or lunches and opportunities can be sought to meet with groups of MPs with an interest in a particular subject. All-party and backbench committees can be useful in this respect. They meet regularly generally in the House of Commons, and although MPs are inclined to come and go there is a valuable opportunity to influence a number of relevant MPs quite quickly.

A trade association should also make its information services available to MPs, but they must ensure that they have a place in a system which will deal promptly with MPs requests for information whether by telephone or in writing. In this respect MPs are not unlike journalists and often work to similar timetables because of an issue which is being raised in Parliament.

What has been said in this section about MPs is, for the most part, also applicable to peers. They are less political than MPs in that there is not the fierce political debate in the Lords that there is in the Commons. Unlike MPs, peers cannot lose their seats so there is the opportunity to build long term relationships. Most of the politically active peers are former MPs, and contacts made at that stage will continue to be useful.

UNIVERSITIES AND RESEARCH BODIES

Academics might seem remote from the work of trade associations and the vast majority are. However, there are a small number of academics who influence the big policy debate both directly and indirectly. Indirectly, academic research can be used to assist trade associations in putting forward a case to government, and equally it can be used to assist pressure groups and others seeking to change the practices of an industry against the wishes of a trade association. The housing field is a good example where academic studies have been used to support public policy arguments. Some academics will deliberately seek to participate in the public policy debate, and their independent academic status can give them credibility.

The point was made in the section on the opposition that it relies to some extent on academics. In this respect academics are more directly involved in the political debate.

78

A trade association should identify those academics with an interest in its subject and maintain contact with them. It should ensure that they have any regular publications and that they are given any information that they seek to help in their research. It can make sense to involve them in trade association activities, for example seminars and conferences. Also, academics can be invited to social functions to meet practitioners in the industry.

Trade associations can be pro-active with academics. They can commission studies to help them pursue certain arguments. This itself will help draw the academics closer to the trade association although without prejudicing their independence. Some trade associations fund research scholarships and some also fund academic posts. Generally, an association will benefit in proportion with the number of good academics there in their particular area. However, as with so many other areas this is a question of resources. Funding a university chair or a fellowship is so expensive such that most associations cannot contemplate it. Funding research studentships is much cheaper but correspondingly brings less benefit to an association. As association can probably best spend its money by providing a good quality service to those academics in the field already, drawing on those academics for "quick and dirty" studies when these are needed. The better informed the academics are to begin with the more they can contribute to the public policy debate.

Over the last decade or so the role of research institutes in the public policy debate has grown considerably, and now a trade association will probably pay as much attention to these bodies as it will to academics in universities. There are in any event strong links between research bodies and universities.

Two long standing "think tanks" have direct relationships with the political parties. The Bow Group and the Fabian Society have links with the Conservative Party and the Labour Party respectively. These institutions have operated with a very small staff, their publications being written by their members and they are very political in nature. Many authors of Bow Group and Fabian Society pamphlets have gone on to become senior government ministers.

The Institute of Economic Affairs is one of the long established think tanks. It is an unashamed free market body, which has commissioned a huge range of publications on every aspect of public policy. The Institute was at its strongest in the 1970s and early 1980s when it contributed in no small part to the ascendancy of the free market argument. As other think tanks have developed and as the IEA's views have become more established so, paradoxically, it has probably lost influence.

The largest think tank today is the Policy Studies Institute (PSI) which describes itself as one of Europe's largest independent research organisations undertaking studies of social, economic and industrial policy and the workings of political institutions. The PSI is not associated with any political party, pressure group or commercial interest. It was formed in

1978 through a merger between Political and Economic Planning and the Centre for Studies in Social Policy. It describes its mission as being to inform the policy making process through the conduct of high quality research and active dissemination of research results. It undertakes research only on the basis that the results will be made public. In the year to 30 September 1994, the Institute received grants of £4,256,000. It publishes three or four substantive publications every month. Its researchers also publish articles in other publications.

The Institute of Fiscal Studies specializes in tax matters and operates in a similar way to the Policy Studies Institute although in a narrower field. Its objectives are to promote and disseminate research into the economic implications of tax and fiscal policy in Britain and elsewhere and to bridge the gap between practitioners, economists and policy makers. Its annual budget is in the region of £1,500,000.

Two think tanks have connections with the Labour Party. DEMOS, established in March 1993, has the objective of helping to re-invigorate public policy and political thinking "which was felt to have become too short term, partisan and out of touch". It has an annual budget of £400,000. The Institute of Public Policy Research was established in 1988 by leading figures in the academic, trade union and business community "to promote an alternative to free market think tanks". While it has no formal connection with the Labour Party it is influential in the development of Labour Party policy.

The PMS Guide to Pressure Groups gives details on about 30 think tanks which it describes as influential. In addition to those already described, following is a brief listing of other think tanks particularly relevant to trade associations -

(a)   The Action Centre for Europe has an annual budget of £150,000 and aims to demonstrate that there is an approach which can put Britain at the heart of Europe.

(b)   The Adam Smith Institute, the objective of which is to promote free market economics and to conduct and publish economic research.

(c)   The Centre for Economic Policy Research which promotes independent objective analysis and public discussion of open economies.

(d)   The Centre for Policy Studies, formed by Margaret Thatcher and Keith Joseph, which is free market orientated.

(e)   The Centre for the Study of Regulated Industries investigates how competition and regulation are working in practice in the UK and globally. This is particularly relevant to the utilities.

(f)   The David Hume Institute, based in Edinburgh, promotes research and discourse on the economics and legal aspects of public policy issues.

(g)   The European Policy Forum provides a focus for positive thinking with an emphasis on decentralising power and promoting market led solutions to policy problems.

(h)   The Royal Institute of International Affairs promotes the study and understanding of all aspects of international affairs.

(i)   The Social Market Foundation seeks to develop an orderly method of exploiting the key shifts in economic and political thinking which took place in the 1970s and the 1980s. PMS comments: "Established in 1989, SMF has become one of Britain's most influential think tanks. It has been responsible for some of the pioneering work in the study of internal markets, the consideration of the government's role as regulator, the development of ways to provide choice in education and health, and the pricing of externalities."

No "think tank" has a guaranteed position of influence. For a variety of reasons, generally connected with the chief executive or the backers of the institute, they can suddenly gain or lose importance. It is therefore necessary not only to seek to work with research bodies but also to be able to identify which ones have influence and which do not.

PRESSURE GROUPS

Many trade associations do not need to give any consideration to pressure groups because there are none which have any bearing on their operations. However, the bigger associations invariably have contact with pressure groups and need to have a relationship with them. There are some pressure groups whose activities are related to specific industries while other pressure groups have more wide ranging interests which may from time to time impinge on the work of a trade association. Before considering these points in more detail it is helpful to describe briefly the difference between a pressure group and a trade association. Unlike a trade association a pressure group does not represent organisations in a common line of business; rather it represents people, and sometimes institutions, with a particular point of view. For example, the Housebuilders Federation is a trade association while Shelter is a pressure group. The National Farmers Union is a trade association while the Ramblers Association is a pressure group. The Electricity Association is a trade association while the Consumers Association is a pressure group.

At national level the Consumers' Association is an important pressure group. Its main function is to conduct high quality research for its members, but it also has a campaigning function related to its research. The National Consumer Council is a government funded body which conducts research and campaigns on certain issues. The National Association of Citizens Advice Bureaux draws on the work of local citizens advice bureaux to campaign of particular points.

In recent years there has been a steady increase in the number and influence of one-issue pressure groups and their role in the public policy debate has become somewhat controversial. Perhaps the growth of these organisations reflects an increasingly affluent society in which many people have time and money to spend on pursuing particular causes. One-issue pressure groups, because they are highly focused, get their message across fairly easily and some are willing to use civil disobedience in order to do so. By concentrating on a very specific objective they may help that cause but generally with little consideration to wider issues. For example, a pressure group campaigning for poor people to have subsidised food or transport or fuel may inadvertently contribute to the problem of the poverty trap whereby as poor people enjoy an increased income so they loose a greater amount in benefits.

The *PMS Guide to Pressure Groups* lists no fewer than 400 pressure groups. It is helpful to list a few examples with their very narrow objectives from which it will become clear that they will be very relevant to some trade associations -

(a)   Advocates for Animals seeks to prevent the infliction of suffering and cruelty to animals.

(b)   Alarm UK presses for a sustainable transport policy.

(c)   The Anglers Conservation Association seeks to use common law against polluters of water.

(d)   The British Road Federation campaigns for a safe and efficient road system.

(e)   The Child Poverty Action Group promotes action for the relief of poverty amongst children and families with children.

(f)   The Council for the Protection of Rural England promotes and encourages the protection of the English countryside.

(g)   Keep Sunday Special Campaign seeks to preserve the special character of a Sunday.

(h)   The Right to Peace and Quiet Campaign campaigns for noise abatement.

Whatever the justification for pressure groups, whether they be one-issue groups or wider groups, trade associations cannot afford to ignore them. Often they may be highly professional organisations, well resourced, and drawing on academics and others on the one hand and using the media and MPs to put forward their views on the other. The best tactic is to seek to work with such organisations by providing them with information, meeting them to discuss their concerns, and encouraging them to think through the consequences of what they are doing. However, this does not always work, and sometimes a stand off develops with any communication between the pressure group and the trade association being through the media.

TRADE ASSOCIATIONS

Trade associations need to have a relationship with other trade associations precisely because they are all opinion formers. As the barriers between institutions and markets have broken down over the years trade associations have needed to co-operate more closely given a very substantial overlap of members and interests. On some issues trade associations have joined together in formal or informal coalitions to present a case to government. At the very least trade associations should keep each other informed of the responses they are making to consultation documents and of submissions they are making to the government generally. Some trade associations have formal contacts with each other but more often it is a case of informal contacts between the secretariats and regular meetings at each others annual lunches, dinners and so on.

ORGANISATION OF THE PUBLIC AFFAIRS FUNCTION

It is useful to conclude this chapter with a brief discussion of how the public affairs function in a trade association should be organised. It is function which has to be centralised. There is no scope, for example, for various sectional groupings to have their own public affairs function or for, say, the legal affairs department or the fiscal affairs department to have a public affairs function. Specialist staff are needed to deal with the press and parliamentary liaison. They will be expected to handle all of the routine work in monitoring what is going on, providing information, dealing with enquiries and so on. However, all the senior staff in an association must play their part in public affairs work and this means talking from time to time with journalists, politicians and other opinion formers. It is also a function that has to be staff rather that committee led. Long term relationships are vitally important and properly trained people have to be responsible for the public affairs function. Allowing an amateur from a member company to take the lead in dealing with the media or politicians is likely to be dangerous.

The nature of a trade association is such that if it is involved in key public policy matters the chief executive must be fully committed to the public affairs function. He or she will be expected to be the principal spokesman for the association and personally to deal with key opinion formers, in particular politicians. This is a function which cannot be delegated. The big trade associations generally have a head of external relations or public affairs who will be one of the senior management team and who will share with the chief executive the representative work. This person may also have a direct responsibility for some of the less technical public policy issues which do not fall within the province of the more technical departments.

The size of the public affairs or external relations department will depend on the size of the association and the importance of public affairs work within it. Sometimes the whole department will consist of only two or three staff who have to share all of the work. In the biggest associations the staff may be divided into a number of sections -

(a)   Media - responsible for monitoring the press, issuing press releases and dealing with all routine press queries.

(b)   Political - monitoring what goes on in Parliament, issuing parliamentary briefings, responding to requests for information from politicians.

(c)   Consumer affairs - producing consumer literature, maintaining liaison with consumer bodies and pressure groups and dealing with consumer queries.

(d)   Research and statistics - producing regular bulletins and other publications, doing in house research and commissioning external research. In some associations this function will be so big that it will be a department in its own right.

A number of trade associations use consultants to help them in their public affairs work. An agency might be used to prepare and distribute press releases.

The use of political consultants is controversial among trade associations. However, there can be no doubting the growth of such consultancies and the use that is made of them. It is estimated that the political consultancy market in the UK now has a turnover of some £60 million a year. The Public Policy Unit has published a guide to using consultants which is drawn on in this section. The paper states that the work of political consultants can be broadly divided into five categories -

(a)   Intelligence gathering and monitoring.

(b)   Policy, legislative and regulatory research in case building.

(c)   Political public relations and contact building.

(d)   Political, policy and legislative problem solving.

(e)   Commercial problem solving.

Political consultancies employ a mixture of public relations specialists and former civil servants, MPs, ministers, local councillors, special advisers and others trained within the system. The consultancies work under contract, usually on a retainer basis for longer term work, or a simple agreement on fees. The trend recently has been away from retainers.

One of the key issues to consider is whether the consultant should make representations. The Public Policy Unit publication suggests that it was the accepted law that the client should always represent itself for three reasons -

(a)   It looked odd if major organisations are not able to advocate their own case.

(b)   It used to be the case that most consultants had neither the background nor the skill to master complex arguments.

(c)   Few consultants had sufficient credibility with government.

The guide goes on to argue that given the rise in the quality of the consultant this is no longer the case. It states: "The view in Whitehall in particular is that it is often easier to deal with a knowledgeable broker who understands - or, better, comes from - the system and whose integrity is unchallenged rather than an organisation which is always presumed to be putting "its case"."

Most large trade associations would not accept this line of argument and there is a widespread view that political consultancies have been "oversold". The real problem is the misunderstanding of the political and policy making process on the part of trade association executives and their members which allow the political consultancies to claim more than they can actually achieve. This has been helped by the media which has implied an almost mysterious and semi-corrupt process by which consultants have substantial influence with MPs in particular.

Most large trade associations would not allow a consultant to represent them and indeed few smaller ones would opt for this route. Rather, they use consultancies for intelligence gathering and for advice, for example on which MPs and special advisers should be targeted, and some may use them to help prepare a strategy. Some may also use consultants for a one-off heavy lobbying job in the same way that consultants generally are used to handle peaks and troughs in workload.

BIBLIOGRAPHY AND FURTHER READING

Choosing and Using Political Consultants (London: The Public Policy Unit, undated).

Guide to Pressure Groups (London: PMS Publications Ltd, 1995).

Nicholas Jones, *Soundbites and Spin Doctors* (London: Cassell, 1995).

CHAPTER 9

Representation at the European Level

Developments at the European level are now vitally important for many sectors of industry and commerce in Britain. Some legislation is made directly at the European level and almost every new law or regulation is constrained by European requirements. Most trade associations now regard European activity as an extension of domestic activity rather than as a subject to be handled by a separate department. Representational work at the European level has to be conducted through a number of channels, the most important of which are the UK government and European trade associations.

HISTORY OF THE EUROPEAN UNION

To set the context for this chapter it is helpful to give a brief historical introduction to the European Union. This and the following two sections draw heavily on *Vacher's European Companion* and a publication of a UK law firm, Clifford Chance.

The Union has its origins in the immediate post-war years when it was felt that if the economies of the European countries could be integrated then the dangers of war would be sharply reduced.

The first concrete step was taken in April 1951 when the Treaty of Paris established the European Coal and Steel Community (ECSC) between Belgium, Germany, Italy, France, Luxembourg and the Netherlands. This Community came into effect in 1952. In March 1957 the Treaty of Rome established the European Economic Community (EEC) and the European Atomic Energy Community (EURATOM). The same six countries were signatories to the Treaty. The three Communities were run as separate organisations, and it was not until the Merger Treaty of 1965 that provision was made for a single Council of Ministers and a single Commission. These came into effect in July 1967.

In January 1972 the Accession Treaty provided for the entry of three new members, Denmark, Ireland and the United Kingdom (Norway was a signatory to the Treaty but membership was rejected by a referendum). The three new members formally joined the Community in January 1973. By July 1977 the nine member states were in a customs union. Some of the earlier analysis assumed that all that was needed to be done to create a community was to remove tariffs. As tariffs were reduced so non-tariff barriers to trade became more apparent and indeed generally were more significant than tariffs. Much of the Community's work subsequently has been to remove these non-tariff barriers. Greece joined the Community in 1981 and Portugal and Spain in 1986, bringing the number of members to 12.

In February 1986 the Single European Act was signed, marking a concerted attempt to remove the barriers to international trade between the Community countries. In 1991 the Maastricht Treaty (more properly, the Treaty on European Union) was signed providing for the Community to become the European Union and also for economic and monetary union to be established, albeit with the British "opt out". The "Single European Market" technically came into operation at the beginning of 1993 although this date is little more than symbolic. A number of the single market measures have still not been fully implemented.

In 1992 the European Community and the European Free Trade Area, then comprising Austria, Norway, Sweden, Switzerland, Iceland, Finland and Liechtenstein, jointly established the European Economic Area, effectively applying the single market provisions to almost the whole of Western Europe.

In January 1995, Austria, Finland and Sweden joined the European Union to make a Union of 15 countries, Norway again having rejected membership in a referendum.

The Union has continually been deepening and broadening with there sometimes being a conflict between the two. This is now more apparent as any broadening is likely to include the countries of Central and Eastern Europe which have very different economic and social structures from the existing members and which economically are considerably more backward. Already there are formal applications to join from Switzerland, Turkey, Morocco, Cyprus, Malta, Hungary and Poland.

The functioning of the European Union, as established by the Maastricht Treaty, will be reviewed at an inter-governmental conference in 1996.

INSTITUTIONS OF THE EUROPEAN UNION

There are four major institutions in the European Union.

The Council of Ministers directly represents the member governments. Each government has one seat on the Council. The foreign ministers comprise the Council on major issues, but on issues relevant to a specific subject then the relevant ministers will comprise the Council. For example, if an agricultural matter is being discussed then ministers of agriculture will comprise the Council of Ministers.

The Council is the Union's principal decision making body, although technically it acts on Commission proposals only. Unanimity is the general rule but there is increasingly provision for decisions to be taken by a qualified majority. The presidency of the Council is held for six month terms by each member in turn. This means that the chairmanship of all Council committees changes on a six monthly basis which presents some problems for continuity.

The members have to devote substantial resources to the European Union while they hold the presidency which can be a strain for some of the smaller countries and can also present problems when there is political instability in the country holding the presidency.

Twice a year, the Council of Ministers becomes the European Council, comprising the heads of government of the member states, which decides on and reviews the overall policy of the European Union.

The secretariat of the European Union is the Commission. This has twenty members, two from each of France, Germany, Italy, Spain and the UK, and one from each of the other member countries. They are appointed jointly by the fifteen governments, now for a five year term. The President of the Commission, a very powerful position, is also appointed jointly by the member governments. Commissioners are obliged to act in the Union's interests independently of their governments. In practice this does not happen with commissioners sometimes quite overtly representing their countries and generally maintaining close contact with the government of their home state. However, it is not unknown for some commissioners to "go native". The Commission's administrative functions are carried out by 24 directorates-general and a number of central services.

The Commission proposes and executes the Union's policies. It also acts as a mediator between the governments and it can take governments or firms to court for breaches of European law. The Commission normally meets weekly and takes decisions by a simple majority. The Commission technically is answerable to the European Parliament although in practice this accountability is very loose compared with, for example, the accountability of the British government to the UK Parliament.

The third European institution is the Court of Justice. This comprises fifteen judges assisted by nine advocates-general. The Court rules on questions of Union law and whether actions by the Commission, the Council of Ministers, member governments and other bodies are compatible with the treaties. The Court also has an advisory function. It may be asked to give opinions on external agreements which the Union plans to conclude with states or international organisations.

The final institution is the European Parliament which comprises 626 members directly elected by the citizens of the 15 member states for a five year term. The UK, together with France and Italy, has 87 members of the Parliament. Germany now has 99. The members sit in party political groups rather than national delegations. The groupings maintain close contact with their parent political parties domestically.

The Parliament does not have legislative powers in the same way as, for example, the British Parliament. However, the power of the Parliament has been increasing over time. The opinion of the Parliament is now sought before European law is made and the Parliament now has at the least a delaying power. It is also now in its own right an opinion forming body and influences the climate of opinion on some issues at the European level.

It would be sensible if all of the institutions of the European Union were located in the same city. They are not, largely because of the need to satisfy a number of national governments. Brussels is the centre of the European Union. The Commission is based in Brussels and the Council of Ministers normally meets in Brussels. The Court of Justice, which has less need to be located near the other institutions, is based in Luxembourg. The European Parliament has its plenary sessions for one week in each month in Strasbourg. However, the Parliament's secretariat is in Luxembourg while committees meet in Brussels. The nomadic existence of the European Parliament is considered to be a major factor holding back its development. Members of the Parliament regularly seek to move more of the Parliament's functions to Brussels but this meets with strong opposition from the French and Luxembourg governments.

In addition to the four formal institutions, an important part of the European decision making process are the permanent representatives of the member states. Council meetings are prepared by the Committee of Permanent Representatives (COREPER) which comprises the member states' ambassadors to the Union. Each of the European Union countries has its own office in Brussels headed by a permanent representative who would generally be one of the most senior diplomats. The staff of the permanent delegations handle a great deal of work and generally act as a link between the Union's institutions and national governments.

TYPES OF EUROPEAN LEGISLATION

It is necessary to describe briefly the categories of European legislation as these are different from national legislation, and there is often misunderstanding about them.

Both the Commission and the Council of Ministers can, in specified areas, issue regulations which are binding and directly applicable throughout the European Union without the need for any legislation at the national level. Most regulations are concerned with matters such as day to day aspects of the common agricultural policy and do not cover broad areas of policy. However, there are also, for example, regulations interpreting the competition rules of the Treaty of Rome. There will normally be consultation with interested parties before such rules are issued.

Directives are the most important form of European legislation, and also the form about which there is most misunderstanding. A directive is binding on member states but only as far as the end result is concerned. It is for member states to decide how to implement the directive. It is frequently said, for example, that a European directive "comes into effect" at a certain date and the national institutions have to abide by it. This is not generally the case.

National institutions have to abide only by the law of their land and it is the responsibility of governments to ensure that that law conforms with directives. If it does not then the Commission can take action in the European Court against the national government. However, Court of Justice case law has shown that individuals can rely on directives as against their governments if a directive has not been implemented or if a directive has been implemented incorrectly.

National governments differ considerably in how they implement legislation. One option is to incorporate the text of the directive into national law. This does not work well with the British legal system as directives are insufficiently precise. The British practice is to transpose directives into legislation, often in some detail, a subject which is the cause of some controversy in the United Kingdom as many feel that the British government is over-zealous in implementing European legislation while other countries are more inclined to pay lip service while carrying on as before.

The Commission and the Council can also make decisions which are binding on those to whom they are addressed. These are rarely used.

Finally, the Commission and Council can make recommendations and opinions which, as their names suggest, have no binding effect. Recommendations may well be issued where it is impossible to agree on a directive.

The Single Market - Theory and Practice

It is frequently said that there is now a single European market. To the extent that there are no longer legal barriers to institutions in one country operating in another and that tariffs and many non-tariff barriers to trade have been removed, this is true. However, markets are not determined solely by legislation and there is a limit to which legislation can remove real barriers between national and even local markets. The position can be illustrated by comparing two industries. There is in effect a global market for jumbo jets. National governments have not signed any treaties to the effect that this should be the case. Rather, the economics of the jumbo jet market, with huge fixed costs and massive economies of scale, are such that the market has to be global and even then there is room for only two or three suppliers. The mainframe computer industry is not dissimilar. By contrast, the hairdressing industry is local. Whatever directives might be made at the European level, over 99% of the population will use hairdressing services within five miles of their home or place of work.

A single market can more easily be created for physical goods than for services. A good which works in one country is likely to be able to work in another with little adaption. This is true, for example, of almost all household goods and electrical equipment. All that might be needed are instructions in more than one language. Indeed, most electrical equipment now comes with instructions in several languages. Occasionally, modifications might be needed before products which work well in one country can be sold in another. This is true for motor vehicles because most countries drive on the right hand side of the road while Britain and Ireland drive on the left hand side. Manufacturers traditionally see export markets as a means of spreading their overheads. The cost of supplying an export market is considered to be little more than the marginal cost of producing the good which may be substantially below the average cost.

Most services are different. A service that works in one country is unlikely to work in another without substantial adaptation (although hairdressing is perhaps a good exception). For example, a mortgage contract which works in Britain will not work in France because of different land law. Services also need more servicing than goods. For example, it is difficult to sell most financial services without a presence in the country and also a substantial after sales service. With many financial services it is not therefore a case of spreading overheads by moving into another country but rather creating a new business with its own overheads. Very little progress has been made in integrating the financial markets of the European Union countries at the retail level because of such factors. The language factor is also important. It is a genuine barrier to international trade where an ongoing relationship is needed between producers, suppliers and customers. Managements also have less control over foreign operations if a different language is spoken.

However, the question of a single market must not be viewed wholly from the British perspective. Where countries share a land border and a common language (UK/Republic of Ireland, France/Luxembourg/Belgium and Germany/Austria) then a true single market is more realistic than in a UK/continent context.

Generally, it is wrong to talk of a single market in the European Union. Having said this, European Union activity has resulted in a significant shift towards a single market for many goods and services. There is a complete spectrum from there being global markets for some goods and services where there are very substantial economies of scale (such as jumbo jets, motor vehicles, mainframe computers and large capital raising exercises) to national markets (for example, for the newspaper, radio and TV industries) to regional markets (for example, shopping centres and sporting activities) to very local markets (such as fast food restaurants and hairdressing).

As people move more across national borders, particularly within the Union, and as certain aspects of national life become Europeanised then inevitably some services get pushed from the national to the European or international level. This has applied, for example, to television where there are now European and international channels as well as national channels. It is also beginning to apply in industries such as retailing and transport. This trend will continue. There will never be a single market in the European Union but there will be continued greater integration of the markets, although generally it is difficult to see that the European Union provides any distinct trading block. It is significant in this context that Switzerland, still outside the European Union, is the base for a number of large banks (Credit Suisse, UBS and SBC in particular), insurance companies (Zurich, Winterthur and Swiss Re in particular) and also engineering companies.

WHY TRADE ASSOCIATIONS SHOULD BE INVOLVED AT THE EUROPEAN LEVEL

It is self evident that trade associations representing large sectors must be involved at the European level, because legislation, regulation and taxation are increasingly set at that level. Once a directive has been agreed then it has to be implemented, and the British government tends to implement rigorously. It is not open at that stage for any trade association to say that it does not like the directive and seek for it to be changed. That has to be done prior to the directive being agreed, and that can be done best by working both at national level with the relevant government department and at the European level.

It is important to emphasise that trade associations need to be involved at the European level not because of any interest in operating in other markets of the European Union but rather because of the effect on the domestic market. In many trade associations there have been those who have argued that resources should not be devoted to Europe because only a few members are interested in setting up European operations and therefore they should pay for any work that has to be done. This is wholly incorrect. Every single company in the country is affected by legislation which has originated at the European level. Huge aspects of British life are now in effect settled at the European level, and the option of seeking to influence developments at national government level only is one that simply is no longer available.

There are other reasons why action at the European level is appropriate.

Increasingly, the public policy debate is at the European level with developments in one country affecting others. Governments will frequently point to experience in other European countries when seeking to bring about a change in their own country. For example, the government has recently issued a consultation paper on identity cards noting that these exist in almost every other European country. In seeking to levy Insurance Premium Tax the Chancellor mentioned that Britain was the only European country without any such tax. There are some areas where the debate is now predominantly at the European level. This applies, for example, to environmental liability and genetic testing. Trade associations cannot afford to ignore an important debating forum on issues which may be of relevance to them. Involvement at European level also gives the opportunity for building alliances and influencing opinion formers, particularly trade associations in other countries.

Trade associations also need to look forward. It is possible to predict what issues are likely to develop at the European level. Taking the financial services sector, the tax issue is bound to become more important. People are now free to invest their money wherever they wish in the European Union. This is beginning to raise problems over taxation. Take, for example, a German national working for a French company in Britain who invests his money in Luxembourg and Ireland. Who is to be responsible for ensuring that income tax is paid on the returns obtained from the investments? It is already the case that British life insurers have set up subsidiaries in tax favoured areas such as the Irish Republic and Luxembourg because they can produce tax efficient products which can then be sold into the British market.

A third reason for involvement at the European level is that there remain market access problems as are well reported in the press from time to time. Notwithstanding the existence of directives, national governments and industry and commerce can use considerable ingenuity in effectively creating barriers to entry, for example, by laborious customs procedures, slowness in issuing licences and the imposition of special inspections by various regulatory authorities. Trade associations need to protect the interests of their members when they seek to operate in the other countries of the Union.

A final point in this section is that almost all industrial sectors now have a European-wide trade body which is recognised by the European Union and others as the representative body for that sector. What that industry body says will have a material effect on legislation emanating from Brussels. If British institutions are not involved then they could suffer the consequences of what the trade body is doing at the European level.

How trade Associations Influence Activity at the European Level

Chapters 7 and 8 of this book explained how the representative function is exercised in the United Kingdom. Civil servants are all-important on the majority of issues. Ministers are obviously important on key issues, while MPs are probably less important than is commonly suggested but nevertheless are influential when legislation is passing through Parliament and also in influencing the climate of opinion generally. The decision-taking process in the British political system is fairly simple. A trade association may make a proposal to the government or the government may make a proposal through issuing a consultation paper. Consultation papers are generally well thought through, frequently offering fairly firm conclusions for consideration. Once the government has taken a decision to legislate or to introduce a change of policy generally then normally this will happen with trade associations and other interest groups being able to influence the decision only at the margin.

At the European level the situation is looser. The Commission is responsible for bringing forward proposals. It operates in a very open way making public (or rather not preventing documents being made public) policy papers at a fairly early stage. This can cause concern if the policy documents are not thought through and has contributed to much anti-European feeling. Consultation documents issued by the European Commission are much "greener" than green papers issued by the British government. This is not always realised and some people take draft Commission proposals too seriously.

The decision-taking process is more protracted at the European level than the national level. There are many more parties involved, many more abortive proposals put forward and generally substantially greater resources need to be devoted to European issues for a given output than is the case for British issues. Indeed, the resources that can be devoted to activity at the European level could be infinite on a demand-led basis. There are endless reports, announcements, speeches, proposals and so on which can generate massive work but most of which are irrelevant. Judgement needs to be exercised in considering which issues are important at the European level, and time and resources generally should not be wasted on controversial proposals which should come to nothing. Many trade associations are excellent judges at which issues are and are not significant. The British government invariably can be helpful in indicating which proposals are likely to make progress and which will be put on the shelf. Some consultants also provide this service although generally it is not as accurate as informal advice given by the civil servants.

The nature of decision taking at the European level is such that the sensible trade body will use a number of different channels for obtaining information and influencing developments.

Perhaps surprisingly the single most important channel for trade associations to influence activity at the European level is the British government, particularly when matters are before the Council of Ministers. Each European directive is in effect an inter-governmental treaty and accordingly representative work can effectively be done at the national level. Trade associations should work in partnership with government departments at the European level. They can provide helpful briefing material and always need to ensure that the British government is fully aware of their case. In return the British government can usefully indicate to trade associations what is likely to happen in their particular area, areas where more resources are needed, perhaps areas where research is needed and so on. Often the British government is overlooked in European representative work with people feeling perhaps that activity has to take place in Brussels. Certainly much of it has to but that activity may be better done by the British government than by a British trade association.

A particular part of the British government that is relevant to trade associations is the Office of the UK Permanent Representative in Brussels, known as UKREP. The civil servants who staff it are generally among the most able, most being on secondment from civil service departments in the UK. UKREP staff will represent the British government at some meetings where it is not felt necessary to send someone over from the UK for the occasion. They also monitor what goes on generally and are an excellent source of information and advice for trade associations. UKREP staff are willing to see trade associations when they are visiting Brussels and generally to keep closely in touch with them. Again, this channel of communication is insufficiently used by many British trade associations.

The European Commission is of course a channel of communication and a target for representational work. There are some (particularly some European trade associations) who argue that the European Commission will not listen to any national organisation but rather will work only through European-wide trade bodies. This is not correct. In fact the Commission is often willing to talk to individual companies as well as national trade associations. The sensible association will maintain direct contact with relevant directorates-general of the Commission, in particular former British civil servants who, notwithstanding their obligation to work in the interests of the whole European Union, generally can be relied on to help the British cause in many areas. A brief visit to the relevant Commission staff and perhaps an informal discussion over lunch or dinner can be helpful in keeping a trade association in touch with developments at the European level, and perhaps helping to ensure that that association may be consulted directly when certain information or analysis is needed.

Members of the European Parliament (MEPs) are a further channel that needs to be used in European representative work. It is fair to say that MEPs have over the last few years moved from being almost totally irrelevant and ignored by trade associations to being relevant on European matters, and they are likely to become more important as time goes on. They were strengthened as a result of the Maastricht Treaty, and with direct elections being held at the same time in every country there is now a feeling that it really is a parliament rather than a talking shop. Although it remains relatively ineffective in that it has few powers the Parliament is becoming increasingly influential. It has good quality MEPs from some countries and these MEPs are well resourced with research facilities. At the very least, MEPs influence the climate of debate, particularly on issues that apply throughout the Union, in the same way that British MPs influence the climate of debate quite separately from their importance in the legislative process. Contact can be maintained with MEPs whether in Britain or in Brussels or Strasbourg.

Most large trade associations are members of the Confederation of British Industry which in turn is a member of the European employers' organisation, UNICE. The CBI is particularly influential on what might be called macro issues, such as employment legislation and initiatives on matters such as deregulation. On such issues the CBI can be used as a very effective channel of both information and communication.

There are many consultants offering services to trade associations and individual companies. A few trade associations consider it worthwhile maintaining an office in Brussels. Many rely on consultants as a source of information and to help them obtain meetings when necessary with the Community institutions. It is perhaps significant that *Vacher's European Companion*, heavily used earlier in this Chapter, has a full name of *Vacher's European Companion and Consultants' Register*. Eighteen political consultants are listed as well as some specialist consultants, in particular legal firms.

There is one specialist consultancy firm that merits particular mention. In 1971, the Confederation of British Industry established an office in Brussels to act as a contact point for the policy specialists working for the CBI nationally and to be the CBI's permanent representation to the European organisation, UNICE. In the early 1990s it was felt that a number of organisations wished to have a greater presence in Brussels due to the increasing amount of legislation but did not wish to set up an office and maintain staff. Accordingly, a half way house was established by the CBI in the form of the British Business Bureau (BBB). While this is located within the CBI it is independent in terms of finance and policy. After four years in operation it now has eighteen members, most of which are trade associations. The main activity of BBB is the collection of information and the dissemination of this information to members. It does not confine itself to published information; rather it also covers the many "non documents" circulating in Brussels at any one time. In order to provide this information service, BBB maintains close contact with the Commission and the Council of Ministers. BBB also arranges meetings in the UK for its members and will arrange meetings with, for example, the Commission in Brussels and MEPs in Strasbourg.

The final channel for obtaining information about Europe and influencing developments at the European level are European trade associations. These now exist for all industrial sectors. Many UK trade associations are not wholly satisfied with their European associations, regarding them as bureaucratic, expensive and often unduly influenced by the Germans who devote very substantial resources to activity at the European level perhaps because they are less able to influence their national government. All too often people who represent trade associations are not top quality although Britain is less guilty in this respect than other countries. Meetings are often held at exciting venues and therefore take more time than is necessary thereby deterring the best people from attending. Having said this, it is recognised that European trade associations do have considerable clout and cannot simply be ignored. European associations are covered in more detail subsequently in this chapter.

The Manchester Metropolitan University study, described in Chapter 3, found that 50% of respondents claimed to be in regular contact with the European Commission. In a series of questions regarding representation in Europe, 80% of respondents regarded the Commission as important to the work of their association although not as many actually provided representation to Europe. However, of this representation to Europe, 40% of respondents provided it directly to the body concerned, 22% indirectly through a larger UK organisation, 7% indirectly through the CBI European Office, and 50% indirectly through a European trade association. Not surprising those associations contained within this latter 50% were generally the same associations affiliated to a European trade association.

THE ORGANISATION OF EUROPEAN WORK IN A TRADE ASSOCIATION

The question of how work at the European level is to be organised by a trade association has caused considerably controversy and some anguish over the years. Initially, most trade associations did not take European activity too seriously. Often, someone was appointed with a specific European remit. In some trade associations a bureaucracy developed comprising relevant staff members and also company representatives who enjoyed their status and frequent trips, not just to Brussels but also to attend meetings of European trade associations generally held in exotic locations. Gradually, it has become necessary for European work to be fully integrated into national work. It makes no sense to have one person responsible for dealing with the work leading to the establishment of a directive and then a totally different person being involved in the work to implement that directive into national legislation.

Most trade associations have now moved fully to integrating European matters fully into their domestic work. This means, for example, that the person responsible for tax policy in the UK will also handle tax policy at the European level. There remains a need for co-ordination of European work and for the maintenance of contact with European trade bodies and other national associations. One senior person is generally delegated with this responsibility.

Trade associations have recognised the importance of having top rate people on committees that deal with European issues, and now generally there is be a close overlap between industry practitioners who handle domestic issues and those who handle European issues as well as there being total integration at the secretariat level.

Most associations have considered establishing an office in Brussels. It is argued that this facilitates the flow of information back to the UK and provides a permanent lobbying resource. Few associations however have felt able to justify the huge expense that would be involved in setting up a Brussels office. It would need to be well staffed with top quality people but in most sectors the job would not be challenging, mainly involving monitoring and keeping in touch with people. Those associations which have established offices in Brussels are generally those for which activity at the European level is most important, for example agriculture.

Retaining a European consultancy or subscribing to the British Business Bureau are options that are frequently followed.

Involvement in European trade associations creates problems for many British associations. Some European bodies want only one member from each country yet there may be several competing trade associations in Britain. Sometimes more than one will join while in other sections the various industry bodies get together in an umbrella body for European purposes. As a good example, in the insurance industry the British Insurers' International Committee has been established comprising representatives of the Association of British Insurers, Lloyd's and various other market bodies. The ABI provides secretariat services and obtains some funding from the other members. This arrangement ensures that there is a uniform British voice at the European level albeit at the expense of an additional level of bureaucracy. This is, of course, not only a British problem. For example, there are five German mortgage lending associations represented in the European Mortgage Federation.

EUROPEAN TRADE ASSOCIATIONS

The need for European trade associations can be analysed in much the same way as the need for associations in Britain or internationally. European associations however fill a distinct market niche that is different from either national or international associations. National associations exist because there are national laws and national markets. International associations exist primarily as a means of exchanging information which is increasingly important given the globalisation of the economy. The rationale for European associations is now that much national legislation and regulation in the countries of the European Union is settled, at least in outline, at the European level. Accordingly, if an industry wishes to influence legislation then it needs to be active not only at national level but also at European level.

The importance of a European trade association will partly depend on how well it is organised but also on certain market factors. There are some industries which are more influenced than others by developments at the European level. The obvious example is agriculture where there is a common agricultural policy. Coal and steel are other industries which have also been greatly influenced by European activity. By contrast, a number of service industries, for example hairdressing and catering, still operate either nationally or even locally and are relatively untouched by European legislation. In these cases, to the extent that there are European associations then there will be smaller and weaker.

In the same way as a single voice at the national level is more influential than a number of competing voices so a single voice at European level is more influential than each national association pushing its own line with the organisations of the European Union. Moreover, European trade associations have been given encouragement by the European Commission which has made it clear that it will give greater weight to representations made by European-wide bodies than it will to representations made by national bodies. In almost every sector of industry and commerce European associations are therefore relatively strong, and the British play an active part in them.

A major difference between national and European associations is that the members of the latter are generally, although not exclusively, trade associations themselves and frequently no more than one from each country. A number of European associations do allow individual companies into membership but generally the governance of the associations is by representatives of the various national bodies. In a way this makes European associations easier to manage than national associations, simply because there are a small number of members which are themselves active in the representational business and therefore understand how to influence the decision-taking process.

Unlike national associations, European associations generally have virtually no role in providing services to their members. Rather, they are confined to representational work and to a limited extent to the exchange of information although related to the representational work. The focus of the representative work of European associations is fairly tight. The target audience is predominantly the European Commission but also the other European bodies in particular MEPs, the Economic and Social Committee and also the secretariat of the Council of Ministers.

At first sight, European associations should be effective as they have a natural market for their representative work and also their members are themselves trade associations which know the business. In reality however managing European associations is fraught with difficulty and there is dissatisfaction with the way many of them are run. European level associations face a series of problems that either do not exist or are more muted in national associations.

The first and most difference is that members may have different interests because of different national markets. This can be well illustrated by reference to the mortgage market. In Britain the mortgage market has been completely open with any institutions being welcome to enter the market from any part of the world without the need for authorisation and able to operate in any way they wish whether by taking deposits or raising loans on the bond market and lending on whatever terms they wish. Many foreign institutions entered the British mortgage market although, for market reasons, a number have now withdrawn. By contrast, the German market is dominated by specialist institutions, mortgage banks and Bausparkassen, which operate under specific legislation and which to a large extent enjoy a protected position. The mortgage banks issue a particular type of instrument, the mortgage bond, which is unknown in Britain. Given these sort of differences it is intrinsically difficult for the British and Germans to agree a common line. There are similar differences in other markets with the British often standing apart from many of the European countries because of the liberal market structure which is open to foreign competition.

There are also different national approaches to representational work. British trade associations generally enjoy a close working relationship with the British government and use the government effectively to put forward their views at the European level. British associations also tend to make much better use of informal contacts, with representatives being given considerable freedom as to how they go about trying to achieve the objectives of their national association. In other countries, in particular Germany, a more formal approach to representative work is adopted, the positions being agreed nationally, which representatives then have difficulty in departing from. Some national associations do not enjoy a good working relationship with their national government and therefore need to put more emphasis on work at the European level. This can lead to conflicts as the Germans in particular are often thought to exert undue influence on European associations to push forward their point of view.

A third problem facing European associations is the language one. The need to translate documents and to provide for simultaneous translation facilities for meetings is expensive and time consuming. There is also a danger that people are sometimes chosen to represent their national association because they are good at languages rather than because they know anything about the subject.

Related to this point is that many European associations are laborious in their method of operation. Some have made the same sort of transition as many of the big British associations to a small tightly focused secretariat that takes the lead and acts as the representative voice, but many are still basically bureaucracies with a secretariat serving committees and often the wrong people on committees. Top people in an industry may well not feel they have the time to attend meetings at the European level especially as there is a tendency for meetings not to take place in Brussels but rather in all the member countries of the European association with often there being competition between the members to provide more and more elaborate hospitality in more and more exotic places that require longer and longer away from the office. A vicious circle therefore sets in with a trade association becoming ineffective because it has got the wrong people which in turn makes it more ineffective. By contrast, those associations which concentrate their activity where most things happen, that is in Brussels, with a highly professional secretariat, will be successful in getting top people to attend meetings if those meetings are meaningful.

The final problem facing European associations is that most are expected to operate with a small budget yet have to cover a wide range of activity. This makes it difficult for the secretariat to be able adequately to cover all the subjects and inevitably there must be greater use of national representatives. Often this can work well but sometimes the wrong people assume a dominant status and then can be difficult to dislodge. There is often a need to divide up committee chairs and to have a rotation for the chairmanship of the European body by nationality and this can often mean the wrong people being selected. It is not unknown for national associations to use positions at the European level as a sort of consolation prize for those who just miss out on becoming an officer at the national level.

All of these factors mean that the value of some European associations is open to question. National associations have found that contrary to what they have sometimes been told, the European Commission is willing to talk to them, particularly if they are effective in representing their industry and the European organisation is ineffective. It is not dissimilar from the position at national level. If a trade association does not adequately represent the members then the government will listen to the most effective members directly. It may not be satisfactory for the others but it is better than using an ineffective trade association as the voice of an industry. Some national associations have found it advisable to have a permanent staff in Brussels, particularly in industries where activity at the European level is of overriding importance such as agriculture. These offices which are expensive to run may be seen to be competing with the subscription to the European body. If the national office is more effective in obtaining information, arranging meetings and making representations then the merits of paying a subscription to a European body will be called into question.

The CBI, through establishing the British Business Bureau, has greatly helped trade associations in their European representative work by, in effect, providing an office in Brussels and an information service for a fraction of the cost that would be incurred if each association did the work individually.

The tensions inherent in a relationship between British trade associations and European associations is well illustrated by the experience of the Building Employers' Confederation. Set out below is an extract from the *Annual Report* of the Confederation for 1994 -

"European Affairs
The European dimension to BEC's work has been recognised as of major importance for some considerable time. The Confederation remains constantly concerned that beneficial influence is brought to bear on proposed EC legislation and that members are properly advised over the impact of such legislation on their activities.

In the year under review there was strong evidence suggesting that the European Construction Industry Federation (FIEC) was failing to meet the standards of service required by the BEC. Genuine and active attempts to achieve change were unfortunately unsuccessful and, since January 1, 1994, BEC membership of FIEC has ceased.

However, the Confederation has taken a wide-ranging series of initiatives designed to strengthen its links with Europe:

first, BEC intends to join the European Builders Confederation (EBC) which is recognised by the EC as an important representative of "small and medium-sized enterprises", by which the Commission means companies with fewer than 500 employees or less than £50 million capitalisation which covers the great majority of BEC members;

second, the Confederation is increasing its involvement in the European Main Contractors Forum to promote the interests of larger contractor members within the National Contractors Group, which will be linked with its equivalent bodies in the rest of Europe;

third, BEC has subscribed to the British Business Bureau (BBB) which has been developed by the Confederation of British Industry to supply an independent Brussels-based service for clients. The Bureau provides an extensive information service, early warnings of relevant legislation and assistance with lobbying and campaigning. Membership of the BBB, together with the Confederation's traditional links with the CBI's European activities, will guarantee better contracts with UNICE, the European equivalent to the CBI;

fourth, BEC is establishing new European links with the prominent international law firm, Masons, which will be assisting the Confederation in its representational work within the European Union. This work will include monitoring legislative and other developments affecting BEC members' interests; fostering relationships with EU institutions and other European contractors' associations and developing BEC's European lobbying capacity and effectiveness. Most particularly, a telephone 'hotline' was established as from March 1 to assist members with queries on such matters as actual or proposed EU legislation and factors affecting work in other European countries. This 'hotline' service will be provided through Masons' Brussels office.

These new links will enable BEC to seek clarification of the EC's intentions over late payments, in securing amendments to the Acquired Rights Directive affecting the TUPE Regulations and in developing intelligence on the EC Structure Funds.

To ensure that BEC's new package operates efficiently and effectively, there is to be greater staff co-ordination and member involvement on European activities."

BEC's Annual Report for 1994-95 reported on the progress of the new arrangements -

"On 1 January 1995 the BEC passed its first anniversary following withdrawal from the European Construction Industry Federation - FIEC. As a result the BEC has become much more active, rather than simply reactive, in its European work and is gaining even greater expertise and influence in its dealings with the European institutions. The assistance provided by the British Business Bureau and Masons (Brussels) has been invaluable in putting BEC firmly on the European map. With their help, BEC has not only tackled a wide range of individual legislative issues, but has also begun the vitally important process of developing close relationships with individual officers from the European Commission and United Kingdom Permanent Representation (UKREP) and members of the European Parliament."

STRUCTURE OF EUROPEAN ASSOCIATIONS

European associations all have a broadly similar structure, and there is not the diversity in terms of size, constitution and method of operation that there is in the UK. Almost all European associations are based in Brussels simply because that is where most of the European Union activity takes place. Membership of European associations generally is from all members of the European Union. Some associations, perhaps for historic reasons, also have other countries in membership and most allow an associate or observer status from countries associated with the European Union or potential members. In some industries the European and international associations have been combined. Recently, most associations have sought to develop links with the countries of Eastern and Central Europe given that most of these countries are likely at some stage in the future to join the Union.

Generally, membership of European associations is confined to national bodies although in some cases where there is no appropriate national body individual institutions might be allowed as members. Some associations allow individual institutions to have a corresponding or associate relationship whereby they obtain directly all literature from the association. A typical subscription scale has a sliding scale withthe four largest members (Germany, France, Italy and the UK) each paying around 15% of total costs and other countries paying smaller amounts.

The supreme governing body of most European associations is a council comprising representatives from each member of the association. The council may meet no more frequently than annually and may have little more than a formal role. The real governing body will be an executive committee or a committee of vice presidents, in which all of the major countries will be represented. The titular head of the association will be a president with the normal rule being that there will be some form of rotation system designed to give the larger members a bigger share of the presidency with the smaller members having a turn from time to time. Some associations have three or four office holders, for example a president, a senior vice president and a junior vice president with a stipulation that they must all come from different countries and at least one must come from a smaller country. There are the usual range of standing committees and panels in much the same way that there is in national associations. European associations are headed by a secretary general, generally with a fairly small staff. It is obviously important that the staff of a European association have a good knowledge of languages but equally important that they have a good knowledge of their subject and of European work. Obtaining all of these qualities in a trade association is never an easy task and not all European associations have succeeded.

BIBLIOGRAPHY AND FURTHER READING

Building Employers Confederation, *Annual Report 1994*.

Clifford Chance, *The European Union - Understanding and Influencing Policy and Law-Making* (London: Clifford Chance, 1995).

Andrew Moore, Trade Associations for the 21st Century - Representation in Europe, paper given at CBI conference, 3 February 1995.

Vacher's European Companion and Consultants' Register (Berkhamsted: Vachers Publications, quarterly).

CHAPTER 10

The Service Function

Trade associations are in a strong position to provide services to their members where these are related to their mainstream representative function or, to a lesser extent, where the members wish to take collective advantage of economies of scale. The provision of services can make a significant financial contribution to a trade association. However, it can also expose an association to risk. Services have to be provided in an efficient way increasingly in competition with commercial suppliers.

CRITERIA FOR PROVIDING SERVICES

Trade associations do not have a monopoly in providing services to their members. Commercial organisations, for example lawyers, accountants, management consultants and public affairs consultants, can provide many of the same services and have a corporate structure that is more appropriate for providing commercial services than are the committee based structures of trade associations.

If a trade association is seeking to provide services to its members then it must be in a strong position to do so more efficiently than others. Associations are best placed to provide services where these meet one or more of three criteria -

(a)   They are based on the representative function, that is the provision of information to members is closely connected with the association's work in providing information to opinion formers and in making representations to the government and official bodies.

(b)   They are closely related to membership of the trade association, for example an annual conference, seminars, exhibitions and statistical schemes. Here the association can rely on lower marketing costs than commercial organisations and at the same time is able to secure better speakers for its conferences, more exhibitors for its exhibitions and so on.

(c)   They are based on the expertise of the association's secretariat either because this has been developed over a period of time or because it naturally stems from the representative work.

THE INFORMATION SERVICE

All trade associations must have as one of their principal functions that of providing information to their members. Associations are in a strong position to provide information.

They are closely involved in discussions with government and regulatory agencies about legislation and regulations, and are, therefore, in the best position to provide their members with timely, accurate information. A government department or a regulatory agency will often be prepared to work with a trade association to help provide information to members. This service would not as easily be given to commercial organisations or to individual members of the trade association. Indeed, it is common for trade associations to be used as a channel of communication between government and an industry.

Trade associations also have information through their public affairs work. They will, for example, monitor the press and they may well issue regular bulletins about industry trends. They may collect statistics from their members which can then be used both for public affairs work and also for giving aggregate statistics back to members. The trade association is uniquely placed to obtain access to information from government departments, and again it will expect to be treated more preferably in this respect than commercial organisations or individual companies.

Six separate types of information which trade associations provide to their members can be identified -

(a)   Factual information on relevant legislative, regulatory and related matters.

(b)   Guidance on legislative, regulatory and related matters.

(c)   Aggregate statistics of members.

(d)   Other statistics and market information.

(e)   Information on general policy developments.

(f)   Miscellaneous information.

In making information available to members, an association should seek to work to the following six standards -

(a)   Information should be timely. Ideally it should be provided as soon as possible after it is available. For example, where the government has published a consultation paper of interest to all members then that paper should be provided to members within a day; often it is possible to come to an arrangement with a government department for bulk supplies to be provided. Where guidance is being provided then there is a strong case for providing "quick and dirty" guidance within a matter of days and immediately establishing a firm timetable for when detailed guidance will be provided. Sometimes within an association there is a tendency not to provide information to members until the association is 100% satisfied that it is complete and accurate. Members however have to continue to do business meanwhile and much prefer having some guidance from the trade association as this is likely to be more accurate than their own initial assessment.

(b)   Information should be easily accessible. It should give members everything they need to know. Members should know where information will appear and should be able to obtain copies. Information should be kept up to date and consolidated as necessary. New guidance should, where possible, consolidate existing guidance rather than being in the form of an amendment to it. Staff within member companies will predominantly judge an association on the accessibility of information. Often, this is given insufficient weight and much benefit is lost as a result. Those associations which are not good at making their information accessible may find commercial organisations repackaging their information, selling it to members at a substantial cost and gaining a good reputation at their expense.

(c)   Information should be user friendly. It should be well written, free from jargon as far as possible, logically set out and with the contents described at the beginning. It should assume that the reader has no prior knowledge of the subject. Any stand-alone document of more than a few sides should include an introductory paragraph stating the purpose of the document, to whom it is aimed and whether it is for action or information, and a summary. Lengthy documents usefully should have an executive summary at either the beginning or the end.

(d)   Information should be high quality. It should give members everything they need to know. It should include a brief history, the problem being addressed, the relevance of the issue to members, and the action taken by the association.

(e)   Guidance needs to be settled at a sufficiently senior level in the organisation. Normally this will be a senior executive and occasionally the chief executive. In exceptional cases committee approval may be needed.

(f)   Queries from members should be handled promptly. Where a query is received from a member then ideally instant replies should be given by telephone, fax or letter. Again this is an area where an association will be judged by members' staff. An association that responds quickly to queries will develop a good reputation throughout the members. Some larger associations have developed member service hotlines where fully trained staff can deal with the majority of queries instantly and know where to pass on queries that they cannot handle directly. Use of modern computer technology has greatly facilitated giving a high quality service to members in responding to queries.

SEMINARS, CONFERENCES AND EXHIBITIONS

Information is best given to members in writing as this ensures that they will all receive the same information at the same time. Specialist workshops, seminars or forums for members can complement the provision of written information. They can be particularly important on highly topical issues. They can on occasion be used for giving fairly confidential information to members when it is thought wise not to put it in writing. They allow members to raise questions with the staff and committee members dealing with an issue and will give important feedback to the association on how members view a particular issue.

Moving on from this type of seminar, which is part of the information function, associations are well placed to run seminars and conferences for their members. An association can use its own staff who are expert in their subject. Also, where an association is organising a seminar or conference then it is generally easier to obtain high quality speakers, for example from government departments and research bodies. Generally, associations can run seminars and conferences for perhaps half the price of commercial organisations and still cover the direct costs and make a significant contribution to overheads. This is largely because the marketing and production costs are much lower than those of commercial organisations.

Some associations generate substantial income from conferences and seminars but there is scope for conflicts within an organisation. There is a danger that resources may be diverted away from the more important work of exercising the representative function in order to participate in conferences and seminars because these are seen to earn income whereas the representative function does not. Preparing for conferences and seminars can be time consuming, and associations need to balance carefully the demands they make on their senior staff for such functions as against their mainstream work.

Conferences and seminars can also be seen as part of the public affairs function. They may be opened wider than the trade association membership and in this respect are part of the representative function. Sensibly, a trade association will also become involved in other conferences and seminars, including those organised by commercial organisations. It can make sense to assist in the development of conference programmes for these organisations so as to ensure that ill-informed speakers are not invited and that the industry is well represented. There are some excellent commercial conference organisers who, because they are independent, can organise the sort of function which an association cannot, including speakers who are likely to be critical of industry practices.

A number of associations have annual conferences although these have tended to decline in importance over recent years and in some cases have disappeared. The traditional conference lasted perhaps three days (and was preceded by a day of golf), was held in a seaside resort, and partners were invariably invited. Not surprisingly these sort of conferences are going out of fashion. Where annual conferences still exist these are now generally much shorter, generally no more than a day, and often in London.

Where bigger associations have major annual conferences these are often combined with a business exhibition. The exhibition provides a meeting place for the conference delegates and also enables delegates to meet the various exhibitors who are likely to be suppliers to the industry or customers of it. Little actual business is done at exhibitions but their role in providing a meeting place is now generally acknowledged. Some associations make significant profits out of running the annual exhibition which effectively subsidises the rest of the organisation. However, this is a somewhat dangerous position to be in. If, for any reason, the profit from an exhibition declines, for example because in a recession there are fewer delegates and fewer exhibitors, then the association may have to substantially increase subscriptions to make up for the shortfall in income. Members will not readily understand this.

STATISTICAL SCHEMES

There are three levels at which trade associations can be involved with statistics. The first is where the association has no statistical capability itself but rather represents its members to the extent that is necessary with organisations which do collect statistics and uses what industry statistics are available in its representative work. Small associations typically work at this level.

Trade associations are greatly strengthened if they are seen to be suppliers of good quality, relevant statistics about industry activity. Similarly, members need aggregate statistics for the industry so as to be able to assess industry trends and also to judge their performance against their competitors. For these reasons many associations run statistical schemes. Broadly speaking, these involve collecting statistics from members, aggregating them and disseminating them to members, generally analysed by various sub groups. Aggregate statistics are also published and generally made use of in the association's representative work. A basic PC and standard spreadsheet are adequate for many of these statistical exercises. The problem is to ensure that accurate data is being provided by members.

Operating at this level is generally both advantageous for an association and risk-free. The service is valued by most members and the aggregate statistics are useful for the representative function. Typically, members would not be charged for providing statistics for these schemes but then the cost of running the schemes is fairly modest.

It is a big step to the third level of statistical work, that is the operation of detailed statistical schemes with a huge amount of data being provided by members, aggregated and analysed by the trade association and then disseminated back to the members on a confidential basis. For example, the Association of British Insurers runs comprehensive statistics for claims for a variety of risks. The exercise involves millions of transactions and a large staff is needed. Members generally are charged for operating such schemes on the basis that the information is not available to those who do not participate.

Such schemes can make a valuable contribution to overheads if these are fully charged to the members. They may also provide useful additional aggregate statistics that can be used in the association's representative work. However, providing such a service is inherently risky. There are other commercial organisations that are dedicated to providing these services and are ready to take over if the association is not able to maintain an adequate quality of service. The association may also be at risk if members withdraw from the statistical schemes for one reason or another. They may be left with a computer and staff without adequate income to meet the expenses. As business has become more competitive over the last few years so members generally are less willing to contribute to such large statistical schemes.

TECHNICAL SERVICES

What have been described so far are all fairly obvious trade association activities. The provision of technical services does not obviously fall within the competence of a trade association but a number of associations do provide such services. They may include, for example, basic research and quality control and inspection systems.

The research function is most likely to be performed in associations comprising relatively small members who see merit in pooling resources and prefer this to be done by a trade association. Where there are a number of large companies in an industry then they are likely to be reluctant to see their trade association, which they will be predominantly responsible for financing, operating collective research schemes which can only enable the smaller members to obtain data that larger ones are having to pay considerable sums for.

One association which has research as a major function is the British Leather Confederation which now interestingly operates under the name of BLC - The Leather Technology Centre. The staff structure covers a scientific services group, an environmental and technical services group, a membership services and development group and a corporate and information services group. In the final group one of three sections is "commercial information" which deals with lobbying and other trade association activities. Most of the rest of the staff of the Confederation are concerned with research services. This is reflected in the committee composition. In addition to a Council and an Executive Board, the main committees are the Research Management Committee, the Technical Monitoring Committee, the Marketing Committee, the Training Committee and the Health and Safety Committee. The

Confederation lists the following products and services it provides to its members -

(a)   Confidential consultancy and audits on environmental, microbiological, process, quality or product performance related issues.

(b)   Contract research and development, if necessary on a strictly confidential basis.

(c)   Independent testing services.

(d)   Environmental consultancy.

(e)   Training and development of human resources.

The organisation's concentration on research is reflected in its financial position. In the year to 30 September 1994, of its total income of £1,586,000 only 33% was in the form of income from members and associates; 31% was income from joint projects with sponsoring departments, 7% was net project income, and 23% was income from services.

This arrangement seems to work well for the British Leather Confederation.   It is predominantly a service organisation with the trade association function perhaps resting heavily on this. The chief executive's report for 1993 emphasised these points -

"Keeping members competitive through technical innovation, improvements in leather quality and performance and reducing costs are key objectives of BLC's collaborative research and development programme. Over £1 million of our resources were deployed to this end in 1993 for the benefit of the membership as a whole."

"The basic rationale for the collaborative programme is to undertake work that is beyond the resources of individual Members.   The necessary investment in highly qualified scientists, leather technologists, environmental engineers and professionals, backed by state of the art equipment at BLC, provides a core of expertise that is also available for trouble shooting and technical service work for individual tanneries on a strictly confidential basis."

Reflecting the nature of its business, BLC now has an extensive international membership. Significantly its 1994 annual report makes no reference at all to representational work.

A second association which provides a significant amount of services is the Freight Transport Association. Its promotional leaflet, *This is the FTA*, usefully explains the position -

"FTA's dynamism doesn't reflect the normal image of a trade association. There is one other important difference. Usually trade associations rely on subscriptions for the majority of their income. In FTA's case 80% of its income comes from the services it provides direct to members. Services tailor-made to meet the needs of industry. You pick the services you want and as FTA is a non-profit making organisation, the rates are the most competitive you will find."

Among the services which the FTA provides are -

(a)   Training - over 200 courses a year are run.

(b)   A vehicle inspection services, which carries out over 100,000 checks on vehicles and equipment each year. The point is made that as FTA's staff never carry out repair work they have no interest in finding faults.

(c)   FTA's Freightcheck service, which carries out over 1,300,000 tachograph chart inspections a year.

(d)   A VAT reclamation scheme for VAT incurred in other European Community countries.

(e)   International shipping and documentation services.

(f)   A full range of insurance and financial services.

The FTA also runs a consultancy service.

The FTA's accounts helpfully give a table showing the gross turnover, direct costs and gross surplus for its various activities. The figures for 1994 are reproduced below.

Table 10.1 Freight Transport Association, Turnover and Gross Surplus, 1994

	Gross Turnover £	Direct Costs £	Gross Surplus £
Membership fees	2,334,867	-	2,334,867
Vehicle Inspection Service	4,242,395	2,980,730	1,261,665
Freightcheck	1,437,123	947,203	489,920
Training courses	1,793,817	1,321,006	472,811
Publications and advertising	876,670	452,760	423,910
Other membership services	635,973	250,122	385,851
Sundry income	330,055	173,710	156,345
Total	11,650,900	6,125,531	5,525,369

It will be seen that more than half the gross surplus of the FTA is accounted for by services rather than membership fees.

PROFESSIONAL AND CONSULTANCY SERVICES

A number of trade associations offer professional services directly linked to their particular sector. A good example is the Legal Assistance Scheme operated by the National Farmers Union. This has given help to well over 6,000 members. The scheme is funded by members' additional voluntary contributions. Through the Scheme the NFU stands behind its members in cases which are thought to have wider implications. The NFU operates the Scheme with a panel of recommended solicitors and its own legal advisers. In 1994 members' subscriptions to the Scheme totalled £784,000. Grants were made totalling £643,000 and administration costs were £134,000.

EMPLOYMENT CONDITIONS

Chapter 1 in this book briefly explains the difference between the functions of an employers' association and those of a trade association. Many trade associations have no function at all in respect of employment matters whilst employers' associations may have very little trade association functions. As this book is concerned with trade associations, only a brief account of the employer association function is necessary here and in this context only as one of a number of services which a trade association might provide.

Dealing with employment matters can be confined simply to providing information to members, sharing information on salary settlements and so on, and running training courses. At another level it can extend to negotiating with trades unions pay and conditions for the whole of an industry. As employment practices have changed, in particular the reduction in national collective bargaining, so the role of employers' associations in settling pay and conditions has inevitably diminished. However, there has been an expansion in training needs, influenced by government policy, and some associations have now developed a major role as "lead bodies" and "industry training organisations".

MARKETING

While most trade associations would recognise promoting the industry and its products as legitimate activities, few become more directly involved in marketing although this subject is frequently discussed among the governing bodies of trade associations. At first sight there is a fairly attractive argument along the lines that collective marketing efforts, through economies of scale, can help all members of a trade association. However, in practice it is difficult to satisfy all members that any such campaign will benefit them equally. The larger members are likely to argue that they will be meeting the bulk of the cost of the campaign but will benefit proportionately less than smaller members. Not every member produces exactly the same products and any campaign will inevitably favour some more than others. Finally, marketing campaigns run by trade associations are frequently run by committees which inevitably makes them less effective than a sharply focused campaign specifically targeted to one company. Having made these points, there are examples of trade associations which work successfully to market the products of their members. Some trade associations run exhibitions which can be regarded as part of marketing and a number specifically seek to promote exports.

PROMOTING COMPETITIVENESS

Most trade associations would consider that all of their activities help to promote the competitiveness of their members. However, they would not have a separate service under the heading of "promoting competitiveness". That is they would not seek to take direct action to identify competitive weaknesses among their members and to seek to remove those weaknesses and build on strengths. However, the Department of Trade and Industry clearly considers that this is a function in which trade associations should be involved. In a speech on 17 June 1993 the President of the Board of Trade said that trade associations ought to be playing a much bigger role in promoting the international competitiveness of their member companies, including UK subsidiaries of foreign owned companies. He wanted associations to become more knowledgeable about what their principal world competitors were doing and for them to give expert advice on how their sector should respond to new challenges.

In a second speech to the CBI in February 1995, the President mentioned some of the initiatives that trade associations had come up with since his first speech -

> "The society of British Aerospace Companies - the SBAC - has picked up the gauntlet in launching in November last year its competitive challenge initiative. This encourages benchmarking and the spread of best practice, particularly among the small and medium sized enterprises within the aerospace sector. The Society of Motor Manufacturers and Traders - the SMMT - early last year launched its own industry forum, both to improve its effectiveness within the very important automotive components sector and to tackle the key competitiveness issues within it.

> And the Federation of Electronics Industry - the FEI - and six of the most successful telecoms companies have launched the Telecoms 2000 initiative. This will help the small supplier companies in the industry to respond to competitive challenges in the future. It will form part of the Electronics Industry Forum which will be launched shortly following the model of the SBAC and the SMMT."

It is worth examining in a little detail work which the SBAC, FEI and other trade associations have been doing in respect of promoting competitiveness.

The SBAC commissioned an in-depth analysis entitled *Building on Success, A Strategy for UK Aerospace*, which identified the key success factors influencing the performance of the industry and chartered the way ahead for the industry to maintain its place as world leader. The study has been used as a basis for briefing of government ministers. The Society has followed up the study by establishing a Strategy Committee made up of senior representatives of the industry. This Committee will work to update the study, to communicate its recommendations to members, and will pursue the programme of briefings to government and others.

Working within the recommendations of the study and supported by the DTI, the Society launched its Competitiveness Challenge in November 1994. The Society's Annual Report for 1994-95 describes the Challenge -

"The Challenge represents an opportunity for aerospace companies to assess their performance, compare practices and better understand the route to improve their competitiveness.

Managed by a team of SBAC officials and industrial secondees, it is intended that the Challenge activities will cover the broadest range of topics to help educate and advise companies on ways to improve performance ... All the Challenge events are tailored to the specific needs of aerospace and use knowledge and experience already held within some companies to the benefit of the broader industry. The Challenge also draws on the experience of other industries where it is relevant and useful. As the programme progresses, the Challenge will rely on the input of its members to direct its activities to the most useful and important areas of their businesses."

Seminars and workshops have been held covering topics promoting best practice within the industry, such as procurement issues, new product development and supplier development. A company self assessment programme is also being run. Over 150 companies participated in this self assessment programme.

The Federation of the Electronics Industry, a relatively new association established by a merger in 1993, has established the Electronics Industry Forum, with the objective of encouraging best practice within the industry. An independent survey of a sample of the IT, electronics and communications industry carried out for the FEI identified the main areas in which companies would appreciate help. This has led the FEI to structure its Electronics Industry Forum accordingly. The Federation supports and publicises widely among the membership and members of the Forum details of all DTI programmes aimed at introducing a culture of best practice and continuous improvement. The second plank of the Forum is a self assessment package to enable companies to measure their performance against the best in the world. This is held to be of particular interest to smaller companies. The third aspect is to provide members with publications, seminars and consultancy on methods of presenting cases for obtaining investment funds from the variety of sources available. Finally," a Make the Most of IT" initiative has been introduced.

The Society of Motor Manufacturers and Traders has probably done more than any other industry to promote competitiveness within the industry. The Society's work is usefully summarised in its review for 1994-95 -

"Britain's component manufacturers have critically benchmarked their own performance in a unique government-backed initiative helping them reach world-class quality standards.

The first annual conference of the new Motor Industry Forum highlighted concerns about current levels of quality and productivity and how to develop 'a critical mass of like-minded companies' all intent on improvement. Confidential reports on questionnaire answers have been sent back to the respondents, detailing strengths and weaknesses. Participants are being invited to 'diagnostic seminars' examining the gap between themselves and world-class performance, and helping them target improvements.

The Forum is open to SMMT member and non-member companies of all sizes - the catalyst for a sector-wide process aimed at securing profitability, long-term survival and a bigger share of global markets. Its pioneering process of self-assessment has been adopted by the aerospace, electronics and insurance industries. A key benefit will be in developing common practice among suppliers serving a number of business areas.

Michael Heseltine, Board of Trade President, welcomed the Forum as an important landmark. 'SMMT is already recognised as a very effective voice for the industry,' he said. 'Trade associations have a major role to play in helping to improve the competitiveness of their industrial sectors.'

The SMMT Industry Forum produces a regular newsletter, and a comprehensive report on the relationships between vehicle manufacturers and suppliers has also been prepared.

FINANCIAL ASPECTS

The financial aspects of providing services to members are frequently the subject of considerable debate within the governing body of a trade association. There are no hard and fast rules but rather judgement is needed in respect of what services to provide and how they should be charged for.

The basic assumption should be that a trade association, in seeking to provide services to its members, should do so on a non-profit seeking basis. If the intention is to generate a significant profit then those members who buy the service are in effect subsidising those members who do not as subscriptions would be lower than would otherwise be the case. Similarly, services cannot sensibly be run at a loss otherwise those members who buy them would be subsidised by others. While these basic points might be accepted there is considerable room for debate as to what constitutes running a service at a profit. Does this simply mean covering marginal costs, making no allowance for staff time, or does it at the other extreme not only cover the staff time plus on-costs for staff but also make a significant contribution to the overheads of the organisation? A commonly used approach is for all direct costs to be charged together with staff time plus on-costs and a modest contribution to central overheads.

Where a service is being provided to outside organisations, for example seminars and conferences and literature, then it should be charged for at the full commercial rate regardless of the costs of production. A number of associations successfully market their literature to professional firms with an interest in the sector, in particular lawyers and accountants, and here commercial pricing is fully justified.

Some associations are heavily dependent on commercial income. The Society of British Aerospace Companies, for example, has noted in its Annual Report that it is vulnerable to any downturn of income from its biennial Farnborough exhibition. The Association of British Insurers faced a problem when a number of members withdrew from its statistical schemes leaving it with staff, office premises and equipment which cost more than could be recovered from the remaining members of the schemes. The Institution of Environmental Health Officers, a professional body rather than a trade association, ran into severe financial difficulties because of trading activities which went wrong.

Generally, an association should consider very carefully the financial aspects of all of the services it provides, ensuring that a reasonable pricing policy is being followed and that the maximum opportunity is taken to earn income from selling to non members. Where a substantial investment in a service is being provided then the downside risk should be carefully evaluated. If necessary members should be tied in to purchasing a service for a given period of years so as to prevent the association facing a problem should some members seek to withdraw from the service.

MANAGEMENT ISSUES

There is scope for conflict between the trade association function and the function of providing commercial services to members. Already it has been noted in the section on seminars and conferences that this clash can occur at what might be called the micro level. However, at the macro level there is a danger of an even bigger clash of cultures. Much of the best work of a trade association is unseen and intangible. The members may never know

117

about it. By contrast commercial activity is visible and may assume a disproportionate importance. If the commercial side is going well the members may be inclined to put more resources into commercial activities in the hope of earning a greater profit, and the trade association function will then be down valued. It is also necessary to recognise that different skills are needed to run commercial activities from trade association activities and this can lead to a clash within the senior management team.

Most trade associations manage these potential conflicts well. In some cases the best decision might to hive off the commercial activities into a separate organisation. One professional body which has taken this course of action is the Chartered Institute of Housing where the previous director now runs the commercial business which is totally split off from the professional body itself. Indeed, that business is now a subsidiary of a regional newspaper group.

THE EXTENT TO WHICH SERVICES ARE PROVIDED

The study by Manchester Metropolitan University in February 1994, described in Chapter 3, showed the proportion of associations which responded to a questionnaire providing various services. The figures are set out below.

Table 10.2 Percentage of trade associations providing services

Service	Percentage
Contact with other firms	81.9
UK government representation	84.9
European representation	76.5
Environmental advice	51.2
Technical advice	73.0
Legal advice	57.0
Training	52.8
Export promotion	25.3
Standards	66.5
Home sales promotion	39.8
Market information	67.0
General advice	88.1

With the exception of training, standards and market information, the vast majority of these services were funded out of subscription income. These services were ranked by respondents in order of their perceived importance to members. The results show that members regard UK government representation as the most important service on offer. In second place came

118

technical advice, and tied for third were the services of contact with other companies and European representation. The most popular publications provided for members were (annual) reports and accounts, as well as (monthly) news bulletins; each sent by over 75% of respondents.

BIBLIOGRAPHY AND FURTHER READING

T C May, J McHugh and T Taylor, *UK Trade Associations in the 1990's: A Research Note* (Manchester: Manchester Metropolitan University, unpublished, 1995).

CHAPTER 11

Influencing The Market

Many trade associations were established with the intention, explicit or otherwise, of seeking to influence the market to the benefit of their members. This function has now largely disappeared because of a combination of an increasingly competitive environment generally and restrictive trade practices legislation. To the extent that trade associations now seek to influence the market they do so through promoting high standards and operating codes of practice.

THEORETICAL ISSUES

Trade associations exist in order to promote the interests of their members. Accordingly, it can be argued that anything which increases the profitability of members is a legitimate function for a trade association. In any industrial section profitability can be increased if output can be reduced and new entrants prevented from entering the market. Some of the larger trade associations have in the past tried to use both of these devices, in some cases with a fair measure of success. This is no longer possible because of restrictive trade practices legislation but nevertheless the principle still merits examination.

Some trade associations have attempted to fix prices. The Building Societies Association, for example, had as its most well known function for many years that of fixing savings and mortgage rates, this arrangement being exempted from restrictive trade practices legislation. The Association also negotiated fixed scales of fees with the professional bodies for lawyers and surveyors. Price fixing on this basis can work only if supply is limited. In the case of the building societies the mortgage and savings rates were both set and therefore provided they were fixed at the right level the supply of and demand for mortgage funds achieved some sort of equilibrium, albeit one invariably with a shortage of mortgage funds.

Such price fixing arrangements can break down either because of pressures from inside or pressures from outside. Some participants within the price fixing arrangement might prefer to increase their market share and will find various ways of getting round the agreed prices. If there are no barriers to entry into a market then newcomers can come into the market undercutting existing market participants. Those trade associations which have operated cartels invariably try to prevent new entrants into the market, perhaps by encouraging government to impose regulatory obstacles or perhaps using unfair tactics such as putting pressure on suppliers not to deal with new entrants. It is easier to keep new entrants out where there are substantial economies of scale and where therefore huge investment is needed in order to justify attempting to break into a market which is already well served.

It is helpful to illustrate this section by describing in more detail the collective arrangements which the Building Societies Association operated for interest rates and how these broke down. In 1939 the Council of the Building Societies Association began to recommend interest rates which should be charged to borrowers and offered to investors. This system worked well in the 1950s and 1960s partly because interest rates were fairly stable. The recommendations were not binding but all the large building societies automatically followed them. As interest rates became more volatile in the 1970s so the recommended rates were changed more frequently.

Following a rapid rise in interest rates the building societies entered into a memorandum of agreement with the government under which the largest societies agreed to support recommendations made or advice given by the Council of the Building Societies Association in the light of reports from a newly established joint advisory committee on mortgage finance. This comprised representatives of the industry and of the government departments with an interest in housing finance. The general understanding was that the larger societies would be bound to follow the recommendations of the Council in respect of interest rates. In the mid-1970s internal competitive pressures led to new forms of investment accounts being offered which were outside the terms of the recommended rate system, in retrospect the first sign of the breaking down of the cartel. In the event, in 1977 it was decided to recommend rates of interest for all investment accounts. There followed a period when there were considerable disputes as to what was and was not covered by the agreement. On the mortgage side building societies started charging higher rates for larger loans. The overall effect of the cartel was that the margin between borrowing and lending rates was maintained at a higher level than the most efficient needed, as a result of which there was non-price competition, particularly in the form of branching.

The recommended rate system came under further pressure in the early 1980s. In 1980 the banks had been freed from the balance sheet constraints under which they operated. They saw the mortgage market as being the way to re-establish themselves in the personal finance market, and rapidly increased their mortgage lending. They concentrated in lending at the top end of the market where they could undercut the building societies who were at the time still charging higher rates for larger loans. Competition grew within the building society market and there was continual pressure on the recommended rate system. The report of the Wilson Committee on financial institutions in 1980 added some intellectual respectability for loosening of the interest rate arrangements. In 1981 there was a loosening to the extent that only one form of share rate was recommended and the requirement to notify changes in rates was relaxed. In 1983 one of the largest building societies gave notice of its intention to withdraw from the undertaking to notify rates. It was decided to replace recommended rates by advised rates, a not wholly semantic point, and to replace the undertaking to notify interest rates by a simple information agreement.

In 1984 the government gave notice that the arrangements for settling interest rates would no longer be exempted from the Restrictive Trade Practices Act. Subsequently, the arrangements increasingly fell into disarray. A number of devices were attempted including, for example, a recommendation that rates should be lowered or increased by a particular order of magnitude rather than actual rates being set. Finally in April 1986 the Council of the Building Societies Association recognised reality and decided that it should no longer seek to influence building society rates. This was a good example of price fixing which market participants thought benefited the consumer but actually benefited the building societies ultimately becoming unsustainable because the building societies could not prevent new entrants into the market and also because of competitive pressures within the building society industry itself.

There are now few examples of such price fixing arrangements and where they do exist they are subject to rigorous regulatory scrutiny from the UK authorities and the European Commission. In any event in almost every market there are aggressive competitors who are not likely to accept any price fixing arrangements and who will take advantage of those arrangements which do exist to increase their market share.

RESTRICTIVE PRACTICES REGULATION

The one Act of Parliament which is of specific relevance for trade associations, particularly those that seek to regulate the conduct of their members, is the Restrictive Trade Practices Act 1976. The Act requires restrictive agreements to be notified to the Director General of Fair Trading. Even informal arrangements and unwritten understandings may be registrable. The Director General has a general duty to refer registrable agreements to the Restrictive Practices Court for a ruling on whether the restrictions are against the public interest.

The Act has differing rules relating to agreements in respect of goods and agreements in respect of services. A goods agreement must be registered if two or more persons party to it carry on business in the UK producing or supplying goods or applying a manufacturing process to goods and two or more of the parties accept restrictions on -

(a)   prices or charges, or

(b)   the terms or conditions on which people are to do business, or

(c)   the quantities or descriptions to be produced, supplied or acquired, or

(d)   the manufacturing process to be used or the quantities or descriptions of goods to which such a process is to be applied, or

(e)   the persons with whom business is to be done, or

(f)   the areas or places of the business.

As will be obvious, if a trade associations attempts to influence the terms or conditions on which goods are supplied by its members in almost in any way then this agreement must be registered with the Director General.

Section 11 of the Act provides that a services agreement must be registered if two or more persons party to it carry on business in the UK supplying services and two or more of the parties accept restrictions on -

(a)   charges, or

(b)   the terms or conditions on which people are to do business, or

(c)   the extent (if any) to which, or the scale (if any) on which services are to be made available, supplied or obtained, or

(d)   the formal manner in which services are to be made available, supplied or obtained, or

(e)   the persons with whom business is to be done, or

(f)   the areas or places of the business.

The Office of Fair Trading publishes a booklet, *Restrictive Trade Practices - Provisions of the Restrictive Trade Practices Act 1976*, which has a brief section which applies specifically to trade and services supply associations. This is set out in full below.

"Trade and services supply associations
An agreement among the members of a trade or services supply association may exist by virtue of the association's constitution, rules, regulations, by-laws or resolutions, or those of one of its sections or committees.

If an association makes a restrictive agreement with another person (or association), its members are treated as parties to that agreement, so that each member accepts any restriction accepted by the association. And so, too, does any person not directly represented on the association but bound by its rules.

A **recommendation** - stated or implied - made by an association to its members (or to a category of members) may well have to be registered. For example, a recommendation to charge a minimum price, to charge for services in accordance with a scale of charges, or to do business subject to certain standard terms or conditions, would be registrable.

Whether a recommendation is 'implied' depends on the circumstances. For instance, the issue by an association to its members of standard conditions may be an implied recommendation to use them - even if the association does not directly recommend that they should be used.

The Act regards an association's constitution as containing a provision that its members agree to comply with any recommendation the association may make. Consequently a restriction on members can arise from such a recommendation - whether or not they follow it in practice."

The OFT requires two copies of all documents setting out the terms of the agreement, one copy of each to be signed by the person providing them and a statutory certificate to accompany the documents. There are time limits within which the documents must be provided. The OFT requires the following details of any agreement which is to be registered -

(a)   The names and addresses of all persons party to the agreement. (For an agreement made by a trade or a services supply association the parties include all the association's members but if there are more than 100 there is no need to give names and addresses. An approximation of the total membership is sufficient.)

(b)   All the terms of the agreement, not just those dealing with the restrictions that make it registrable.

In the case of an unwritten agreement, two copies of a memorandum setting out all of its terms are required.

The OFT publication has a short section on further points for trade and services supply associations which is set out in full below.

"Further points for trade and services supply associations
Where an agreement made among the members of a trade or services supply association is contained in its constitution, the rules, regulations, by-laws or resolutions of the association (or - where appropriate - those of one of its committees or sub-committees) must be provided.

If specific recommendations are made by, or on behalf of, an association to its members (or to any category of members), the agreement to establish that association is deemed to contain a term under which the members agree to comply with those recommendations. In this case the documents which must be provided are:

• the agreement by which the association is formed;

• a list of all members' names and addresses (or, if there are more than 100, an approximation of the total membership), whether or not the recommendations are made to all of them; and

• a copy of any recommendations issued to members (usually by circular letter) with the relevant extracts from the minutes - if any - authorising those recommendations."

On receiving details of a registrable agreement and after checking it to ensure that it complies with various requirements, the agreement is entered in the register. Whether an agreement is registrable is a matter of law, and the decision is based on legal advice. Registration does not imply that the OFT regards the agreement as undesirable in any way. Once an agreement has been registered the Director General must normally refer it to the Restrictive Trade Practices Court for a decision on whether the restrictions it contains are contrary to the public interest. There are four situations where such a reference is not required -

(a)   In certain limited but important circumstances the Director General may recommend to the Secretary of State that an agreement does not need to be referred.

(b)   If he thinks it appropriate, taking account of any relevant provisions of the European Community and any authorisation or exemption they may have granted to an agreement, the Director General may refrain from taking proceedings.

(c)   The Director General may also refrain from taking proceedings if the agreement has ended or if all the restrictions which make it registrable have been removed or have ceased to have effect.

(d)   In the case of some agreements by professional bodies recognised under the Financial Services Act and by the members of such bodies, the Secretary of State may direct the Director General not to make a reference to the Court.

It is the first exception that is most relevant to trade associations. Under the terms of the Act the Director General may recommend to the Secretary of State that an agreement not be referred to the Court only if the restrictions are not significant. The OFT booklet goes on -

"In assessing that, important considerations are whether the restrictions are likely to reduce competition to an extent that would be harmful to the public, or whether they would be likely to produce discriminatory or other unfair results. For instance, any agreement to fix prices would almost certainly be considered to contain restrictive restrictions. Other matters the OFT examines include:

(a) the extent to which the parties are generally subject to competition from other firms that are not parties to the agreement;

(b) the relative bargaining strength of the parties in relation to trade customers or consumers;

(c) in the case of recommendations by associations to their members on standard terms and conditions, whether those terms and conditions
   - are reasonably fair to the parties;
   - are not likely to mislead those who will use them;
   - do not unnecessarily exclude variations to meet special circumstances."

The OFT booklet comments specifically on two matters of considerable relevance to trade associations - codes of practice and standard terms and conditions. These sections of the booklet are set out in full below.

"Codes of practice - Trade associations, services supply associations and professional bodies often produce codes of practice or codes of conduct for their members to follow. Sometimes a code will have been drawn up in consultation with the OFT, which may therefore already have had an opportunity to consider the implications of any restrictions it might contain. In such a case, this part of the association's agreement may be immediately suitable for a representation to the Secretary of State.

Codes introduced without consultation with the OFT frequently contain provisions for self-regulation which do significantly restrict competition - typically in such matters as advertising, canvassing for business, and remuneration. It is likely that restrictions of this kind will have to be modified or abandoned before such a code is suitable for a representation.

Standard terms and conditions - Trade and services supply associations often recommend their members to adopt standard terms and conditions for the supply or acquisition of goods and services. Such standard terms and conditions may be in the interests of both customers and suppliers - especially for small firms with little or no legal expertise, which might otherwise enter into legally unenforceable contracts. The benefit to customers must, however, be set against the detriment that they are not free to secure any more favourable terms than those inherent in the restrictions. Consequently, the OFT always examines standard terms and conditions very closely.

Standard terms and conditions commonly incorporate provisions on liability under contract for loss or damage. Whether a limitation of liability is acceptable depends on individual circumstances. For example, it may be more economical for a customer to insure and for the supplier to reflect his reduced liability in his charges - or the customer may already be covered by insurance. Standard terms and conditions should allow for such variations.

Provision for surcharges on overdue accounts is another feature of some standard terms. It is often difficult to assess what is a reasonable rate of interest - where one is specified - but the Director General would not be able to make a representation on surcharges which included any element of penalty.

Some standard terms also provide formulas to adjust contract prices if costs should change before goods are delivered. In some trades such formulas may be desirable because they give customers a broad idea of how much extra they might have to pay, but any such formula must be fair and reasonable. The OFT generally considers them acceptable if they are based on official government indexes of labour and material costs. For some goods where raw materials are subject to severe and frequent price fluctuations the formulas may be based on cash sums rather than percentages of the contract price. Such cash-sum formulas are not necessarily a bar to a representation - but they do require more detailed investigation."

The Restrictive Practices Court consists of fifteen members - five High Court Judges and ten lay members chosen by the Lord Chancellor. The Court must declare a restriction contrary to the public interest unless it is satisfied by the parties that the restriction meets one or more specific criteria set out in the Act - usually known as the gateways. However, even if a restriction passes through a gateway the Court must be satisfied that the restriction is not unreasonable having regard to the balance between the advantage provided by the gateway and any detriment to the public which arises or is likely to arise from the operation of the restriction.

The gateways are set out in section 19 of the 1976 Act. They can be summarised as follows -

(a)   The restriction is to protect the public against injury.

(b)   Removal of the restriction would deny the public specific and substantial benefits or advantages.

(c)   The restriction is needed to counteract measures taken by another business to restrict competition.

(d)   The restriction is needed so that the parties can negotiate fair terms with a user or a supplier who controls a preponderant part of the business.

(e)   Removal of the restriction would be likely to have a serious and persistent adverse effect on the general level of unemployment in an area or areas in which a substantial proportion of the business is carried on.

(f)   Removal of the restriction would be likely to cause a reduction in export business, when this is substantial in relation to the whole business of the particular trade or industry, or to the export business of the United Kingdom as a whole.

(g)   The restriction is needed to maintain another restriction found not to be contrary to the public interest.

(h)   The restriction does not directly or indirectly restrict or discourage competition to any material degree in any relevant trade or industry, and is not likely to do so.

127

REGULATORY ISSUES

Most trade associations do not attempt to influence the conduct of their members. At first sight this seems paradoxical and indeed much press comment and public attitude seems to start from the assumption that trade associations are almost regulatory bodies and should be influencing the conduct of their members. The fact is however that they can have only limited power over their members and if they attempt to exercise that power they may suffer a loss of membership or even risk action under the restrictive trade practices legislation. One can however develop a fairly simple set of criteria which should govern whether trade associations should attempt to regulate the conduct of their members, for example through codes of practice, and if so how they are to operate these arrangements.

An industry is likely to seek to regulate behaviour of market participants where by so doing it will improve the image of the industry, increase sales and perhaps fend off statutory regulation which invariably is seen as being worse than self-regulation, although this is an assumption which is open to challenge.

The industries where self regulation is most appropriate are those which deal directly with the public and where the product is difficult to evaluate. There is for example little need to regulate transport and the sale of food other to ensure that basic safety standards are met. Problems occur where the public have little knowledge of what they are buying. This applies particularly to some financial services, building work and car repairs. In the case of some financial services there is a statutory framework for regulation through the Financial Services Act, and therefore there is little need for the trade bodies themselves to become regulators. Having said this, the deposit taking institutions and the insurance companies have established code of practices which fill in the gaps left by the absence of state regulation and may well at some stage in the future be replaced by more formal statutory regulation. Building, car repairs and estate agency are areas where self regulation remains dominant.

The problems for trade associations being regulators are basically those of ensuring that everyone in the market is covered, how any regulations are to be enforced and also possibly ensuring that restrictive trade practices legislation is not used against them. All such arrangements are potentially unstable and perhaps are held together predominantly by the fear of more onerous statutory regulation. It is helpful to illustrate these points by examining the position in a number of industries.

Dealing first with banks and building societies, the two sets of institutions are regulated respectively by the Bank of England and the Building Societies Commission. However, they are concerned with prudential regulation rather than regulating the conduct of business, although at the extreme abuses in respect of conduct of business can be grounds for regulators taking action under their respective Acts of Parliament. The Consumer Credit Act 1974 has a bearing on the sale of mortgage loans, but deposit taking and money transmission business are unregulated. It can be argued that regulation is not necessary as the products are fairly clear unlike, for example, car repairs and building work. However, there appears to be a different attitude towards the sale of financial services than there is towards the sale of other goods and services such that providers are almost obliged to sell the product that is in the best interests of the consumer.

The banks, building societies and finance houses got together to produce a code of practice for the advertising of deposits to ensure that all advertising was on a similar basis. This fairly simple code has proved effective in practice. The banks set up a voluntary ombudsman scheme with all the major banks being members. The building societies have a statutory requirement to belong to an ombudsman scheme, and the question of self regulation does not therefore arise although the industry itself was responsible for setting up the scheme. Following considerable disquiet about certain practices in respect of money transmission services, in particular the levying of charges, the banks, building societies and also the Association for Payment Clearing Services got together to produce a code of banking practice. All of the major deposit taking institutions subscribe to the code which includes in its requirements belonging to an ombudsman scheme. Compliance is achieved largely by requiring the chief executive of each institution to sign an annual statement that his institution has fully complied with the code. Transgressions are reported to a monitoring committee and investigated if necessary. In the event the code has proved to be self-policing.

Turning to the insurance companies, investment services are regulated by the Financial Services Act, and the trade associations play the proper trade association function of representing their members' interests in discussions with the regulatory bodies. There is no similar regulation of the sale of non-life insurance products. Insurance brokers have to be registered under the Insurance Brokers' Registration Act but any institution can perform the function of an insurance broker without being registered. To deal with this seemingly illogical position the Association of British Insurers agreed to operate a code of practice for the selling of general insurance which applies to all intermediaries other than those registered under the Insurance Brokers' Registration Act. The requirements under the ABI code are fairly similar to those of the Act, and the arrangement works well although the two tier arrangement has been criticised. Insurance companies operate a voluntary ombudsman scheme which gives another powerful element of protection to the consumer.

In the estate agency field, the National Association of Estate Agents operates rules of conduct. They are a condition of membership. Members have to agree to abide by them through their application form and they also must abide by the disciplinary procedure regulations. In summary, the code of conduct requires -

(a)   A duty to maintain separate clients' accounts.

(b)   A general duty to abstain from acts of dishonesty.

(c)   A duty not to carry on business with inadequate working capital.

(d)   A duty not to carry on business without stipulated security.

(e)   A duty not to describe class of membership.

(f)   A duty to abide by the aims and rules of the Association.

(g)   A duty not to seek business by improper means.

(h)   A duty to ensure that agency terms are fair and that clients are aware of them.

(i)   A duty to protect and promote clients' interests.

(j)   A duty to prevent conflicts of interest.

(k)   A duty not to accept secret commissions.

(l)   A duty to allow inspections of accounts.

(m)   A duty to assist in disciplinary investigations.

The disciplinary procedure provides for penalties ranging from a caution to expulsion.

The rules are reasonably comprehensive but as always there is room for debate as to what they mean. For example, the rule relating to carry on business without working capital simply states that "a member shall not carry on business if he lacks sufficient financial resources to operate successfully without undue risk to the interests of clients and applicants". This is a vague requirement and does not stipulate any capital sum that is required or any bonding arrangements. Similarly, the duty in respect of ensuring that agency terms are fair requires that "a member shall not propose to a prospective client terms and conditions for the supply of services, including lettings, management and commercial, which are otherwise than fair and reasonable." To help back up its code, the Association operates an insurance guarantee bonding scheme.

These arrangements undoubtedly give some protection to the consumer. However, only a minority of estate agents belong to the National Association of Estate Agents. Indeed, anyone can set up business as an estate agent without any qualifications and without belonging to any body. The NAEA has its own rules of conduct but there are different rules in operation from the two relevant professional bodies, the Royal Institution of Chartered Surveyors and the Incorporated Society of Valuers and Auctioneers.

Turning to the building industry, there is an effective self regulatory scheme in operation through the National House Building Council. In the 1950s and 1960s there was concern at the quality of some housebuilding, particularly when the builder disappeared after completing and selling a poor quality house. The unfortunate purchaser may have found that he had committed a huge amount of money but had no redress when things began to go wrong. The government, rather than legislate, persuaded the building societies to mortgage new houses only if they were built by a housebuilder registered with the National House Building Council (NHBC). Under the NHBC requirements all houses were inspected during the course of construction, had to meet the quality standards of the Council and in the event of the builder going out of business the NHBC itself arranged the necessary repair work. The NHBC formally is constituted as an insurance company. Almost without exception mortgage lenders will lend only on the security of new houses where there is NHBC cover. This is a good example of self regulation working in the interests of the consumer and also enhancing the image of an industry.

It is well known that there are major problems in policing small building work such as repairs and extensions. There have suggestions that an NHBC type of arrangement might be extended to cover small building work. In practice this is not feasible because much work is not financed by mortgage lenders. However, one of the trade bodies, the Federation of Master Builders, which represents predominantly medium and small builders, does operate a warranty scheme. Set out below is a description of the scheme taken from the Federation's publication *Focus on FMB* -

"The building industry has been subjected to unfavourable comments about poor workmanship for many years and this situation needed to be addressed. As a result it was agreed to give protection to the client from poor workmanship and inferior materials. The National Register of Warranted Builders was established in 1980, the perception of quality has been achieved and it is a great success.

The Scheme is the market leader in insurance backed guarantee schemes. It is supported by Government Departments and Local Authorities and is highly regarded by consumer groups. It has been examined by the European Commission as a basis for future European legislation. Indeed, the United Kingdom Government has a declared policy that Local Authorities should be able to provide applicants with details of local builders who are able to carry out repairs and improvement works to the appropriate standard. In drawing up a list of such builders, Local Authorities are urged to have particular regard to those firms which have an insurance-backed guarantee scheme.

Whilst membership of the Register is voluntary at present, more and more builders are joining the scheme because it is proving to be a winner with clients when seeking a builder to carry out home improvements, repairs and maintenance work.

The Warranty Scheme is insurance based, and has variable premiums depending on size of contract. Current costs are available by enquiring to the Federation's Head Office. By being able to display the Federation, EBC and Warranty logos members of the Federation have a clear advantage over other builders when seeking contracts and are more likely to be selected by clients to carry out work because of the security of an insurance based warranty scheme being offered with the contract."

The Association of British Travel Agents (ABTA) has an important regulatory role and protects people from the consequences of travel agents going bankrupt. In its promotional literature to the public, ABTA states that there are four benefits in dealing with one of its members -

(a)   ABTA members operate under strict codes of conduct.

(b)   ABTA travel agents and tour operators are required to provide financial protection to their customers.

(c)   ABTA members are required to give comprehensive advice on matters such as insurance, visas, passports, health requirements and alterations to travel arrangements.

(d)   ABTA maintains a complaints resolution procedure.

ABTA members must have capital of £50,000, total net assets after deducting intangible assets of not less than £50,000 and a working capital surplus of £15,000. There is a minimum bond level of £50,000 and, in addition, a contribution has to be made to the Travel Agents Bond Replacement Scheme amounting to £500 for each head office and £50 for each additional branch. The bond is a formal undertaking from an approved bank or insurance company to pay a sum of money to ABTA in the event of the member's financial failure, primarily for the purpose of reimbursing customers who would otherwise lose money which they had paid. All members of ABTA are required to submit to ABTA audited accounts and quarterly turnover statements. There are different rules for tour operators.

BIBLIOGRAPHY AND FURTHER READING

Mark Boléat, *The Building Society Industry* (London: Allen & Unwin, 1986).

Office of Fair Trading, *Restrictive Trade Practices - Provisions of the Restrictive Trade Practices Act 1976* (London: HMSO, 1993).

CHAPTER 12

Government Policy

Unlike in many other countries there is in Britain no specific legislation on trade associations. There is no requirement on them to be registered and they can take almost any or no legal form and there is no specific legislation which applies to them. Recently the DTI has been attempting to promote a rationalisation of the trade association structure and the development of more effective associations.

THE LEGISLATIVE FRAMEWORK

In some countries there is specific legislation governing trade associations and other trade organisations, and even a requirement on institutions in a particular sector to belong to them. In Britain there is a laissez faire attitude. There is no legislation that refers specifically to trade associations, no requirement on them to be registered, no requirement on them to publish accounts and so on. Trade associations can take any legal form. The majority are companies limited by guarantee but a significant minority are unincorporated organisations while a small minority are companies limited by shares.

Many trade associations are also employers' associations, and those associations are subject to specific legislation, currently in the form of the Trade Union and Labour Relations (Consolidation) Act 1992. Part 1.1, section 122 defines an employers' association for the purposes of the Act -

> "In this Act, an "employers' association" means an organisation (whether temporary or permanent) -
>
> (a) which consists wholly or mainly of employers or individual owners of undertakings of one or more descriptions and whose principal purposes include the regulation of relations between employers of that description or those descriptions and workers or trade unions; or
>
> (b) which consists wholly or mainly of -
>
> (i) constituent or affiliated organisations which fulfil the conditions in paragraph (a) (or themselves consist wholly or mainly of constituent or affiliated organisations which fulfil those conditions), or
>
> (ii) representatives of such constituent or affiliated organisations.

and whose principal purposes include the regulation of relations between employers and workers or between employers and trade unions, or the regulation of relations between its constituent or affiliated organisations.

References in this Act to employers' associations include combinations of employers and employers' associations."

Sections 28-37 and 43-45 of the Act make certain provisions in respect of employers' associations -

(a)   A duty to keep accounting records.

(b)   A duty to keep records available for inspection.

(c)   A right of access to accounting records.

(d)   The requirement to send an annual return to the Certification Officer.

(e)   A duty to appoint auditors.

(f)   Eligibility for appointment as auditor.

(g)   Appointment and removal of auditors.

(h)   The auditors' report.

(i)   The rights of auditors.

(j)   Provisions in respect of newly formed associations.

A Certification Officer was established in 1975 to oversee the operation of legislation in respect of trade unions and employers' associations. Part 1.1 of the Trade Union and Labour Relations (Consolidation) Act 1992 states that the Certification Officer is responsible for maintaining a list of employers' associations, and for ensuring that the statutory requirements concerning accounting records, auditors, annual returns, political funds and the statutory procedures for amalgamations and transfers of engagements in respect of employers' associations are complied with.

Any employers' association can apply to have its name included in the public lists maintained by the Certification Officer. Listing, however, is voluntary. At the end of December 1994, 117 employers' associations were on the list. In 1994 there were an additional 123 employers' associations which submitted annual returns to the Certification Officer but which did not seek to be on the list.

The one Act of Parliament which is very significant for trade associations is the Restrictive Trade Practices Act 1976. The Act requires restrictive agreements to be notified to the Director General of Fair Trading. Even informal arrangements and unwritten understandings may be registrable. The Director General has a general duty to refer registrable agreements to the Restrictive Practices Court for a ruling on whether the restrictions are against the public interest. The provisions of the Act are explained in detail in Chapter 11

GOVERNMENT POLICY - THE HESELTINE SPEECHES

Until fairly recently there was no discernable government policy on trade associations. The situation changed on 17 June 1993 when the then President of the Board of Trade, Michael Heseltine MP, made a speech on trade associations at a CBI conference. The President briefly outlined the roles that trade associations play, particularly representation but also including research, setting of technical and professional standards, supplying commercial and technical information to government, and explaining new regulations and guidelines to members, providing legal and economic services, and seeking to have an impact on policy formation. He went on -

"All these are self-evidently important tasks, for which member companies are prepared to pay. Yet remarkably little objective assessment appears to have been made about the effectiveness of these activities, or their practical value to member companies.

There is a general assumption, for example, that trade associations in Britain are weaker and less influential than their counterparts in the US, Japan and many industrial sectors in Europe. How well-founded is that belief? And if true, how much does it matter in terms of the quality of input into government policy and our overall industrial competitiveness?

Could trade associations play a much more significant role here than they do at present?

Clearly the ideal would be to have a highly effective trade association network which is fully responsive to customer needs. But how closely does that really correspond to the present situation in Britain?"

The President went on to mention briefly the Devlin Report and he asked what had changed since then. He said -

"But in far too many sectors, there appears to have been little change since Lord Devlin reported. It is widely believed that many trade associations simply do not have the resources they need to be effective - because of a fragmentation in coverage, because key companies are not members, or because the industry they serve is not prepared to provide the funds required.

135

So we still face the familiar vicious circle: some top companies won't join, whilst others won't pay more because they take the view that the trade associations representing their sector provide only a very limited service. As a result, we have too many associations who do only provide a limited service because they lack the resources to offer anything else. The inherent tragedy of this situation is that many officials of under-resourced associations - and even some of their members - continue to inhabit a kind of make-believe land. They believe they are effective, when it is all too brutally clear that they are not."

The President spelt out three minimum services he thought trade associations should be providing -

(a) They need to be in a position to influence government policies and the quality of public services. He said this requires both resources and expertise and it followed that trade associations need sufficient capability to keep track of developments within a European and other international contexts.

(b) Trade associations ought to be playing a much bigger role in promoting the international competitiveness of their member companies, including UK subsidiaries where these are foreign owned. He wanted associations to become more knowledgable about what their principal world competitors were doing and for them to give expert advice on how their sector should respond to new challenges. He wanted to see them identifying new market opportunities.

(c) Trade associations should be more influential in contributing to new government initiatives.

The President said that many trade associations were failing to meet these requirements and that been leading to growing dissatisfaction both in industry and in government. He went on -

"Bluntly the standard of representation from associations which we receive in government still varies from the good to the very poor. In sharp contrast with the well-researched and notably positive approach which I should like to see, a good deal of the input from trade associations is both negative and of a low quality. That is disturbing, not least because there has got to be a much clearer recognition that policies resulting from the closer involvement of the private sector in building an industrial strategy can only be as good as the assumptions and advice which are fed into them.

No less alarming, is that only a minority of associations appear to have thought through the implications of the growing European dimension. Few of them seem to have any clear idea of which issues should be pursued in London and which in Brussels - or of how European representation should best be organised.

Also critically in my view, only a minority of associations seem to regard the international competitiveness of the UK companies in their own sectors as a matter over which they have much influence, or for which they have any responsibility.

For all these reasons I believe that change is now urgently needed. It is not my intention to undermine the good work that is being done by the best of our trade associations. But I am determined to consider changes aimed at raising the average performance of the whole network.

The first requirement is that every sector should have at least one well-resourced trade association equipped to serve its members effectively, to engage in serious debate with government and to promote the competitiveness of their sector. That doesn't mean that industry should have a rigid structure of representation in this country, with the CBI as some kind of national federation heading a series of lesser federations below it. I am not persuaded that the Continental pattern would prove ideal, even if it could be successfully transplanted here.

Nor do I believe that every small association necessarily has to be subsumed within a large organisation. Some small associations accept that they are in business to serve niche markets and do a good job - even thought I suspect they could often benefit, without any loss of their independence, by pooling resources and effort within a larger organisation.

I should also make it clear that I see no conflict between strong sectoral associations and strong chambers of commerce acting geographically. I recognise that there is bound to be some element of overlap. I don't have a detailed blueprint to prevent this, indeed I believe they may be mutually reinforcing, rather than duplicating each other's roles."

The President then went on to how change might be brought about. He said that, at present, government departments were perhaps too polite, listening to trade association deputations attentively however unrealistic the argument being put to them. Government did not tell industrialists and associations what they thought of their representations. He intended to change this. He saw the government becoming more frank in talking to industrialists about government views on the trade associations in which they invest their resources as well as speaking frankly to the executives of the associations. He said he was considering adopting a new approach which would mean that where a lead association has emerged in a sector and the subject of proposals is relevant to the whole sector or wider, departmental officials would refer him only to the proposals from that lead association. Other representations would be referred back to the lead association for co-ordination.

The President also suggested that the CBI had a role to play in facilitating restructuring by being candid in giving views on the effectiveness of individual associations and by giving moral and practical support to those companies and associations seeking to promote change in their sectors.

He said that the principal responsibility for bringing about change fell on the companies who were members of trade associations. Companies should be aware of how much they spend and how effective their trade associations were.

The President of the Board of Trade returned to the subject of trade associations in a further speech to a CBI conference on 3 February 1995. He expressed the view that mergers, where appropriate, will lead to more powerful and effective trade associations and that such mergers can be achieved without losing or diluting the interests of particular niche industries within sectors. He asked companies to consider being more ambitious especially where there was a plethora of large and small associations all trying to represent the interests of members in the same sector. He cited the Federation of the Electronics Industry as an example of what could be achieved.

He commented on federations saying that if these led to more effective representation then he would welcome it. However, he also noted dangers if all that a federation did was to introduce another layer of bureaucracy or if it was only a nominal sharing of interests and information or only a paper exercise. He said in these circumstances it would be unwelcome because it would create the appearance of change without the substance.

Generally, the President expressed disappointment that more tangible progress had not so far been achieved. He said he would be asking officials in his sponsorship divisions to consider the issues carefully and that, together with industry, it might be possible to produce workable models for trade associations.

The President urged trade associations to undertake a critical analysis of their sector's performance internationally and the support they received from the government. Generally, he wanted competitiveness to be at the top of the agenda.

The President also wanted trade associations to have a major role in helping companies win abroad. He said he would shortly be announcing details of an export challenge for trade associations.

In February 1996 the DTI followed up the Heseltine speeches by publishing a paper, *A best practice guide for the Model Trade Association*. This is reproduced in full as an appendix to Chapter 16.

THE M90s PROGRAMME

The Department of Trade and Industry has for many years been encouraging management best practice through its Managing 90s Programme - M90s. A range of events and publications has been produced and M90s have also actively supported networking and other interaction between companies. Recently the programme has been extended to trade associations. The DTI have stated that many trade associations have recognised that they are uniquely placed to act as the catalyst for management change in companies throughout their sector. The Department lists the benefits to the sector as being by working together with other companies a company can -

(a) Build on best practice without reinventing the wheel.

(b) Customise existing material to the particular needs of that sector.

(c) Generate sector specific awareness and training material.

(d) Undertake confidential benchmarking so that companies can identify their strengths and weaknesses.

(e) Pool and share resources for mutual benefit.

The Department suggests that the partnership approach directly benefits the trade association by -

(a) Raising its profile among members and potential members.

(b) Providing valuable management information relevant to the future role of the Association.

(c) Helping to attract new members.

(d) Helping to ensure the long term survival of the sector and so of the association.

The Department states that M90s can offer -

(a) Advice based on the experience of other trade association initiatives.

(b) Free access to and customisation of the extensive M90s material produced by industry experts on all aspects of management best practice.

(c)   Advice on the most effective use of the advice and events available including a mobile presentation on competitiveness that can encourage best practice among members.

(d)   A programme of visits to companies within and outside the sector to demonstrate aspects of management best practice.

(e)   Support with launching the sectoral initiative by conference or newsletter for example.

An Evaluation of Government Policy

The two speeches of the President of the Board of Trade have served a useful purpose in stimulating debate about the role of trade associations. However, there is as yet little evidence that the Department of Trade and Industry has sought to encourage rationalisation along the lines suggested by the President of the Board of Trade. The Department generally does not appear to have increased the extent to which it comments on the effectiveness of trade associations, still less has it dealt only with one trade association in a particular field.

There are also grounds for questioning some of the functions which the President of the Board of Trade believes a trade association should have. Some associations would not see it as any part of their function to seek to increase the international competitiveness of their members. This would be true for many smaller associations where international competitiveness is irrelevant. Some large associations also have difficulty with the concept of increasing the competitiveness of their members because their members include foreign companies as well as UK based subsidiaries of foreign companies. As members of an association they are entitled to all the benefits of membership and if a very significant proportion of the resources of a trade association are devoted to what might be seen as the UK members this may not be satisfactory to other members. Having said this, the examples of the Society of British Aerospace Companies, the Society of Motor Manufacturers and Traders and the Federation of the Electronics Industry, quoted in Chapter 10, show that even large associations with an international membership can play a major role in seeking to improve the competitiveness of British industry, the term meaning the industry in Britain, rather than just British owned companies.

Perhaps the main result of Mr Heseltine's speeches in particular, and the DTI initiative on trade associations generally, has been to stimulate interest in the role and structure of trade associations, both within associations and in industry and commerce more generally. Associations are developing initiatives to become more effective, merger talks have been stimulated (for example, between METCOM and BEAMA in the engineering industry), and a number of associations have been employing higher quality staff, particularly chief executives. Associations have also been stimulated to examine the competitiveness of their particular sector and some have launched benchmarking and other initiatives. The DTI initiative has also begun to affect the attitude of other government departments towards trade associations, and it can be expected that both ministers and officials will be adopting a more critical stance in their dealings with associations. If government policy has, as yet, had few direct effects, it has certainly been a catalyst for much needed change and has probably brought forward reforms, in some cases by years. The full effects of the new government policy will take a few more years to show through; also, it will be difficult to disentangle these effects from others, notably the deep recession in the early 1990s, a more competitive environment generally and the increasing influence of the European single market.

REGULATORY ISSUES

Speech on trade associations (untitled) by Michael Heseltine MP, President of the Board of Trade, to CBI Conference, 17 June 1993.

Speech on trade associations (untitled) by Michael Heseltine MP, President of the Board of Trade, to CBI Conference, 3 February 1995.

Annual Report of the Certification Officer 1994 (London: Certification Office for Trade Unions and Employers' Associations, 1995).

CHAPTER 13

Structure And Management

Trade associations are different in nature from other corporate organisations largely because the ultimate governing body comprises people who compete with each other and who are transient in nature. Many trade associations have complex corporate structures involving numerous committees. The role of the secretariat varies from being a simple secretarial function to the dominant position in the organisation. The relative balance between the responsibilities of the secretariat and officers has been the subject of much debate and change over the last few years.

THE SPECIAL NATURE

Trade associations are businesses producing an output in the form of services to their members using inputs, predominantly staff resources. In many respects normal management principles are applicable to the management of trade associations. However, there are some special features of trade associations that are relevant in determining their system of corporate governance and how they operate as businesses.

Unlike most businesses trade associations are not profit-seeking. Some associations are run on the basis of collecting subscriptions at the end of the year to meet the costs incurred during the year. Most operate on a pay-as-you-go basis and few have substantial reserves of any form. The absence of the profit motive means that one of the usual spurs to efficient operation is not present, and equally it is difficult to produce objective criteria for measuring the success of a trade association. The application of techniques that may be appropriate in the members of the trade association, for example rigorous control of costs and profit targets for each division, can be inappropriate when applied in a trade association context.

Perhaps trade associations are most different from most other corporate organisations in respect of the composition of boards. Normally boards of any organisation, be it a large plc, a tennis club or school governors, are united in what they are trying to achieve and have a responsibility to the organisation which does not conflict with any other responsibilities. By contrast, those on the governing body of a trade association are often in competition with each other. While as members of the governing body they should be primarily concerned with the whole trade association and the industry it represents, they cannot ignore their responsibilities to their own company. There are probably some people who have served on governing bodies of trade associations with the specific objective of disrupting the trade association which they see as benefiting their competitors at their expense.

142

The governing bodies of trade associations are also transient and have become more so over recent years. Senior executives are less inclined to spend a long time with the same company culminating perhaps in many years as chief executive. Rather, people move between companies and industries more frequently, and at the very top level many now believe that five years is long enough. In the past the governing bodies of trade associations have generally had on them a number of "elder statesmen" who had passed through the chair and who helped give some stability. Potential chairmen were identified years in advance. This is now less possible, and governing bodies can change from one year to another, often unexpectedly, with there being less scope for forward planning. People generally go off governing bodies when they lose their position in their company, although some continue after that time and become gradually less effective.

A third special feature of trade associations is that there is scope for conflicts between their members including those on the governing body. Not only do they compete with each other but in their method of operation they can be divided into categories which have different interests. For example, in the insurance field in general insurance business there are those companies that write business directly and those that write through intermediaries. In life insurance similarly there are some companies that sell predominantly through independent financial advisers and others that sell directly. These groupings of companies may have different interests on key industry issues, and it is necessary to keep them all reasonably satisfied whilst maintaining an overall sense of direction. It is an interesting phenomenon that almost all members of a trade association believe that a group of members, of which they are not one, has an undue influence.

A fourth special feature is that the secretariat have a greater knowledge than members of where issues are and what forces are at work, as they are dealing with these issues full time, whereas members are only periodically involved. This difference in knowledge and perception can cause tensions between the secretariat and the members.

Finally in this section is the necessity to balance democracy and efficiency. Some trade associations have governing bodies in excess of fifty people. They all know that this is not efficient, but equally they know the importance of democracy. Members wish to feel that they are involved in the management of the organisation, if not directly then by having someone of like mind on the governing body. Special interest groups might be represented by committees but there is the potential for a clash between the views of a specialist committee and the views of the whole organisation. The greater the need to accommodate every conceivable interest through committees and governing bodies the less efficient the trade association will be. Yet at the same time the members will be seeking results and an efficient operation generally.

These features of trade associations need to be recognised by all those responsible for their management. They are not insurmountable. The skill of trade association executives and officers is in managing these special factors.

143

CORPORATE STRUCTURE

In the United Kingdom trade associations can take any corporate structure. There is no requirement for associations to be corporate bodies or to be specifically registered or authorised by any government organisation. This is in contrast to some countries, for example the USA and Belgium, where trade associations cannot exist in unincorporated form.

For many trade associations, particularly smaller ones, an unincorporated association is a satisfactory business form. This provides maximum flexibility. The constitution can be brief, changes can be made easily without the necessity to involve lawyers, and the accounting concepts are also simpler. Even quite large trade associations such as the Building Societies Association and the Association of British Insurers take the form of unincorporated associations. Appendix 1 sets out in full the constitution of the Council of Mortgage Lenders as an example of a simple, but effective, constitution for a major trade association which is an unincorporated body.

For those associations which are incorporated the basic options are to be limited by guarantee or limited by share capital. A survey of larger associations shows that the option of being limited by guarantee is the most common.

The formal corporate structure which trade associations have today probably depends on a mixture of history and accident. A newly established association, particularly a smaller one, is likely to take the form of an unincorporated association because this is cheapest and most flexible. Where associations are unincorporated or limited either by guarantee or by share capital there is little incentive for them to change their corporate form.

Where trade associations are not incorporated they cannot own property and enter into certain contracts. In practice this is not a problem as it can be overcome for example by using a member company or by using a trust company.

GOVERNANCE

Every trade association will say that the ultimate governing body is an organisation representative of members. This can go by a variety of names, the most common of which is council. In other cases the governing body might be called a board or an executive committee. The word "council" is more likely to be used where there is a large governing body; in some cases this might be recognised by terms such as "grand council". The governing body of the association must be representative of the members. How this is achieved depends on the nature of the membership.

In the case of those associations that are confederations, typically the governing body will comprise a representative or representatives of each of the member associations. For other associations there is a variety of methods of selecting the governing body. One option is for the governing body in effect to elect itself. This is similar to the process in large plcs. A committee of the board will identify future candidates for the board who will then be co-opted to the board and perhaps formally elected by the members. Where this method is used the governing body needs to be careful to ensure that all sections of the membership feel that the composition of the governing body is fair.

Some associations have provision for the largest members automatically to have a right to nominate a member of the governing body. This is in recognition of the subscription which they pay and also the need to ensure that the largest members are fully involved with the affairs of the association. Where a trade association represents an industrial sector which can be divided into a number of different sub-sectors then there might be provision for each sub-sector to select or elect members. Sometimes the division can be by type of organisation. For example, the Council of Mortgage Lenders has a constitution which provides for its governing body to be made up set numbers of building societies, finance houses, insurance companies, banks and other mortgage lenders. In the case of associations with a large number of members and with regional affiliates then election by the regional organisations is common and is a good way of ensuring that smaller members in particular are represented. In associations with a smaller number of members election nationally is feasible.

There are variations on these broad systems; the method chosen will depend on a mixture of the particular characteristics of the industry and past practice. Example are -

(a)   The Association of British Insurers has a board which technically is elected by the members but which in practice is nominated by the board itself.

(b)   The Building Societies Association has a council comprising those members (currently four) with assets of more than 5% of the industry total, six nationally elected members and one member elected by each of the three regions.

(c)   The Electricity Association has automatic membership of the board for larger companies; smaller companies can form groups of ten to elect a Board member.

(d)   The council of the Chemical Industries Association comprises representatives of the eight companies paying the highest subscriptions, nine members elected by companies paying a subscription above a threshold, three elected members for minimum subscription companies, two committee chairmen and five regional chairmen.

(e)   BEAMA has a council comprising the President, Deputy President, five counsellors, the Chairman of the Finance Committee, the Chairman or President of 18 federated associations and 17 co-opted members.

145

Perhaps the key point is not the structure of the governing body but rather the necessity to ensure that it is managed. In practice there may be little difference between the system in which the governing body elects itself and the system in which there is nomination by the largest members and election by the smaller ones. A group of people, who must in practice be on the governing body itself, have to get together to ensure that the governing body is appropriately representative of the members and has people on it who can take on the various offices. Where voting is weighted according to subscriptions as is common then the big members can through their voting power ensure that the "right" people are elected. However, the system also has to be seen to be democratic in that each member must be satisfied that the governing body fairly represents the interests of all of the members. Frequently this condition can be fulfilled only by a very large governing body. This is particularly true where there are a number of separate identifiable interest groups within the membership or where there is a large membership.

Where governing bodies get beyond a certain size then they cannot be effective in managing the association's affairs. Most trade associations that have governing bodies above, say, 15 or 20 people therefore also have a smaller grouping with more executive responsibilities. That grouping may be called the executive committee, the finance and general purposes committee, the chairman's committee or the president's committee. In addition to or in place of an executive committee there may be a smaller group of three or four centred around the chairman. The chairman may be vested with certain powers to act on behalf of the governing body but many trade associations find it helpful to have an inner core, perhaps the chairman and his deputies if there are any or the chairman and the past chairman or the chairman and one or two other members, who can act on behalf of the governing body on matters of urgency and between meetings.

There are some core functions of a trade association which must rest with the effective governing body. These include agreeing the annual budget and subscription scale, agreeing the long term strategy and annual operational plan, and settling the terms and conditions of employment of the chief executive. The governing body will also have specific responsibility for policy issues relevant to the whole association.

Almost every trade association has a chairman or president as a principal office holder. That person will be from the industry and will act in an unpaid capacity for a limited period. (There are a few exceptions to this general rule, notably the Newspaper Publishers Association which appoints a prominent public figure as its chairman.) Some trade associations have as their titular head a patron or president, generally an eminent public figure, whose activities are confined to presiding over the annual meeting and perhaps some social functions. However, attention should properly focus on the key industry office holder.

The selection of the chairman of a trade association is of critical importance. A good chairman can do much to enhance the performance of a trade association and the image of the industry. A poor chairman can be disastrous, especially when combined with a weak chief executive. The process of selection of chairmen of trade associations has undergone considerable change over recent years.

The point has already been made that the nature of business has changed with people staying at the top of companies for shorter periods than previously. Competitive pressures have also grown, and companies are now less prepared to share information with their competitors and allow their executives to devote considerable time to good causes but which are not seen, rightly or wrongly, as contributing directly to the bottom line. In the past in many industries it was accepted, particularly among the larger members, that they had a duty to provide a chairman of the association from time to time. A potential chairman could be identified years in advance and might spend ten or more years on the governing body of the association before going through to be chairman. This system generally worked well although there was the danger of the "buggin's turn" principle producing a poor chairman because he or she was expecting it, no-one having the courage to change the established course of events.

As business practices have changed so this traditional route to the chairmanship has changed. While many trade associations have found themselves in difficulty in securing someone of adequate calibre to be chairman, some executives have devoted considerable time and energy to a trade association perhaps with the objective of becoming chairman. In some cases this has been at the expense of running their own company and sadly there are examples of companies led by the chairmen of trade associations failing and of chairmen of trade associations being removed from companies, or in some cases removed in effect but not in name until after their period of office had finished. The best people in an industry are less willing to take on the chairmanship partly because they fear that the time commitment will prevent them from doing their job properly, and partly because they fear they may be compromised in competing with other companies in the industry.

The general reaction to this development has been to reduce the time commitment on a chairman both in respect of term of office and duties. Typically, a person served for two years as incoming deputy chairman then for two years as chairman and perhaps a year or two as immediate past chairman, each one of which had a major time commitment. It would be necessary to approach somebody to ask them about becoming deputy chairman the following year for a two year stint and then chairman for a further two years. This five year time horizon is now generally unrealistic. Many associations have responded to changing market conditions by reducing the period of office from two years to one or removing any run-in period. The old argument that someone needed a year to know the ropes has been seen to be incorrect in practice and has always been questionable in theory. If someone is good enough to head a major company and has the capacity to head a trade association as well then they should not need a long run-in period. The time requirement on a chairman during his or her period in office has been reduced through the delegation of much responsibility to the secretariat, a point which will be developed subsequently.

There is a fairly standard process for selecting the chairman of a trade association. Very few have meaningful elections in which there are competing candidates (although this has been the case increasingly in professional bodies, including those for lawyers, accountants and architects, in recent years). Rather, a potential chairman will be identified and approached, and then announced to the membership and formally elected in due course. This might be done internally on an informal basis with the incumbent chairman taking on this role. Most large associations have a more formal selection or appointments committee which will have the task of identifying the incoming chairman.

The role of the chairman will vary substantially between trade associations. Some will have almost an executive responsibility particularly where by accident or design there is a weak secretariat. In the larger associations and those with a strong secretariat the role can now be fairly tightly defined -

(a)   Managing the business of the governing body and resolving differences between the members.

(b)   Representing the industry where representation at top practitioner level is essential.

(c)   Ensuring that the secretariat manages the affairs of the association appropriately.

(d)   Chairing the AGM and hosting and attending appropriate social functions where the members are entitled to expect that the elected chairman will be present.

In a well run organisation these functions can be undertaken with a relatively small time commitment unless something goes seriously wrong - for example, a major split between members, perhaps some resigning, or the need to appoint a new chief executive, or, even more significantly, to remove an existing chief executive. Some chairmen wish to become much more involved particularly in exercising the representative function. Here the working relationship with the chief executive is important. Unlike in plcs and most corporate bodies the chief executive has to get used to a different chairman each year or every two or three years. Some will wish to have a hands-on approach even to the extent of being on a personal ego trip while others will see it as a duty which they will perform leaving it as far as possible to the secretariat to get on with the job. The creative tension between the two can often produce good results but in some cases is so great as to present serious problems. A chief executive may for example be hired on the basis that he or she will be the principal policy adviser and spokesman for the industry only to find a year or two later that a different chairman has a different view and that he or she becomes marginalised. This point is considered in more detail subsequently in the section on management structure.

COMMITTEE STRUCTURE

In the previous section the point was made that trade associations have a governing body, typically called a council, and if it is above a certain size then there will be a smaller grouping, perhaps an executive committee. Many associations also have a inner group comprising the office holders, say the chairman and deputy chairman or the chairman and chairmen of sub-committees, which may or may not have a formal status but which in practice exerts considerable influence particularly on day to day matters. Beyond that, trade associations have a network of committees. Some are concerned with the running of the association itself. Again the point was made in the previous section that there may be a formal selection or appointments committee which will determine who the next chairman will be. Some such committee is also needed to consider the terms of employment of the chief executive and perhaps other executives; frequently these can be combined. Some associations have a finance and general purposes committee to deal with administrative matters but increasingly these are now delegated to the chief executive.

The key policy committees of a trade association can be based either on disciplines or functions or a combination of the two. Where the activities covered by a trade association can be divided into fairly discrete categories then committees representing each category are appropriate. For example the Association of British Insurers has a Life Insurance Council, a General Insurance Council and an Investment Committee. There are also some committees that deal with more specialist areas such as creditor insurance and private medical insurance. Where the activities covered by the trade association are more homogenous then committees are more likely to be concerned with functions, for example, taxation, regulation and external relations. Often a combination of the two will be needed. The danger is of having a huge number of committees and that they may take a narrow sectional interest in conflict with the views of the organisation as a whole.

There is a difficult question of the extent to which responsibility is delegated down to such committees or rather whether their function is to make recommendations to the governing body of the association. If it is the latter then there is frustration if those recommendations are turned down; if it is the former there is a danger of committees generating a life of their own and doing and saying things which are not in accord with what the association generally has been saying. Committee chairmen are just as capable of going on an ego trip as chairmen of associations. To some extent this problem is dealt with by ensuring, for example, that chairmen of committees are on the executive committee or the governing body. This has advantages but brings with it a greater time commitment of the people who serve as committee chairmen, and also perhaps leads to the supreme governing body or executive committee being too large.

Examples of the major committees of some of the larger associations are set out below -

United Kingdom Petroleum Industry Association: Council; Executive Committee; committees on health environment and safety; fuels; legal affairs; public affairs; rail; retail; road transport; security; statistics.

Water Companies Association: Council; Executive Committee; committees on economic regulation; external strategy; quality and standards.

Chemical Industries Association: Council; Employment Affairs Board; Business and Trade Board; Chemical Industry Safety, Health and Environment Council; Science Technology Committee; Public Affairs Committee; Finance and General Purposes Committee.

Engineering Employers Federation: Council; committees on economic policy; education; training and recruitment policy; finance; health; safety and environment; representation.

Food and Drink Federation: Council; Executive Committee; committees on finance; environment; external relations; food policy and resources; food service, grocery trade liaison; scientific and advisory.

Federation of Civil Engineering Contractors: Council; committees on external affairs; legal affairs; wages and industrial; training; safety, health and welfare; environment; technical and research; open-cast coal.

In addition to committees dealing with policy issues many trade associations have technical panels made up of people who are recognised as being technical experts in their particular subject. Much of what they deal with may not be of huge policy significance but nevertheless important for the member companies. Again, there is a danger that some such panels will develop a momentum of their own and will stray into policy areas without fully thinking through the implications and what the views of the association as a whole might be.

Many trade associations have had to reorganise drastically their committee structures over the past few years. This has been an increasing acceptance that a multiplicity of committees results in a bureaucratic system with a great deal of paper being generated and no clear ownership of issues. As committee structures have become less effective so the quality of representation on them has declined. Some companies have adopted the practice of sending the same person to a number of committees; often such a person will be someone who is not highly regarded in his or her own company.

It is essential in running a trade association to ensure that the best people are on the committees. This will be done only if there are clear responsibilities for committees and if the time commitment is kept to a minimum. This is being achieved in a number of ways. The first is to abolish a large number of committees particularly those with titles involving words such as joint, co-ordinating and liaison. Secondly, wherever possible instead of there being a permanent committee an ad hoc working group should be established to deal with a particular subject. The working group is then stood down when its work is completed. This avoids the proliferation of unnecessary committees which some people then enjoy being on, perhaps because it gives for them a power base and perhaps the opportunity for regular visits to London at somebody else's expense.

Most importantly, more sensible use of committees must go hand in hand with greater delegation to the secretariat. It is the secretariat's task to do intelligent staff work to facilitate decision-taking. If it is the secretariat's responsibility to prevent committees getting out of line and adopting policies which are inappropriate then the need for some committees, in particular co-ordinating and liaison committees, is reduced. If the affairs of the committee are well managed then the time commitment on the members is reduced. If it is clear what the committees can and cannot do and if they are seen to be important then people of the right calibre will attend. The process is a circular one. Time-wasting committees attract time-wasters. Effective committees attract effective people.

The process of reducing committee numbers is painful. There is a fairly typical pattern. The top people in an industry will come to the view that there are too many committees and will order there to be a sharp reduction. The secretariat (or in some cases even a newly established committee) will draw up proposals to merge certain committees and abolish others. This will be warmly welcomed by the governing body but will meet with criticism by some of the committees. The proposals will then be reconsidered and watered down. The devious association may take steps to stand down committees in effect if not in theory, by ensuring that they never meet. The process is often two steps forward and one step backwards, and it needs very firm leadership from the top if it is not to fall foul of the vested interests of certain members of committees.

Effective committees are central to the operation of trade associations. They provide the vital practitioner input which is unlikely to come either from the members of the governing body or from the secretariat. The process of selecting or electing members of the committees is important. This is probably carried out in practice by the secretariat, if in theory by the governing body. The experts in the industry must be identified at an early stage and involved in the affairs of the association. There must be seen to be a two-way benefit. The association must benefit from their input, but equally they will derive a benefit by having an early warning of some impending developments and being fully familiar with certain industry issues before their competitors. The importance of being on trade association committees is recognised in many companies, as is the cost. It is not unknown for some large members of a trade association to complain one day that too many of their staff are on the committees of the association, and to complain the next that they are not represented on a newly established committee on a major issue.

ROLE OF THE SECRETARIAT

The role of the secretariat in a trade body will depend to a large extent on how large it is. Some trade associations have only one or two members of staff, who can be expected to be no more than administrators leaving the key work to be undertaken by the members. The trade associations representing significant industrial sectors have a full-time secretariat, often a large one. As a general rule the big associations have around fifty staff involved in which might be called trade association work; other staff may be engaged on commercial activity or services which are self-financing. The analysis in this chapter deals predominantly with those associations with large secretariats.

Obviously one function of trade association staff is to serve committees. This function used to be the most important. The skills required were those of a committee clerk, that is drawing up and distributing agendas, attending meetings, faithfully taking the minutes and communicating with others about the action to be taken. This task is important but less so than it was, partly because of the sharp reduction in the number of committees in many trade associations. People who are skilled only at being committee clerks are not needed if there are fewer committees to clerk. The committee clerk function has also changed as more responsibility has been devolved to the secretariat. Often the secretariat will have complete responsibility for drawing up the agenda and producing the minutes with there being no involvement of members or even of the chairman. It is no longer good practice to seek the chairman's approval for anything to happen and to ask various people to vet the minutes before they are distributed to members of a committee.

The trade association staff have to run the business. Managing the finances, managing the office building and managing the staff are all business functions. In some cases responsibility is delegated to the secretariat while in others committees become involved. Increasingly the practice is for the chief executive to be given responsibility over all administrative matters including, for example, all matters relating to staff within broad guidelines given by the governing body, and all other matters that are connected with the running of the business. It is no longer the case that cheques have to be signed by officers rather than by executives, or that officers are involved in interviewing staff below chief executive level.

The most important work of the trade association secretariat is to do the business of the trade association, that is representing the members and providing services to them. This is a management discipline that has developed greatly over the last few years, but it is still one that has not reached all trade associations including a number of the larger ones. The key trade association staff must no longer be reactive, waiting to be told what to do by committees; rather they have to identify the issues with which the trade association should be concerned. They have to have a major responsibility in developing policy together with practitioners using their knowledge of the policy process and what is feasible and what is not. They have to co-ordinate the work of the trade association. The point was made in the previous section that committees can develop a life of their own and can work contrary to the interests of the trade body as a whole. Increasingly it is recognised to be the secretariat's responsibility to have an overview of what is happening in the committee structure and to ensure that no committee is going beyond its responsibilities and that where it is considering policy issues it does so in the full knowledge of the overall policy of the association.

The implementation of policy is increasingly a matter for the secretariat. Once a decision has been taken it should be left to the secretariat to implement it in its entirety. This may involve finalising the drafting of a policy paper, forwarding it to officials and then having discussions with them. It may be necessary to involve practitioners in this but the key responsibility should be with the secretariat.

MANAGEMENT STRUCTURE

The management structure of a trade association partly reflects the nature of the association and partly the extent to which the philosophy of delegating matters to the secretariat has been adopted. The key person in any trade association is the chief executive. In some very small associations with a staff of only one or two the chief executive properly has the title of secretary and that is the function. Where a trade association has a significant staff then traditionally the title of the chief executive was secretary general, recognising the important secretary role. As more has been delegated to the secretariat so the title has changed over time and most large associations now have a director general or a director. Some use the simple title, chief executive.

The principal functions of the chief executive are -

(a)   Management of the association including all staff matters.

(b)   Principal policy adviser to the association.

(c)   Principal spokesperson of the association, although in some cases this may be the responsibility of the chairman.

153

In any trade association all staff must ultimately report to the chief executive. In many associations the practice, if not the theory, was for some staff to report to committees. In addition to causing confusion between the responsibilities of committees and the ultimate governing body, this practice also caused management problems. It is essential that organisations are not allowed to build up within organisations and that there is a proper pyramid structure in place.

The large associations tend to have a broadly similar management structure. There will be a department concerned with the provision of central services such as personnel, finance, accommodation and office administration. A second department will be responsible for external relations or public affairs, with the former title now being the most common. This will deal with the media, consumer organisations and the like, and will also be responsible for some co-ordination of essential representative work with the government and appropriate regulatory bodies. The key policy departments are likely to be divided into fiscal and legal matters. Where the association has identifiable interest groups then departments may reflect these, particularly where the core issues such as regulation conveniently split into groups. The big associations generally have an economics and statistics department although this function might be part of an external relations department. Some associations have separate departments to deal with European or international matters, although increasingly European matters are now integrated into the normal work of the association. Generally, it is necessary to be pragmatic. From time to time it may be justified to have responsibility for all matters in a market, eg the USA, resting with one member of staff.

The big associations, those with, say, fifty staff, are likely to have an inner management team of five or six people. One of the departmental heads may be designated as deputy chief executive or alternatively someone might have this as a specific job title without any functional responsibilities.

The organisational structure below the departmental heads will be little different from that in similar sized organisations. There is the same scope for debating whether there should be a flat management structure or the more traditional pyramid approach. However, there is little which distinguishes a trade association in terms of management structure from other organisations.

Set out below are the job titles of the executive teams of a number of associations usefully illustrating the typical structure described above.

    Association of Unit Trusts and Investment Funds
        Director General
        Director of Legal and Fiscal Affairs
        Director of Communications

Association of British Insurers
  Director General
  Deputy Director General and Head of Public Affairs
  Head of Legal and Fiscal Affairs
  Head of Life Insurance
  Head of General Insurance
  Head of Central Services
  Head of Investment Affairs

British Bankers Association
  Director General
  Director, Operations Matters
  Director, Banking Supervision, Regulation, Accountancy and Taxation
  Director, Statistics
  Director, Banking Information Service
  Director, Administration

Building Societies Association
  Director General
  Deputy Director General
  Head of Legal Services
  Head of Research and External Affairs
  Head of Financial Policy
  Head of Personnel, Finance and Administration

Association of the British Pharmaceutical Industry
  Director
  Director of European and Commercial Affairs
  Secretary and Director of Intellectual Property and Legal Affairs
  Director of Public Affairs
  Director, Centre for Medicines Research
  Director of Medical, Scientific and Technological Affairs

Paper Federation of Great Britain
  Director General
  Director, Business and Environment
  Company Secretary
  Director, Administration and Training
  Head of Industrial Relations
  Manager, Communications
  Manager, External Services

Newspaper Society
  Director
  Deputy Director/Head of Government and Legal Affairs
  Head of Employment Affairs
  Head of Development, Education and Training

British Printing Industries Federation
  Director General
  Deputy Director General
  Director, Corporate and Policy Affairs
  Director, Employment Affairs
  Director, Finance
  Director, Membership Services
  Director, Sections

STAFF REQUIREMENTS

As the nature of trade associations has changed, with more being delegated to the secretariat, job requirements have also changed.

The chief executive needs to be capable of leading an organisation. The managerial skills needed to head a complicated organisation are more important than in similar sized organisations because of the unique nature of trade associations described in the first section of this chapter, in particular the absence of a profit motive and a transient governing body. He or she must have the appropriate standing so that they can talk on equal terms with the members of the governing body and also be of such standing that they can represent the association publicly whether it be through making speeches or through representations and media appearances at whatever level is appropriate.

There is no obvious career path to become a chief executive of a trade association. It is not similar to the way that people can work their way up through a company or the civil service. Some of the best trade association chief executives have spent much of their working life in a trade association field and have made a career of it. Some of those who have come from outside have been civil servants or have worked in a quango thereby having a good knowledge of public policy issues. Some have come from within the industry, often in the belief that a good knowledge of industry issues is essential. Traditionally, many have come from the armed forces.

The key to obtaining the right chief executive is to offer the appropriate remuneration package and to adopt a sensible selection process. The two run together. Appointing a deputy to succeed a chief executive on retirement may make sense in many cases but it is not something which should be done automatically. Increasingly the big trade associations use head hunters whilst smaller ones advertise and perhaps use some professional assistance. There is much debate over the appropriate remuneration package. Trade associations traditionally have been poor payers and as a result have attracted poor executives. Where a chief executive has turned out to be good he or she has often moved on to more remunerative employment perhaps in the industry, perhaps with another trade association or perhaps in a totally different field. This has been increasingly recognised over the last few years and the salaries of chief executives have risen accordingly. Among the City trade associations the typical salary range for chief executives is now from £120,000 to £150,000, and some of the larger associations representing manufacturing industries also pay their chief executives over £100,000 a year. A CBI survey of mainly large trade association salaries in November 1995 showed a median salary of £78,500 for chief executives. Interestingly, there was little differentiation by size of association in terms of number of staff employed. The main determining factor is the size of the sector being represented.

The requirements on the senior management team of a trade association are not too dissimilar from those of the chief executive except that the vital leadership and management skills are not quite so necessary. The CBI survey in November 1995 showed a median range of £43,325 to £56,125. There are a number of senior staff earning salaries in excess of £80,000.

The larger trade associations typically have a senior management team of between five and seven and then perhaps fifteen to twenty other staff who have a responsibility for policy areas, disciplines or particular functions. Those staff will need all the usual skills and expertise for someone in their position. It is worth emphasizing however particular requirements for staff in trade associations. They must have excellent communication skills in respect of standards of written English, the ability to draft quickly, appropriate oral communication skills, in particular effective and authoritative contributions at meetings, high quality personal skills and the ability to think laterally. They need to have sufficient knowledge of the industry with which they are dealing. They do not need to be experts because they can readily call on experts within the industry, but they must understand the basics. Most of the policy issues with which they will be dealing are not related to detailed aspects of the industry but rather are concerned with broader issues where perhaps legal or tax expertise is needed or simply where there is a difficult public policy issue.

The most important requirement however is that there should be a willingness and an ability to "own" particular issues and projects. They cannot hide behind committees and regard themselves as mere committee secretaries; rather they have to become the industry expert on the issue and take the lead in developing policy and making representations. They need to be able to guide committees rather than simply serve them. This work involves the communications skills referred to earlier but also requires diplomatic skills. The members may well be wrong but they are after all the members. If an issue is handled properly the members of whatever committee or board a paper is put to are likely to come to the right decision. There will be some individuals and members who are particularly awkward. The skilled trade association executive can deal with these people, perhaps helped by a committee chairman or the chairman of the association. It may be a case of giving way on a relatively small point or simply persuading the member that although their views are respected and are valid they are not shared by the majority of members.

A trade association equipped with a good director general, a top rate senior management team and other senior staff with the skills outlined in this section will be very effective. For the staff concerned there is great job satisfaction in taking responsibility for a subject and also in being involved at the highest level both with the members and with other bodies such as government and parliament. By contrast there is nothing more frustrating than good staff work being thrown away at a first meeting with, say, civil servants or ministers at which company representatives take the lead or staff, on instruction, attempt to dictate or bully.

Appendix 2 to this chapter sets out the formal requirements for the senior managers of the Association of British Insurers as a good example of what is required on senior staff.

CONTRACTING OUT MANAGEMENT

Trade associations are invariably relatively small organisations compared with the size of member companies. The staff have to cover a wide range of areas. This can present problems because the work load may suddenly increase in one area, and it is not possible easily to augment staff resources if particular skills are necessary. The management of trade associations can be assisted by contracting out some work.

At one extreme some associations contract the whole of their management to other associations. Typically a large association may have affiliated to it a number of small associations representing special interest groups with the whole of the management of those small associations being carried out by the larger one. In practice there may be very little difference between this sort of arrangement and one in which there are special interest committees within the structure of the main association. As an example of a large association servicing others the Paper Federation services six related associations, the British Association of Trade Computer Label Manufacturers, the British Box and Packaging Association, the British Disposable Products Association, the Catering Industries Liaison Council, the Environmental and Technical Association for the Paper Sack Industry and the Packaging Distributors Association. An External Services Department of the Paper Federation is responsible for these management services.

An alternative arrangement where there is no obvious "parent" association is for the management to be sub-contracted, for example to a specialist firm of association management companies (of which there are only two or three), a firm of chartered accountants or solicitors. In such cases the managing agent generally performs an administrative function with the members themselves having the policy input. It may be that as the importance of effective trade associations is increasingly realized so there will be a growth of association management companies (AMCs).

(It is instructive here to note the importance of these companies in the American context. This brief description is largely taken from an advertising feature in *Association Management* by William Drohan, President of an AMC. There are currently some 500 AMCs managing more than 1,700 associations. Many of these associations represent specific market segments of a large industry or profession which wish to demonstrate their independence. Associations can contract for total administration, a single service on an ongoing basis, a specific time period, or a single project. Areas of expertise include executive management, public affairs and lobbying, membership development, communication services, financial management and accounting, meetings and convention planning, marketing, education and professional development and management consulting services. Typically an AMC provides an account executive who serves as executive director for the organisation, administrative staff and specialist staff. The AMC offices serve as the headquarters. Fees can be structured on a flat basis or a "time and materials" basis.)

Like other companies trade associations have the option of contracting out services such as building maintenance, personnel, finances and catering.

Trade associations need and will draw on the services of management consultants, academics, lawyers, accountants and others as necessary. It makes sense for a trade association to have a good relationship with professional firms which provide services to members. A trade association can be certain of getting a good service from any company that wishes subsequently to deal with the members. A legal firm for example will be helped in its dealings with members if it also works for the trade association. The association may wish to contract out the whole of its legal services for example or alternatively it can augment its in-house service by going outside when the need arises. There will be occasions when it makes sense to go outside because the members or others are more impressed by an independent outside report than by something produced by the organisation itself. More generally, an association cannot have all the expertise it needs in-house so use of outside consultants is an efficient way to handle issues. Consultants can also be used to deal with problems that would otherwise be caused by peaks and troughs of work in particular areas.

BIBLIOGRAPHY AND FURTHER READING

Mike Hudson, *Managing Without Profit* (London: Penguin, 1995).

Constitution of the Council of Mortgage Lenders

Adopted by the Executive Committee on 30 March 1995

INTRODUCTION

1.   The name of the Council shall be the "Council of Mortgage Lenders" (referred to in this constitution as "the CML").

2.   The CML was established on 1 August 1989.

3.   The CML has the following mission statement -

"The Council of Mortgage Lenders provides a service to mortgage lending institutions by helping to establish a favourable operating environment, by providing a forum for discussion on non-competitive issues, and by providing information to assist them in their business."

OBJECTIVES

4.   The CML shall have the following objectives -

(a) To be a central representative body to put the views of mortgage lending institutions to Government departments and agencies, Parliament, the Bank of England, the European Commission and other relevant organisations.

(b) To be a research and statistical centre, to aggregate and publish statistics, and to provide analysis on mortgage lending and other relevant market information.

(c) To be a technical centre providing commentary, guidance and advice on all legal, fiscal, financial and other regulatory developments of relevance to mortgage lending.

(d) To provide a forum for the exchange of non-competitive information.

(e) To provide a focus for media relations stemming from (a) to (d).

MEMBERSHIP

5.   Membership of the CML is available to institutions which are mortgage lenders, and, in exceptional cases, institutions which, as their principal business, service or finance mortgage loans. Admission to membership is at the discretion of the Executive Committee.

ASSOCIATES

6. The Executive Committee shall, at its discretion, admit as an associate of the CML any organisation which is not a mortgage lender, but which is otherwise interested in the operation of the mortgage market. Associates shall be entitled to receive most publications and other literature prepared under the auspices of the CML, but shall not otherwise be entitled to participate in the affairs of the CML. They shall not advertise or promote themselves as having a relationship with the CML.

FINANCE OF THE CML

7. The financial year of the CML shall be the calendar year but this may be changed by resolution of the Executive Committee.

8. The costs of running the CML shall be met by The Building Societies Association. Each member other than a member of The Building Societies Association shall pay an annual subscription according to a scale which shall be set by the Executive Committee. Such a scale shall provide for a minimum subscription of no less than £2,000 and shall be related to mortgage assets, or mortgage assets under administration (whichever is higher). The total sum to be collected shall be set in consultation with the BSA on the basis of the services provided to the CML by the BSA Secretariat.

9. Associates shall pay an annual subscription fixed by the Executive Committee.

MEETINGS OF THE CML

10. The CML shall hold an annual general meeting not later than four months after the end of each financial year. At least 10 members of the CML, or the Executive Committee, may at any time require the Secretary to convene a general meeting of the CML. In convening such a meeting the Secretary shall give not less than 21 days notice to members.

EXECUTIVE COMMITTEE

11. The affairs of the CML shall be directed by an Executive Committee, the composition of which shall be decided by the Executive Committee subject to the following -

    (a) No more than nine members representing building societies.

    (b) No more than seven members representing institutions authorised under banking legislation.

(c) No more than three members representing insurance companies.

(d) No more than two members representing finance houses.

(e) No more than four members representing other mortgage lenders.

12. Where a trade body exists for a category of member it shall be invited to nominate candidates for the Executive Committee. If there is no trade body wishing to make nominations the Executive Committee shall decide how members in the appropriate category shall be elected or otherwise chosen.

13. Members of the Executive Committee shall be appointed or elected to serve from the first meeting of the Committee in each financial year until the first meeting in the following financial year.

14. A member of the Executive Committee shall cease to be a member if he resigns, or if he ceases to hold office in (or be employed by) the institution in which he has hitherto held office (or been employed) or if a nominating body withdraws its nomination. The Executive Committee shall have the power to fill any casual vacancy after considering any nomination from a relevant trade body.

15. Each member of the Executive Committee shall have one vote. The Chairman shall have a second, or casting, vote in the event of equality.

CHAIRMAN AND DEPUTY CHAIRMAN

16. The Executive Committee shall, at its first meeting in each financial year, elect a chairman to hold office as chairman of both the CML and of the Executive Committee until the first meeting in the following financial year. The Executive Committee shall also elect a deputy chairman, who shall not come from the same group of institutions as the chairman. No person may hold the office of chairman, or of deputy chairman, for more than two consecutive years. In the event of the chairman or the deputy chairman resigning or ceasing to be a member of the Committee, the Committee shall have power to elect a replacement to serve for the remainder of the term, this period of office not counting for the purpose of the requirement in the previous sentence.

SUB-COMMITEES AND PANELS

17. The Executive Committee may establish and maintain sub-committees, and may delegate matters to them.

162

18.   The Executive Committee may appoint technical panels to advise and assist it.

19.   The composition of sub-committees and panels shall reflect the membership of the CML, and any special interests of groups of members.

SECRETARIAT

20.   Secretariat services shall be provided by The Building Societies Association on terms to be agreed between the Executive Committee and the Association. A senior member of that Secretariat will be designated as Secretary to the CML and to the Executive Committee.

REVISION OF THE CONSTITUTION

21.   This constitution shall be amended by the CML, provided that at least 75% of the members of the CML present at the meeting vote in favour of amendments of which prior notice has been given.

ABI Senior Management Requirements

INTRODUCTION

1. Staff in any organisation are entitled to know what is expected of them. This applies equally to senior managers. This paper sets out what is required of senior managers under six headings -

    (a) Insurance

    (b) Professional skills

    (c) Management skills

    (d) Trade associations skills

    (e) Leadership and presence

    (f) ABI business.

    It is recognised that there is a significant overlap between these categories.

INSURANCE

2. All senior managers need a basic knowledge of insurance. A reasonable expectation is that they should -

    (a) Be familiar with a basic text, such as Carter and Diacon's *Success in Insurance*.

    (b) Understand fully the current state of the business, in particular the annual statistics publication.

    (c) Understand the ABI consumer publications.

3. The Director General and the Head of Public Affairs need a greater degree of knowledge so as to be able to undertake the necessary representative work. The Head of Legal & Fiscal Affairs needs knowledge relevant to current issues being handled by his Department, often covering a wide range of matters. Specialist knowledge is needed by the Senior Managers responsible for life and general insurance.

164

PROFESSIONAL SKILLS

4. Some particular professional skills and knowledge are required, generally so as to be able to manage those who are required to have specific skills. More specifically -

    (a) The Head of Legal & Fiscal Affairs needs to be familiar with legal, tax and regulatory issues, including European matters.

    (b) The Head of Investment Affairs must be knowledgeable about the securities markets and corporate governance issues.

    (c) The Head of Central Services needs a knowledge of information technology, statistics, financial control, personnel and building and office services.

MANAGEMENT SKILLS

5. All Senior Managers must be excellent managers; this is the essential requirement for such a position. The required skills include -

    (a) Day-to-day management such that committee papers etc are prepared on time and are of good quality, correspondence and phone calls are handled promptly and efficiently, information is given to members in a timely and user-friendly way, and generally the workload is efficiently managed.

    (b) Planning on a long, medium and short term basis such that work that needs to be done is identified and then managed.

    (c) Staff management, including training, encouraging career development, team building, leadership, motivation and delegation.

    (d) Effective communication to their staff directly or through delegation what is required of them, policy developments, ABI developments, developments in the department etc. They must ensure effective communication within the department and between the department and other departments. Senior Managers are also responsible for upward communication to the Director General and Senior Managers collectively.

    (e) Participating fully as a team player in the senior management team, including commenting within the specified time on papers circulated to Senior Managers.

    (f) Budgeting and financial control within their departments, including annual preparation of departmental budget and monitoring of expenditure.

6.	Managers are held fully responsible for the work of their departments. If there are staff problems, eg poor quality in some areas, poor morale, high turnover, this is the responsibility of the Senior Manager. The excuse of inadequate staff resources, in terms of quality or quantity, is not acceptable for anything other than the very short term.

TRADE ASSOCIATION SKILLS

7.	Senior Managers whose work includes policy issues must have a high level of trade association skills. These include -

(a)	Understanding current public policy issues.

(b)	Understanding the political and regulatory system.

(c)	Appropriate personal contacts with relevant government departments, regulatory bodies, other trade associations and members.

(d)	Excellent written communication skills, in particular in respect of policy representations.

(e)	Verbal communication skills. At a minimum, these must be excellent at the committee level and competent with large audiences. Ideally they should be good to excellent in respect of radio and TV and large audiences.

LEADERSHIP AND PRESENCE

8.	Senior Managers should be distinguished from other managers by the qualities of presence and leadership. Each senior manager should have 'presence' through their appearance, manner, skills and knowledge, that immediately establishes their authority in meetings with staff, members, civil servants, regulators etc.

9.	Leadership refers both to leadership of a department and to ownership of all issues that come within the province of the department. Each Senior Manager must, through his work not his position, command the respect of his department, other Senior Managers, members etc. This must involve 'ownership' of all issues that properly come within the province of the department. This includes identifying issues that should be handled as well as handling ongoing issues. Ownership means taking lead responsibility for an issue and is very different from a committee secretary role. It implies disagreeing with committees at times and guiding them at all times. It is an abdication of responsibility for a senior manager to rely on a committee to identify policy issues or to formulate policy.

ABI Business

10. All Senior Managers should be fully familiar with the business of the ABI and should be managing their departments accordingly. This involves -

   (a) Full participation in the management of the ABI through Senior Managers' meetings and in other ways.

   (b) Understanding the budget and finances generally.

   (c) Understanding fully the ABI strategy, current internal targets and policy priorities and the Annual Report.

   (d) Keeping up-to-date through studying all papers that go to the Board, relevant committees and the staff.

Summary and Checklist

11. Senior Managers must judge themselves and will be judged against the following criteria -

   (a) Knowledge of insurance appropriate to the position, ranging from basic knowledge for the Head of Central Services to detailed knowledge for those responsible for the insurance work.

   (b) Other professional skills as appropriate.

   (c) Management skills covering -

      (i) day-to-day management,

      (ii) planning,

      (iii) staff management, in particular motivation, delegation and communication,

      (iv) participation in senior management team,

      (v) financial control.

(d)   Trade association skills covering -

      (i)   understanding policy issues,

      (ii)   understanding the political and regulatory system,

      (iii)   appropriate personal contacts,

      (iv)   excellent writing skills,

      (v)   good verbal communication skills.

(e)   Presence.

(f)   Leadership and ownership in respect of the department and all relevant issues.

(g)   Understanding of ABI business, strategy and current issues.

CHAPTER 14

Finance

Trade associations are not profit-seeking-organisations. Nevertheless, they need to be run on sound financial lines. Core trade association services are financed by subscription income, and subscriptions scales are among the more controversial parts of trade association business. Commercial activity can generate significant additional income.

OVERVIEW

The previous chapter noted the basic characteristics of trade associations. Most take the legal form of either a company limited by guarantee or an unincorporated association. They exist to serve their members and cannot have corporate objectives independently of their members. Most corporate organisations seek to maximise a combination of their profit and their size measured in turnover. For trade associations this cannot be a legitimate objective; rather they have to provide the service their members want at minimum cost. Capital is also not important for trade associations. Many large trade associations operate with limited, and in some cases, negative capital.

Trade association representative work can be financed only by subscriptions. It is not of its very nature a commercial activity as all members of the relevant group benefit regardless of whether they pay the cost. Typically subscription income accounts for more than three quarters of total income. Most expenditure comprises staff costs and related accommodation costs. Table 14.1 shows a typical income and expenditure account for a large trade association.

Table 14.1 Income and Expenditure, Typical Large Trade Association

	£000
Income	
Subscriptions	3,000
Interest	150
Services and other income (net)	250
	3,400
Expenditure	
Staff	1,750
Property	750
Office	250
Travel, hotels, entertaining	150
Depreciation	100
Other	300
	3,300
Surplus before tax	100
Tax	(40)
Surplus for year	60

There are some basic principles which should govern the financial operations of all trade associations, having accepted the basic premise that they are not profit-seeking organisations.

They have to be run in a businesslike way and this means using the same financial tools as are used in corporate organisations with more commercial objectives. In this respect they are no different from other non-profit-seeking organisations such as charities, educational establishments and public sector institutions. There should be proper systems for making financial projections in the medium term, shorter term budgeting, financial controls and monitoring. Policies are needed in respect of reserves, prices and subscriptions.

Having accepted the basic principles that trade associations are member organisations and are not profit-seeking, a further financial principle follows, that is, trade associations should be run, broadly speaking, on a pay-as-you-go basis. The membership of trade associations will change over time as new entrants come into and some existing participants leave the market. Market shares may change substantially from year to year. On this basis it is reasonable, in any one year, that the subscriptions payable should equal the costs of running the business for that year. If they reflect income or costs that were incurred some time in the past or might be incurred some time in the future there is an inequitable position, and one that might not be easy to justify to all members. An association which seeks to build substantial reserves by making profits year by year is, in effect, transferring resources from today's members to tomorrow's members. Similarly, an organisation being run at a substantial deficit is relying on future membership to pay for past services. These are not stable positions or supportable propositions for the current membership or governing body. However, reserves do enable exceptional items of expenditure to be more easily coped with.

It can be argued that the pay-as-you-go principle might point to subscriptions being levied annually in arrears based on actual expenditure and membership. While there is some merit in this it goes against the objective of running the organisation in a businesslike way and is not a practice followed by most well-run trade associations. Rather, most associations raise subscriptions for a year which will roughly meet planned expenditure in that year.

Unlike many other organisations, trade associations have little need for capital. Some associations, however, do have substantial capital either through initial contributions (as for example with the Electricity Association which has share capital of £16 million) or as a result of the accumulated profits in the income and expenditure account. For many associations there is a divergence between the capital position as disclosed in the published accounts and the true position, because there is no requirement to value property at market value rather than historic cost. Some associations have owned the freeholds of their premises for many years and have no financing costs. Such associations can provide a given level of service for a significantly lower subscription income than those associations paying a market rent. At the other extreme some associations had the misfortune to acquire a long lease at the peak of the property market and are now paying perhaps twice the current market rent. A few associations acquired leases at the peak of the market of properties larger than they needed for their own occupation and are now not only paying above the market rent on their own accommodation but also are carrying a substantial cost of property which is sublet to tenants. An association with no rental costs can run with subscriptions 25% lower than one paying a market rent.

Some associations have had a target level of capital, for example, the Building Societies Association had a policy of maintaining free reserves (defined as net assets less the balance sheet figure for property) at 10-15% of annual expenditure although it has actually achieved a much higher proportion and has now adopted a 25% target. In the USA a typical median reserves goal is 40% of annual operating income with the median actually achieved being 30%.

Table 14.2 shows for a number of associations published data on capital and reserves in relation to the key variables of subscription income and total expenditure. It must be stressed that the table is not comparing like with like because of substantial differences in accounting policies and more particularly because of the property factor described above.

For example, an association with balance sheet reserves and capital of, say, £1 million, might also own the freehold of a property which could be worth £10 million. Conversely, an association which might seemingly have substantial balance sheet reserves might own a property with a market value substantially below its book value or be tied into a long-term lease at significantly above current market rents.

Having made these qualifications, it is interesting that there is such a huge variation of capital positions. There are a few associations whose balance sheets suggest that they are strongly capitalised. They include the Electrical Contractors Association, the British Leather Confederation, the Heating and Ventilating Contractors' Association, the Road Haulage Association and the National Farmers Union. At the other extreme, there are some associations that operate with minimal capital, although again it must be stressed that such associations might be financially strong, depending on their accommodation position.

It would seem to be good practice that at the very least an association should have a stated policy in respect of capital and reserves.

Table 14.2 Reserves and Capital, Selected Associations, 1994 Data

Large associations	Reserves & Capital £m	Subscription Income £m	Total Expenses £m	Reserves/ Income %	Reserves/ Expenses %
National Farmers Union	30.3	14.8	19.9	205	152
Association of British Insurers	3.2	14.1	20.3	23	16
Electricity Association	17.2	5.7	19.8	302	87
Building Employers Confederation	5.7	5.0	5.6	114	161
Chemical Industries Association	0.2	4.1	4.6	5	5
Retail Motor Industry Federation	1.5	3.3	7	44	21
Building Societies Association	1.5	3.3	3.4	45	44
British Printing Industries Federation	1.2	3.2	5.6	37	21
Society of Motor Manufacturers and Traders	2.8	3.0	9.5	92	29
Association of British Travel Agents	4.1	2.9	6.2	142	66
National Federation of Housing Association	1.5	2.8	6.5	54	24
Federation of Master Builders	1.4	2.5	2.8	57	51
Freight Transport Association	4.1	2.3	11.3	177	36
Water Services Association	1.0	2.3	3.5	45	29
Newspaper Society	1.1	2.1	3.6	50	30
Electrical Contractors Association	25.9	1.9	5.5	1328	295
Road Haulage Association	3.6	1.7	2.4	212	148
Association of Unit Trusts and Investment Funds	0.0	1.7	1.9	0	0
Heating and Ventilation Contractors Association	5.5	1.4	5.3	410	104
The Paper Federation	1.3	1.2	1.9	107	67
British Plastics Federation	0.5	1.2	1.3	43	39
Vehicle Builders and Repairers Association	0.7	1.1	2.0	65	36
National Association of Estate Agents	0.6	1.0	1.0	58	61
Total1	**114.9**	**82.6**	**150.9**	**151**	**65**
Median				57	39
Medium Associations					
British Hospitality Association	0.8	0.9	1	87	77
Timber Trade Federation	0.8	0.8	0.9	103	88
British Rubber Manufacturers Association	0.1	0.7	0.7	7	7
British Property Federation	0.7	0.6	0.7	111	107
British Leather Confederation	2.2	0.5	1.5	421	148
Producers Alliance for Cinema and television	0.3	0.4	1.5	98	23
Total	**4.9**	**3.9**	**6.3**	**138**	**75**
Median				100	77
Total all associations	**119.8**	**100.7**	**157.2**	**148**	**68**
Median				87	44

Note: Figures are from annual reports for years ending between 1/7/94 and 30/6/95.

172

Some associations may have a policy of seeking to retain any surplus they earn on income and expenditure account rather than using it automatically to reduce subscriptions in the following year.

This usefully leads on to one important issue in financial policy for trade associations, that is the smoothing of subscription income. Generally, trade association expenditure is quite stable but there can be occasions when, for one reason or another, there might be a significant change in income or expenditure from year to year. For example, professional fees might be very high one year reflecting the need to deal with substantial legislative and regulatory issues. In another year there might be a windfall gain through selling a property at a surplus. A sensible policy is to smooth changes in subscriptions. The maintenance of modest reserves facilitates this as does the policy of retaining the surpluses earned on the income and expenditure account above those anticipated in the budget.

An association sensibly should make medium term financial projections which will indicate whether an increase or a reduction in subscriptions is possible or likely over time. If, for example, it is anticipated that over time subscriptions may well fall then it would make little sense to increase subscriptions in one year merely because of a one-off item of additional expenditure in that year. Members are likely to react strongly to increases in subscriptions. Similarly, there is little point in taking advantage of special circumstances to reduce subscriptions in a year if it is clear that a year later they will have to increase.

Table 14.3 illustrates how the principle of smoothing subscription income can work.

Table 14.3 Subscription Smoothing

Year	Total Expenditure £m	Subscription Income as 90% of Expenditure £m	Smoothing Subscription Income £m
1	3.5	3.15	3.1
2	3.6	3.24	3.2
3	3.0	2.70	3.2
4	3.5	3.15	3.3
5	3.7	3.33	3.4
6	4.6	4.14	3.5
7	4.0	3.60	3.6
8	4.1	3.69	3.7

The table shows that if subscription income is simply set at 90% of expenditure then there could be huge year-to-year variations, for example, an increase of 24% in year 6 and a reduction of 17% in year 3. The smooth scale would be more palatable to the members. However, a policy of smoothing can work effectively only where there are reasonable grounds for knowing the long term trend. It would, for example, be dangerous for any trade association simply to assume that an increase in expenditure in one year is a one-off affair unless it is clear that this is the case.

The smoothing of subscriptions applies not only to the overall subscription income but perhaps more importantly to the average subscription. If an association's membership is increasing then it can more easily afford to increase total subscription income if this will mean no increase in the average subscription. Conversely, a trade association with a falling membership cannot assume that those members who remain are going to be content to pay for those who have left.

Accommodation costs are significant in trade association budgets, and policy on accommodation is therefore important. In practice, however, most associations are long-established and carry with them an historical property position that perhaps is not one which they would seek if they were starting from scratch today.

Having accepted the principle that a trade association should, broadly speaking, operate on a pay-as-you-go basis, it follows that the best accommodation arrangement is one in which, as far as possible, market rents are paid. In the past this could be achieved by the normal renting mechanism which typically provided for upwards only rent reviews after five years. The prudent association would take account of the likely increase in rents at the end of the five year period and would provide for this, for example, by making a modest surplus in the two years immediately prior to a rent review and perhaps a modest deficit in the two years afterwards.

Outright ownership of office accommodation is generally inappropriate for a trade association faced with making an accommodation decision. Almost certainly there will be windfall gains or losses which means that there will be a transfer of resources between those members existing at one time and those members existing at another time. Notwithstanding this, many associations have opted to own the freehold or a very long lease on their property. In practice, for many associations this has been extremely successful, as a result of which they are now occupying accommodation at substantially below a reasonable market rent. To the extent that this has happened then present members are benefiting at the expense of past members. Conversely when property values have declined the costs of accommodation exceed the market value imposing a burden on present and future members and reducing the value of the association to the members.

Having made these points, this discussion is largely academic for those associations that either own their own property or that have a long lease. They may be occupying accommodation at costs substantially below or above the market. It is sensible for this to be recognised in the management accounts of the association, for example, by recording market rent as a cost with the difference between market rent and actual rent being recorded as an exceptional item.

Even where an association has an established head office, the location of that office will be a subject regularly under review either at the instigation of the governing body or the management or the members. Trade associations can be broadly divided into three categories in respect of where their head office has to be located -

(a)   The very large associations whose work is predominantly representation to government and governmental agencies. Of the largest 30 or so associations all but five have head offices in London. Those five are METCOM (which has three head offices - in London, Glasgow and Birmingham), the British Paper Federation (Swindon), the Freight Transport Association (Tunbridge Wells), the Road Haulage Association (Weybridge), and the Vehicle Builders and Repairers Association (Leeds).

(b)   Associations representing industries which are concentrated in a geographical area. Good examples are the British Ceramic Federation, which is based in Stoke, and the British Leather Confederation, which is based in Northampton.

(c)   Smaller associations which cannot easily afford a central London location and which, in any event, have less of a role in exercising the representative function to government than the larger associations. These associations can be based almost anywhere, although a significant number are on the outskirts of London.

It is helpful to analyze why a London location is seen as being important by the largest associations. If much of the time of the chief executive and other senior executives is to be spent on representative work then this will involve meetings with government departments and regulatory agencies, and also MPs and the media. These are all based in London. If the trade association is not in London then either there is less face-to-face contact or an inordinate amount of time is spent in travelling. As importantly, informal contact is a major part of the work of a trade association. The lunches, receptions and dinners that happen every day in London are not simply opportunities for entertaining but more importantly opportunities for making contact, discussing policy issues and getting the industry's message over to a wide variety of opinion formers. If one is based outside London then attending these functions is more difficult.

Where a trade association has nationwide membership then London is likely to the preferred location simply because it is the easiest place to get to and from. While Birmingham may be more in the centre of the Country, getting to Birmingham from, say, Edinburgh, Norwich, Exeter or Southampton is more difficult than getting to London from almost anywhere. It is for this reason that even some of the associations which have their head offices outside London have their meetings in London.

London is expensive because accommodation and staff costs are relatively high. Almost every association will have considered whether to relocate outside London and will have concluded that there could be a substantial cost saving but that this would be counterbalanced by a significant decrease in effectiveness. Some associations have considered the option of keeping only a limited number of staff in London with other staff being in a cheaper location. Generally, trade associations are too small to operate this policy effectively. In an organisation of, say, 400 it may well make sense to have the bulk of the staff in a cheaper location, but in an organisation of 50 this policy is likely to decrease effectiveness for only a modest saving in costs.

BUGETING

The budgeting process in a trade association should be little different from that in any other organisation and only a brief summary is necessary here. The association's corporate plan should have some long term financial projections which will be the starting point for the budgetary process. In practice, medium term financial forecasting for a trade association is relatively simple. There are two major variables. The first is subscription income. It might seem odd that this can be a variable given that it is for the members to decide the subscription level. However, it is helpful to project forward subscriptions on a steady state business and to produce ranges that may depend on the effect of mergers within the industry (particularly where there is a tapering subscription scale) or changes in the size of the industry. Similar principles of scenario testing apply in any business. A projection that subscription income will fall, other things being equal, requires a different short term reaction from a scenario in which, other things being equal, subscriptions will be stable or increase. The second key variable is accommodation. This would be important either where an association is actively considering relocation or where an existing lease is coming to an end. There may be other factors which can be built into long term financial forecasting such as likely changes in income from commercial services.

It must be assumed that the association is operating according to a long term strategy in respect of the services that it provides and that there is continually a rigorous examination of value for money and of all possible methods of reducing costs and increasing income. For many associations for most of the time the budgeting process can be on the steady state assumption, that is that the same range of services should continue to be provided unless a decision has been taken to the contrary.

Assuming that the financial year of an association coincides with the calendar year, it would be normal to set subscriptions in either November or December. The budgetary process needs to begin a few months earlier than this with the preparation of the budget for the year on the basis of continuing existing activity and taking into account any known additional items of income and expenditure.

The budgeting process then has to take into account various key policy issues. For most associations most of the time the working assumption will be that there should be a balanced budget, perhaps constrained by trying to maintain reserves at a certain relationship with income or expenditure. The steady state budget will then throw up a subscription figure as a residual. At this stage policy on subscriptions needs to come into play. If the subscription figure is very close to that for the previous year then it may make sense to hold subscriptions even at the expense of running a modest deficit or surplus. If there has been a sharp increase in membership then it might be best to freeze individual subscriptions thereby increasing total income. If a substantial increase in subscriptions seems likely because of a one-off item of expenditure then the smoothing process described earlier needs to be brought into operation.

It is at this critical stage that judgement is needed. How will the members view the overall level of subscription income, more importantly the average subscription payable? Generally, provided the average subscription payable is not rising, the members may well be not greatly concerned about the shape of the budget at all and even the key committee may give it only cursory examination. By contrast, if there is clearly a need for a significant increase in subscriptions in order to maintain the same level of expenditure (for example, because of a huge rent increase or because of the loss of some large members) then the whole budget will be subject to rigorous scrutiny, and there may need to be significant cuts in order to produce a subscription level that is acceptable to the members.

The process which has been described so far will, in most large associations, be undertaken entirely by the secretariat with a budget being put to the governing body at the appropriate time. In some associations, particularly smaller ones, the process may be in the hands of a committee.

The governing body of the association will be expected to approve the whole budget for the year and the subscription scale that flows from it.

Table 14.4 shows the key table of a typical summary budget statement that might be put to the governing body of a trade association. The statement would be supported by a more detailed breakdown of the figures.

177

Table 14.4 Budget Statement, Typical Trade Association

	1994 Actual £000	1995 Budget £000	1995 Estimated Actual £000	1996 Budget £000
Income				
Subscriptions	3,120	3,140	3,140	3,160
Interest	250	250	220	200
Commercial				
services (net)	<u>730</u>	<u>800</u>	<u>780</u>	<u>820</u>
Total	**4,100**	**4,190**	**4,140**	**4,180**
Expenditure				
Staff	2,600	2,650	2,620	2,650
Accommodation	750	750	750	760
Office costs	300	320	340	350
Publications	200	180	200	180
Professional services	100	150	120	150
Other	<u>50</u>	<u>60</u>	<u>70</u>	<u>60</u>
Total	**4,000**	**4,110**	**4,100**	**4,150**
Surplus	100	80	40	30
Tax	40	32	16	12
Surplus after tax	60	48	24	18

MONITORING

The nature of trade association activity is such that financial monitoring is relatively easy. With commercial organisations a key variable is sales, whereas for trade associations the main equivalent of sales, that is subscription income, is generally determined annually in advance. There is little scope for major changes in most items of expenditure, that is staff and accommodation, assuming that the budgetary process has been undertaken correctly. The most significant variations from budget are likely to occur in respect of professional fees on the expenditure side and net income from commercial services on the income side. The more a trade association seeks to provide services on a commercial basis, as opposed to being an adjunct of the trade association service, the more that income from services is likely to fluctuate both in absolute terms and in proportion to total income.

A typical pattern in many large associations is for the executive to monitor progress against the budget on a monthly basis with quarterly reports to the appropriate governing body identifying, in particular, expected significant variations from the budget. A typical monitoring statement put to a committee would include actual figures for the previous year, the budget for the current year, figures for the year to date and expected outturn. An example of a typical monitoring statement for the half year position, corresponding to the budget in Table 14.5, is shown below.

Table 14.5 Monitoring Statement, Typical Trade Association

	1995 Actual £000	1996 Budget £000	1996 Year to Date £000	1996 Estimated Outturn £000	Variation from Budget £000
Income					
Subscriptions	3,140	3,160	1,580	3,160	0
Interest	220	200	100	180	-20
Commercial services (net)	780	820	450	900	+80
Total	**4,140**	**4,180**	**2,130**	**4,240**	**+60**
Expenditure					
Staff	2,620	2,650	1,300	2,600	-50
Accommodation	750	760	400	760	0
Office costs	340	350	200	360	+10
Publications	200	180	70	200	+20
Professional services	120	150	70	130	-20
Other	70	60	30	70	+10
Total	**4,100**	**4,150**	**2,070**	**4,120**	**-30**
Surplus	40	30	60	120	+90
Tax	16	12	24	48	+36
Surplus after tax	24	18	36	72	+54

SUBSCRIPTIONS

Perhaps the most important financial decisions any trade association can take can relate to subscriptions. The subscription payable to a trade body is a price and serves the same purposes as other prices. The price charged to members for trade association services will affect their attitude towards the trade association, perhaps even to the extent of encouraging some members to resign. For those associations with less than 100% market share the subscription payable will be a key factor in helping to attract new members.

However, the subscription is not exactly the same as any other price. If one wishes to purchase a motor car, for example, one pays the price and has the car. If one does not pay the price then the car cannot be purchased. By contrast, most trade association services are intangible. The representative service benefits not only members but non-members as well, and even the information service can benefit non-members who often can have access to it without paying the full price. To some extent companies in the industry must be expected to "do the decent thing" and pay their fair share of contributions, even though they could take advantage of the product at virtually no cost.

This inherent nature of the trade association can at times conflict with the need to run the trade association as a commercial business. Also, members can be ambivalent in their attitude to the association with some taking the view that it is purely a commercial arrangement while others take the wider view that they are subscribing to a trade association as if out of some sort of duty.

There are three general approaches to setting subscriptions for members of a trade association. The first method is for each member to pay an equal amount. This seems fair on the grounds that each member obtains exactly the same service. The study by Manchester Metropolitan University, carried out in February 1994, showed that 38% of respondents used the flat fee basis. For 30% of these associations the annual fee was £90 a year or under, for 70% it was £500 or under and for 90% it was £1,521 or under. Among the larger associations, the Electricity Association and the Water Services Association adopt this method. However, there are few of the largest trade associations where such a system can work. In the case of the Electricity Association and the Water Services Association, all of the firms concerned are substantial organisations that regard themselves as the equal of each other. Most trade associations have a mixture of large and small members, those providing a wide range of services and those providing a narrower range. The single equal subscription would be inappropriate for them.

At the other extreme is a subscription scale which relates subscriptions proportionately to business undertaken. That business will have to be measured in relation to a variable which is bound to be arbitrary to some extent. The Manchester Metropolitan University Study estimated that 13% of associations calculated fees on company staff levels, 37% used company turnover and 20% used another variable, generally a combination of staff levels and company turnover or a variable specific to the industry in question. The Association of British Insurers, for example, has a scale which directly relates subscription income to insurance premiums. Subject to a minimum subscription of £5,000 and a 45% discount for certain specialist insurers, the 1995 subscription was 174.2 x general insurance premium income in 1993 (£m) + 77.5 x life insurance premium income in 1993 (£m). Put another way, the levy was equal to 0.0174% of general insurance premium income and 0.00775% of life insurance premium income. Such subscription scales can be fairly complex mathematical formulae which in practice has an advantage in that members are less likely to challenge it.

This third method of calculating subscriptions, probably the most common among the larger associations, is a tapering scale with a minimum and a maximum. The minimum figure recognises that there is a minimum cost of providing the basic trade association service, and arguably the maximum figure recognises that there is a maximum benefit. The logic of tapering is that although large members are likely to benefit more than smaller ones they do not benefit proportionately. Indeed, some would argue that they have the resources to undertake much of the work which the trade association does themselves, perhaps to do so more efficiently and without giving information to their competitors. The extent of the taper is often a matter for fierce negotiation and ultimately it is the big organisations which must decide what happens as they bear the bulk of the costs. A good example of this system is the scale used by the Producers Alliance for Cinema and television. The scale is based on turnover with three levels, £485, £605 and £725.

The alternative methods of levying subscription income are illustrated in Table 14.6, which assumes a simple trade association with ten members but of hugely different sizes.

Table 14.6 Subscription Scales

Subscription Base £m	Subscription on Proportional Basis £000	Subscription on Equal Basis £000	Tapering Scale with Floor and Ceiling £000
10	-	200	5
20	1	200	5
50	2	200	5
100	3	200	15
500	15	200	40
1,000	30	200	70
5,000	150	200	250
10,000	300	200	400
20,000	600	200	550
30,000	900	200	660

It is helpful to illustrate this section by looking specifically at the subscription scale of a fairly newly established trade association, the Council of Mortgage Lenders. Table 14.7 shows the actual subscription scale for 1993 for those members which were not building societies and also the relationship of the subscription to mortgage assets for the mid-point of each range and some examples at the top and bottom of the range.

Table 14.7 Council of Mortgage Lenders, Subscription Scale, 1993

Mortgage Assets at End-1991 £m	Point in Range £m	Subscription According to Scale £	Subscription/ Mortgage Assets %
	10	2,500	0.025
Under 100	50	2,500	0.0050
	100	2,500	0.00025
100-200	150	3,000	0.00020
200-400	300	4,000	0.00013
400-600	500	6,000	0.00012
600-800	700	8,000	0.00011
800-1,000	900	10,000	0.00011
1,000-2,000	1,500	13,000	0.000087
2,000-4,000	3,000	18,000	0.000060
4,000-6,000	5,000	22,000	0.000044
6,000-8,000	7,000	27,000	0.000039
8,000-10,000	9,000	31,000	0.000034
10,000-15,000	12,500	36,000	0.000028
15,000-20,000	17,500	54,000	0.000031
20,000-25,000	22,500	72,000	0.000032
Over 25,000	35,000	85,000	0.000021
	45,000	85,000	0.000016

The effect of the taper is clearly seen. Paradoxically, the taper seems to go in reverse for a time at the top end of the scale. This can be explained by the fact that no member came into the £15,000-£20,000 million category, and the only one in the £25,000 million plus category had mortgage assets substantially above that amount.

The Heating and Ventilating Contractors Association uses a tapering scale but based on two separate variables, wage roll and turnover. Table 14.8 shows the position.

Table 14.8 Heating and Ventilating Contractors Association, Levy, 1993/94

Wage Roll £m	Levy £ per £100 of Wages
0 - 0.425	55p
0.425 - 1.0625	45p
1.0625 - 2.125	40p
2.125 - 3.187	35p
3.187 - 4.250	25p
4.250 - 6.375	15p
Over 6.375	5p

Turnover £m	Levy £ per £1,000 of Turnover
0 - 0.6	120p
0.6 - 2.32	79p
2.32 - 14.35	40p
14.35 - 43.05	30p
Over 43.05	10p

The tapers are fairly severe, the smallest members paying proportionately ten times as much as the larger ones. An association with a less severe taper is the Dairy Industry Federation which introduced a new financing system from November 1994. It opted for seven bands, based on throughput of milk, with subscriptions varying from 0.0153 pence per litre for the smallest member to 0.0125 pence per litre for the largest. There is, in addition, a minimum subscription of £250 and the ten largest members pay an additional £10,000 in exchange for having a Council seat.

The Newspaper Society had a maximum scale for 1995 of 52.5p per £100 of wages for the first £8,471,000 of wages and 46.4p for wages in excess of this ceiling. In addition there was a minimum subscription of £675.

The Federation of Civil Engineering Contractors, for 1995, had a basic subscription of 34p per £100 of wages paid, with a minimum of £895, a threshold of £12,580 above which the rate became 26p and a maximum of £34,270.

Changing a subscription scale is bound to be controversial because there will always be winners and losers. Many associations might take the view that their scale is not satisfactory, but there needs to be an overwhelming case for change before a scale is reviewed because the act of reviewing is bound to raise wider issues such as value for money. Some associations may have very obscure scales that have been in existence for years and might wish to replace them with a more sensible structured scale. However, in so doing it would have to be conscious that it could invite problems. The best time to review a subscription scale is when subscriptions are falling so as to minimise the losers.

The analysis so far has assumed that there is a rational base on which to determine subscription income. In practice this is not easy as in many industries there is no single generally acceptable variable. Some measure of turnover is common but for some industries the volume of outstanding business might be more appropriate. There is also the question as to whether the variable should be one that is wholly objective, for example a figure that has to be reported in an annual return to a regulatory body, or rather whether members should be asked to give their own return of the necessary information. Whatever system is used, it is generally the case that subscriptions in, say, 1996 will have to be based on 1994 data as these are the most recent that are available when the budget is agreed and subscriptions levied.

Many associations have an associate category of membership aimed at institutions connected with the business. For example, the Council of Mortgage Lenders has as associates firms of lawyers and accountants, insurance companies and computer companies. Associates have access to information, much of which they could probably obtain by other means, and may be able to participate in some of the activities of the trade association, but they are not generally able to indicate publicly that they have a relationship with the association. The associate category of membership is normally an effective way for associations to raise additional income. Typically, a single figure will be set for associates that is likely to be at or close to the minimum subscription for members. Those eligible for membership should not be allowed to become associates. This could otherwise be seen as a cheap method by which they obtain the advantages of membership without paying the price.

SERVICE INCOME

Trade associations, like other organisations, have been under financial pressure in recent years. Members have sought value for money and have in many cases demanded significant changes in the way associations operate. Those associations which have undertaken or commissioned full scale inquiries into their activities have invariably examined the concept of charging for services. It is necessary to distinguish seeking to charge for the basic trade association services directly rather than through subscription income and running commercial activities as an adjunct to the trade association service.

In practice it is difficult to segment the provision of trade association services although many associations have sought to do so. The representative service must be on behalf of all members. Where a trade association covers activity which can be divided into a number of discreet activities then a separate charge can be made for each activity in which a member has an involvement, but this is merely a refinement of the method of calculating subscriptions rather than charging for a specific service. A member cannot opt in or opt out of obtaining the basic representative service.

Similarly there is little scope to charge for providing any promotional service. If a trade association is seeking to promote a whole industry then if it is successful it will benefit the whole industry rather than those that contribute to a certain campaign.

Information services provide most scope to seek to raise money by charging rather than through the subscription mechanism. For example, a hefty charge could be levied for information on changes in taxation and regulation. The problem with this approach is that the information frequently stems from the representative function and members would argue that they have paid for this and should, therefore, not be paying again to receive the information. Also, it is difficult to confine the information to those who have paid for it. Some members pass on the information they receive to their professional advisers who are not beyond marketing it to others inside and outside the industry.

In practice, the true trade association service cannot be segmented and charged for on a menu basis. It is an all or nothing service that has to be financed out of subscription income. It for this reason that subscription income is the best indication of the size of a trade association. While many associations have experimented with seeking to segment the service and price for various parts of it, few have succeeded and many have abandoned the attempts or do no more than pay lip service to them. This is usefully illustrated in the annual report of the Publishers Association for 1994-95. This stated that during the course of the year it became increasingly apparent that the menu subscription system previously in operation providing for separate optional subscriptions for the Educational Publishers Council and the Council of Academic and Professional Publishers was coming under stress "because of objections by publishers from those sectors at having to pay additional subscriptions on their relevant turnover, and that this was putting memberships at risks". A working party was established to consider the subscription system, in particular the problems of the optional division subscriptions, subscription rates for special categories of publishing and the requirements for group membership. The report goes on: "After careful consideration, the group advise that the menu system should be replaced by a single subscription system, which it was anticipated would have the additional effect of overcoming concerns about the subscriptions payable in respect of special categories of turnover, and that, when companies in operating divisions in groups were bona fide independently managed, Council should exercise its discretion more readily to permit such separate companies or divisions to be members of the PA on their own, without the necessity for all relevant companies in the group to be in membership."

There is, however, scope for trade associations to earn substantial income by marketing services that are related to their mainstream trade association service. The provision of services was described in detail in Chapter 10; some repetition is necessary here to put the financial aspects into context. Trade associations need to understand the market position they are in. There is no reason why they can be any better at providing professional services than, say, a firm of management consultants or lawyers or accountants or anyone else. However, they may well be more efficient at providing a service where they are exploiting their trade association position using their considerable knowledge of their industry and the public policy issues relevant to it. Given an effective secretariat with a reputation for delivering services that are value for money, it is quite easy for a trade association to sell some services to its members and to outsiders at a price that generates perhaps a considerable profit, or in the case of members at least makes a significant contribution to overheads. The range of services that can be provided is fairly narrow. As far as members are concerned the range comprises -

(a) Publications. These can include both publications about the industry (for example, a regular monthly or quarterly bulletin) and bulk supplies of publications which members can use in their own business. This is an area where the trade association must capitalise on its skills as being expert on the various subjects on which it is issuing publications and also having the information earlier than anyone else.

(b) Seminars and conferences. These are very similar to publications. Trade associations have on their own staff and committee people who can make presentations at seminars and conferences on timely subjects. Because the costs of arranging conferences and seminars are low with minimal marketing costs they can often be popular with members. Certainly they are likely to undercut substantially commercial conferences.

(c) Statistical services. Many associations in addition to producing aggregate statistics operate closed user group schemes by which aggregate statistics are given only to those organisations that contribute so as to enable them to compare their position against the industry total and perhaps even against other individual companies.

(d) Market intelligence. A trade association may have to monitor what goes on in the market and perhaps in foreign markets and can sell this information to members.

(e) Press cuttings. Those associations who are in the public eye will almost certainly undertake a press cutting service for their own purposes and this can then be sold to members with delivery either by fax or by mail. This can be expanded into a media monitoring service.

The correct pricing tactic for services sold to members is that they should reflect costs of production together with a reasonable allowance for overheads. There are good grounds for arguing that it is improper to sell services to members at a commercial price especially where the services being sold exist only because of the subscriptions which members have paid. Members resist paying twice for the same product, and are particularly critical if the trade association is selling them a service which they can buy from somewhere else more cheaply. A trade association is in a strong position to sell some services to its members at below the full market price yet at a price sufficient to more than meet its own costs and make a contribution to overheads.

A trade association can also sell services to outsiders. For the most part these will be the same services that are sold to members, that is conferences, publications and seminars. Press releases and statistical reports can also be sold and there is a ready market among consultants and analysts. Here the proper tactic is to charge whatever the market can bear. The pricing decision is no different from that which any other commercial organisation would take. Some associations have earned substantial fee income from selling services to outsiders who in many cases could probably obtain the service anyway through a contact with a member.

A few associations derive a significant part of their income from a major annual conference or convention at which commercial firms take space in an exhibition. Where this works it is an ideal way of funding a trade association in that subscriptions can be held down and members can obtain the basic trade association service for much less than the cost of providing it. However, there are few industries where this is feasible. Also a trade association is vulnerable if it is reliant on income from an exhibition. If that income for whatever reason suddenly dries up it may be faced with having to implement a huge increase in subscriptions to maintain the same service and thereby run the risk of losing members.

Some trade associations have sought to diversify well beyond those services which are directly related to its prime trade association functions. Some, for example, have gone into wider consultancy work competing with professional consultants. Trade associations are not well suited to going into commercial activities that are not related to trade association activity. They do not have the proper governance and management structures and in particular lack the necessary checks and balances. An enthusiastic trade association executive can easily move into a wide range of fairly unrelated activities on the basis of assumptions which look plausible but which might then expose the association to substantial loss if they go wrong.

◢ MANAGEMENT ACCOUNTING

Many trade associations, particularly smaller ones, have no more financial data than the income and expenditure account as presented in Table 14.4. Larger associations need more sophisticated management accounts to be able to understand and manage the business properly. However, preparing management accounts is difficult, largely because overheads are likely to comprise a significant proportion of total expenditure and because allocating expenditure to particular headings is arbitrary. At the very least departmental income and expenditure accounts need to be prepared. Table 14.9 shows a summary of the departmental expenditure analysis for the Association of British Insurers for 1995.

Table 14.9 Departmental Expenditure, Association of British Insurers, 1995

	Department							
	Premises	Central Services	Public Affairs	Legal and Fiscal	Investment	Life Insurance	General Insurance	Total
	£000	£000	£000	£000	£000	£000	£000	£000
Employment	5	1,458	830	333	184	262	492	3,504
External relations	-	23	273	552	1	72	1,124	2,044
Management expenses	-	643	266	137	55	73	138	1,312
Accommodation	2,258	163	418	87	52	65	97	3,392
Total direct	2,263	2,487	1,787	1,109	294	471	1,850	10,260
Total after allocating central services	2,263	1,302	2,020	866	403	738	2,668	10,260

Several points in this table need explaining. It will be seen that there is a separate department called "premises". This is because the ABI, like a number of other trade associations, is occupying property for which it is paying much more than its current market value. Rather than attribute the total cost of the property to the various departments only the current market rent is charged to them with the remainder being allocated to the notional premises department. Secondly, it will be noted that there are some high figures for external relations for the general insurance and legal and fiscal departments. For the most part this reflects funds being collected which are immediately passed on to another organisation, the Loss Prevention Council and the European Insurance Committee respectively. The central services department, in addition to providing head office services such as personnel and accounting, also runs the statistics and computing sections which provide services to members. The mainstream central service expenditure is reallocated to each department resulting in the figures shown in the bottom line of the table.

A further step is to produce income and expenditure figures for the separate functions of the trade association, for example, representation, information, public relations, trading services etc. This requires fairly heroic assumptions on allocations of expenditure. While the figures are undoubtedly useful in illustrating how a trade association spends its money they can be dangerous if they are used a basis for starting new activities or discontinuing existing ones. Often the effect of discontinuing an activity is the loss of the income but with little saving in expenditure because so much of the expenditure is the allocation of overheads or otherwise is expenditure which cannot easily be reduced.

Accounting Issues

This chapter and some of the others use data from the accounts of trade associations. It has been emphasised on several occasions that not too much should be read into differences between associations based on figures in their accounts because there are considerable inconsistencies and differences in accounting treatment. In fact, a number of associations not only do not publish accounts but will not make them available to anyone other than members. Arguably, this is not unreasonable. Trade associations are member organisations and have a duty to provide financial information to their members only. They have no duty to provide it to any outsiders although a number choose to do so. Some associations publish full accounts as a component part of their annual report, but an increasing tendency is for either no financial figures to be given at all or for a summary of the financial data to be given perhaps with the full accounts being available on request.

Those associations that are companies have of course to file accounts with Companies House so that they are more likely to make them generally available. Associations that are unincorporated associations have no obligation to file accounts anywhere and merely have to comply with their own constitution.

Accounting differences between trade associations partially reflect whether or not the association is a limited company. The main areas where there are differences in accounting treatment are -

(a) Interest from bank deposits and other sources can be included either as income or alternatively it can be recorded "below the line" after the operating surplus has been calculated. The Building Societies Association, an unincorporated association, for example records it as income, as does the British Leather Confederation, a company limited by guarantee, whereas the Water Companies Association and the Electricity Association, both limited companies, record net interest receivable as a separate item after operating profit.

(b) Income from the sale of services can be recorded net of expenditure outside the organisation (although not easily net of internal expenditure) or it can be recorded as gross income with the expenditure being recorded gross. Associations that do this will have an inflated figure for expenditure compared with those associations which record a net income figure.

(c) Some associations may have a number of specific reserves (for example, to meet large future items of expenditure such as an international convention or a future rent increase). Other associations may simply budget for such large items without making a specific reserve.

The remainder of the chapter sets out the published income and expenditure accounts for a number of trade associations to illustrate the differing accounting treatments. The figures are taken directly from annual accounts simplified only to remove irrelevant items or reduce the number of items.

The Electricity Association (a company limited by shares) adopts a standard Companies Act format.

Table 14.10 Electricity Association, Year to 31 March 1994

	£m
Turnover	22.7
Staff costs	7.7
Other operating expenses	14.0
Depreciation	0.3
	22.0
Operating profit	0.7
Exceptional items	(1.5)
	(0.8)
Net interest receivable	1.5
Profit on ordinary activities before tax	0.7
Tax	-
Profit for year	0.7

The notes to the accounts give no breakdown of either turnover or other operating expenses. Subscription income cannot therefore be identified.

The Water Companies Association, a company limited by guarantee, has a different approach.

Table 14.11 Water Companies Association, Year to 31 March 1994

	£
Income	
Subscriptions	1,034,215
Administration charge	49,500
Other income	7,684
	1,091,399
Operating expenditure	1,113,805
Operating surplus	(22,406)
Bank deposit interest	26,577
Surplus before tax	4,171
Taxation	6,914
Surplus for the year	2,743

The Timber Trade Federation, a company limited by guarantee, illustrates a further variation.

Table 14.12 Timber Trade Federation, Year to 31 December 1994

	£000
Turnover (continuing operations)	
Subscriptions/contributions	778
Administrative expenses	895
Subscriptions	18
Donations	2
	914
	(136)
Interest receivable	21
Investment income	43
Other operating income	64
Net profits on sale of investments	19
	150
Surplus on ordinary activities before	
taxation	14
Taxation	1
Retained surplus for the year	13

The Chemical Industries Association, also a company limited by guarantee, has an income and expenditure account similar to management accounts. An abbreviated version is set out below.

Table 14.13 Chemical Industries Association, Year to 30 June 1994

	£000	£000
Income		
Membership subscriptions		4,084
Trading income	741	
Less costs relating to trading income	364	
Contribution from trading income		377
Net income		4,461
Expenditure		
Salaries and wages		1,746
Staff related costs		827
Property occupancy costs		881
Operating expenses		1,101
Total		4,555
Deficit on ordinary activities before		
interest and taxation		94
Interest receivable		115
Surplus before tax		21
Tax		(19)
Surplus after tax		(2)

The income and expenditure figures are broken down in detail, operating expenditure for example being divided into 14 categories.

The Paper Federation of Great Britain, a company limited by guarantee, adopts a similar approach but includes interest as income and expenditure rather than separately.

Table 14.14 The Paper Federation of Great Britain, Year to 31 December 1994

	£
Income	
Members' subscriptions	1,179,112
Provision of services	208,495
Creating process NVQs	67,189
Waste and newsprint study	56,233
Special projects income	16,143
Conferences and seminars	204,601
Sales: special statistics	62,071
Publications	7,664
Rents and service fees receivable	36,082
Bank interest receivable	13,712
Other income	5,410
Total income	**1,856,712**
Cost of provision of Federation services and administration	
Staff costs	939,533
Rent and rates	64,087
Other premises costs	38,352
Meeting and travelling expenses	123,014
External relations	7,681
Creating process NVQs	67,189
Waste and newsprint study	56,233
Conferences and seminars	108,481
Publications	25,979
Subscriptions	118,626
Legal and professional charges	14,622
Audit fee	5,750
Computer costs	76,663
Direct costs: special statistics	5,740
special projects	5,111
Postage, telephone and stationery	111,229
Repairs and renewals	616
Other administrative expenses	9,743
Depreciation	85,721
Interest and charges	4,272
Total expenditure	**1,868,642**
(deficit) surplus for the year before taxation	(11,930)
Taxation	(7,267)
(Deficit) after taxation transferred to accumulated fund	(4,663)

The diversity illustrated by these few examples is sufficient to illustrate that no meaningful comparison can be made between trade association accounts. Certainly comparisons of expenditure are meaningless. The most significant variable which can be used for comparison is subscription income, although significantly this variable is not identified in some accounts.

BIBLIOGRAPHY AND FURTHER READING

T C May, J McHugh, T Taylor, *UK Trade Associations in the 1990s: A Research Note* (Manchester: Manchester Metropolitan University, unpublished, 1995).

CHAPTER 15

Strategic Planning

Strategic planning is an essential part of the process of managing organisations. However, it has not featured in many trade associations. Traditionally they have operated with a short time horizon punctuated by irregular fundamental enquiries into objectives, functions and organisation, generally prompted by concern on the part of larger members. Now, it is increasingly accepted that trade associations must operate and plan their future in the same way as more commercial businesses. Trade associations are particularly vulnerable to changes in government policy and in the markets of their members. The planning process must recognise this.

THE NEED FOR PLANNING

Any organisation needs to plan its future. Organisations cannot work on a day-to-day basis partly because some decisions, for example in respect of capital investment, may have a long lead time before they can be implemented and an even longer lead time before there is a pay back. The planning process is designed to enable the day-to-day functions of an organisation to be carried on smoothly and in line with the longer term objectives.

There are numerous publications on strategic planning so all that is required here is a brief summary. The planning process typically begins with a SWOT (strengths, weaknesses, opportunities, threats) analysis. These can be examined internally provided there is sufficient objectivity, with the help of outside consultants or entirely by outside consultants, although obviously drawing on information within the organisation.

Strengths and weaknesses are internal characteristics of an organisation. External circumstances are regarded as threats or opportunities. Set out below is a useful summary of the factors typically taken into account in a SWOT exercise, taken from *The Manager's Handbook* -

Internal - strengths and weaknesses

People	- skills, training, attitude
Organisation	- structure and relationships
Systems/	
Communications	- formal/informal, manual, computer and telecommunication
Products	- quality, life, cost
Production	- nature, capacity, quality
Finance	- balance sheet, profit and loss account, cash flow
Credentials	- reputation, track record, customer perception
Knowledge	- technical, market, competition

194

External - opportunities and threats

Market	- growth, decline, movement, fashion
Technology	- product development, substitution, production technology
Economy	- export/import, sterling strength
Society	- sales practice, employment practice, trade union practice
Legislation	- consumer protection, product liability
Ecology	- energy, raw materials, recycling, environmental protection, control

Such analyses are best kept relatively simple so as to concentrate on the key issues. Often such analyses will throw up the same issues being both a threat and an opportunity or a strength and a weakness. For example, a company that has invested heavily in new technology may regard this as a strength in terms of its ability to produce a competitive product, while the high overheads which have resulted from this may be regarded as a weakness. The rapid growth of a new market gives a new opportunity but at the same time it is a threat if it attracts significant new entrants into that market.

Having undertaken a SWOT analysis a long term plan can then be devised. Again, this is well covered in standard textbooks. The plan will start from the products that are to be produced and then how they are to be produced including for example the need to acquire new premises, the need to make other capital investments, the need to recruit new staff and perhaps the need to raise additional capital. Plans might not always be this positive. Many organisations face a declining demand for their product. In this case the long term plan will be how to downsize, for example by closing plants, withdrawing from certain product lines and so on.

Both the long term plan and its implementation need regular review. It is reasonable to establish annual targets in accordance with the plan and for progress against these targets to be monitored at, say, quarterly intervals. However the plan itself cannot simply be ignored once it has been settled. Plans need to be updated perhaps on a yearly basis in the light of changing circumstances. For example, an organisation might be gearing up to meet anticipated new demand which then fails to materialise. The plan will need adjusting mid-stream.

THE PLANNING PROCESS IN TRADE ASSOCIATIONS

The planning process in trade associations is similar to that in other types of organisation. The same SWOT analysis should be conducted in broadly a similar way. However, there are special features about trade association activity which should be reflected in the SWOT analysis.

It is useful always to start from a "mission statement", something which is now common in all types of organisation. A great deal of work can go into devising mission statements; generally this is unnecessary, and a brief simple statement prepared by management is generally sufficient. The advantage of a mission statement is that it concentrates minds within the organisation and is a useful starting point for explaining the organisation to any outsider.

A selection of mission statements taken from annual reports and promotional literature for various trade associations is set out below -

> The Council of Mortgage Lenders provides a service to mortgage lending institutions by helping to establish a favourable operating environment, by providing a forum for discussion on non-competitive issues and by providing information to assist them in their business.

> METCOM's mission is to be a major industrial confederation within engineering which seeks to raise the image and importance of the Industry, influence the industrial environment and assist in the improvement of the Industry's performance and efficiency for the benefit of all members. (Mechanical and Metal Trades Confederation)

> To represent the views of the property industry, both commercial and residential. The BPF speaks for a broad membership of companies and individuals, protecting and furthering the interests of its members, and working to create a better understanding between the industry and government and the public in general. (British Property Federation)

> The Retail Motor Industry Federation serves and represents the businesses concerned with the provision of motor industry products and services and aims to assist, support and promote members in providing the highest standards of operation for the mutual benefit of themselves and their customers. The organisation seeks to become the strongest, most representative and effective national industrial sector trade federation in the United Kingdom and Europe.

> To represent and support member companies in pursuing profitable and responsible innovation, investment and trade, within a successful, well regarded chemical industry. (Chemical Industries Association)

> To promote and safeguard the UK plastics industry, so enabling it to fulfil its business potential. (British Plastics Federation)

> The Federation of Master Builders is the leading voice for all medium and small sized building companies in the United Kingdom, representing their views to government, parliament, the European Commission, and other sectors of the construction industry and the general public. The Federation also provides a comprehensive quality service to, and a forum for, its membership to work towards unity in the various sections of the construction industry and to raise the status of building standards and skills with consumers.

The Association exists to take the initiative to ensure that the views of the British hospitality industry are strongly represented to the UK government and to policy makers in the UK and internationally in order to ensure that its members businesses flourish. (British Hospitality Association)

To offer a professional, quality service and support to members, to develop their efficiency and profitability and obtain better prices. (Vehicle Builders and Repairers Association)

To promote conditions that will support and encourage the provision of efficient, competitive and profitable transport and distribution and, where appropriate, to seek harmonised operating terms and conditions for transport between member states of the European Union. (Road Haulage Association)

To be recognised as the representative and authoritative voice of insurance brokers and independent financial advisers. To promote the interests of all members. (British Insurance and Investment Brokers Association)

The mission of the Engineering Employers Federation is to promote successfully in the UK, Europe and internationally, the interests of the UK engineering industry.

The mission of the BEAMA Federation is to represent its member associations and companies on major policy issues affecting their business interests and to provide services, all with the aim of contributing to the commercial success of these members. (British Electrotechnical and Allied Manufacturers Association)

To protect and seek to enhance the business prospects of Members in terms of the regulatory and fiscal environment, to advise Members of opportunities for new business, to gain recognition of the FLA membership's contribution to the economy and to promote FLA Members as responsible lenders and lessors with whom it is safe and profitable to do business. (Finance and Leasing Association)

It will be noted that there is a wide variety of mission statements. Some are not mission statements in the accepted sense of the word and some are scarcely literate, which is surprising bearing in mind that if a mission statement is to have any importance it is to communicate succinctly the purpose of the organisation. Some associations have missions which stress the competitiveness of the particular association, for example the Retail Motor Industry Federation seeks to be the "strongest, most representative and effective national industrial sector trade federation in the United Kingdom and Europe."

Perhaps the most appropriate mission statement is that of BEAMA which states in simple clear English the purpose of the organisation -

197

The mission of the BEAMA Federation is to represent its member associations and companies on major policy issues affecting their business interests and to provide services, all with the aim of contributing to the commercial success of these members.

It is helpful to note here an example of a mission statement from an American textbook on trade associations -

> The Association of Median Processors is a trade association that exists to strengthen the economic and political environment for the median processing industry. It works to expand economic opportunities and markets for its members through programs to enhance quality standards; to collect and disseminate pertinent economic, regulatory, and other information; and to increase public and customer knowledge of the industry's products and services and their value to society. AMP also seeks to achieve a governmental climate favourable to the marketing of the industry's products and services, and to inform and assist its members in enhancing their professional skills in the light of advancing technical knowledge.

The analysis of internal strengths and weaknesses will be similar to that of other fairly smallish companies. The variables listed in the previous section are for the most part covered elsewhere in this book. It is helpful however at this stage to briefly summarise some of the key points.

People: the staff of a trade association, like those in other businesses, have to be adequately trained, competent and well motivated. The skills required are not those of, say, a doctor or an accountant or a teacher, but rather in some cases appropriate professional skills which might include law or accountancy, management skills, and, for the most senior staff, trade association skills. In-house training programmes are unlikely to provide these skills. In any event the vast majority of trade associations are too small to employ their own training specialists. Partly for these reasons, and also the nature of trade associations covered earlier in this book, many trade associations are weak in respect of people.

Organisation: trade associations almost by definition have a complex organisational structure. The staff structure may look logical but superimposed on this is a committee structure, and if not well managed there can be a lack of direction and inefficiency.

Systems/communications: unless they are engaged in substantial service activity trade associations do not need sophisticated computer systems but rather the basic systems appropriate to any small office. Communications with members are invariably by post. This is one area where most associations will probably not have significant strengths or weaknesses.

Products: the products of trade associations are intangible. They are predominantly the representative service and the information service. Measuring the quality, volume and cost of these products is difficult as there are no obvious comparatives.

Production: this is largely irrelevant to a trade association as the production system is simply the staff.

Finance: the key variable here is the size of reserves. Other important variables include the predictability of income (an association relying on trading income may have a more unpredictable income flow than one relying solely on subscriptions) and accommodation costs.

Credentials: these are vital for a trade association. An association must have credibility with its members and with the other organisations with which it deals, in particular government departments and official bodies.

Knowledge: in the case of trade associations this is inextricably linked with people. There is little technical knowledge that is required but the staff of an association collectively must understand the market in which they are operating and the products they are providing.

OPPORTUNITIES AND THREATS

More so than most other organisations trade associations have to take a market as they find it and are not able to influence that market to any great extent. Accordingly, a strategic planning exercise must give more weight than is usual to the operating environment within which the trade association works.

Few markets are static. Developments in technology and in consumer tastes can lead to new markets being created or existing markets appearing. To take one good example the increase in crime has led to the growth of a whole new security industry which operates at both commercial and retail level. Other examples are related to improvements in technology, for example the growth of the video industry, the personal computer industry, the software industry. Some industries decline because what they produce is no longer competitive, for example the coal industry. As important for trade associations there is a tendency for markets to merge. This is best illustrated by the finance industry. Fifteen years ago banks undertook banking activities which at that stage did not include mortgage lending to any significant extent, building societies offered deposit and mortgage accounts to individuals and insurance companies provided insurance services. As a result of developments in technology and deregulation the banks have now moved strongly into the mortgage market, the building societies have moved into the mainstream banking market, both banks and building societies have moved into the insurance market, and to a lesser extent insurance companies have moved into the mortgage and savings markets. These developments create problems for trade associations. As barriers between markets and institutions break down a static trade association will represent a smaller and smaller proportion of activity in a market. It may want to embrace different types of institution which have entered the market but existing members may resist this, feeling that their own competitive position will be eroded if they share their long established trade body.

Within markets that change little the members themselves can change substantially. In particular, there can be a reduction in the number of members as a result of mergers, takeovers or companies going out of business. A good example is the building society industry where the number of members of the Building Societies Association has fallen from 450 in 1974 to under 100 today. Mergers present problems to trade associations where there is a tapering subscription scale. The contribution of a merged organisation is less than the combined contribution of the organisations that made up the merger. Conversely, as a result of privatisation some previous monopolies have been broken down into a number of individual companies which have then needed to get together to form trade associations. This is most apparent in the water and electricity supply industries. New entrants into a market are always attractive to trade associations as they are a valuable source of additional income. New entrants in particular are likely to find the service which a trade association provides particularly valuable given their own lack of knowledge, while their subscriptions will be low on the grounds that they have as yet undertaken very little business.

The environment also has to take account of the views of members towards the trade association and generally towards cooperation with each other. In an expanding and profitable industry attitude towards the trade association is likely to vary from strong support to relative apathy, with people happily paying the annual subscription almost on the basis that it is a contribution to a club which everybody joins. When an industry is under some pressure, either because of market developments or because of regulatory problems, then attitudes towards a trade association are likely to change sharply. Members may question the subscription payable and may expect the trade association itself to act in a far more businesslike way. Almost all trade associations have experienced this change of attitude over the past few years, although it has been significantly more pronounced in some than in others.

A final factor in any analysis of environment is government policy. If government has no policy and no involvement in a particular industrial sector then there is only a limited representative service which has to be undertaken. If for whatever reason there is to be a concentration of government activity on the sector then a different trade association might be needed. This can occur perhaps because of legislation which will directly affect the sector or perhaps because there are suddenly major policy issues that need to be dealt with by government. It is fair to say that it is this factor which has led to significant changes in some trade associations over the last few years. It has been recognised that a poor trade association can allow great damage to be done to its industry whereas a good trade association working with government can save its members many millions of pounds.

It is clear from this analysis that the external opportunities and threats part of the planning process will concentrate on changes in the market in which the members are operating and changes in government policy, two variables that may often be related. Until fairly recently, few trade associations would describe themselves as having competitors. Now, because of the breaking down of barriers between markets, associations are more in competition with each other. For example, as banks have moved into mortgage lending and the building societies have moved into banking, so the British Bankers Association and the Building Societies Association have to some extent competed with each other.

ORGANISING THE PLANNING PROCESS IN TRADE ASSOCIATIONS

Because trade associations are not profit-seeking organisations many have not been run in a businesslike way and accordingly the planning process has not followed the textbook formula. Rather, the process has begun with dissatisfaction on the part of major members with the performance of the trade association often coupled with or indeed concentrating on the performance of the chief executive. The larger members may be aware through their own contacts that the industry is not getting its message over and that this is damaging. It is not unknown for civil servants and occasionally ministers to quietly mention to industry leaders that they would get a better deal from government if they were better organised in their trade association.

When the planning process starts in this way it follows one of two forms. The first is to employ a consultant to undertake a full planning process. The second is for a high level committee to be established comprising in particular representatives of the large members and some of those who have not been directly involved in the trade association work.

Reports that come from such exercises are likely to have much in common. They will point to how the market has changed, how there is now a need for a more professional trade body, how the committee structure must be rationalised in order to reduce the time burden on company representatives and how responsibility needs to be transferred to the fulltime secretariat. There may be a recommendation that a "director general" be appointed with a recognition that the previous position, for example "secretary general", no longer either reflected the work that was being done or the requirements of the job.

This is generally not a good way to undertake the planning process. It is expensive, time-consuming and where there is dissatisfaction with the organisation there is a danger that consultants may be poorly briefed and will not get co-operation from the staff; indeed the whole exercise can cause morale problems within the staff. However, often such exercises are the only way to secure the step change which might be needed in a trade association and the initial report may well be a useful basis on which subsequent planning can be based. The report will almost certainly point to the need for an ongoing planning process.

The ideal planning process, one already underway in most well run trade associations, is for this to be handled by the senior executive team with the long term strategy being approved by the governing board and with regular monitoring reports being given to it. Unlike in most other organisations trade association strategies have to be fairly public. They have to be made known to the members which in many industries virtually ensures that they will find their way at least to the trade press. This means that strategy reports have to be written on the basis that they will be read by other trade associations which might be regarded as competitors and by others who might be able to make use of the information in the report to help their own businesses. On the other hand, a public strategy can be helpful to trade associations by reducing the need for regular debates on the same subject. For example, a trade association might well have as part of its strategy that there should be greater delegation to the secretariat and that the chief executive should adopt a more public role in respect of the media, conferences and so on. Once this has been firmly decided by the governing body of the association and published to members then it will be easier to defend if raised by individual members, whereas if something like that simply emerges there will be those who question whether it is appropriate.

Strategic plans and their implementation have important implications for the staff and the accommodation of the trade association. This is another area where trade associations are different from other organisations. In terms of staff they are small bodies compared with the members that they represent. The staff are the major asset. If an association is performing poorly then the chances are that this is because the staff are poor, and the planning process will inevitably reveal this. If the organisation is expensive to run then this might call into question current accommodation both in terms of space occupied and location. These are all very sensitive issues and if not handled well can be damaging. For example, if staff feel that they are not highly regarded then it is the best members of staff who are likely to leave, that is those who can easily obtain a job somewhere else, whereas the poorer members of staff will remain. Some early protracted debate about the location of an office will cause some staff to leave and make it more difficult to recruit.

The special nature of trade associations means essentially that there must be a two-tier planning process. There will be the public process with a document made available to members and therefore in effect anyone else as a consequence of that. The leadership of the association will have some sort of private agenda which may entail significant staff changes, relocation, merger with other trade associations or downsizing.

BIBLIOGRAPHY AND FURTHER READING

Ernst & Young, *The Manager's Handbook* (London: Sphere Books, 1992).

Charles Mack, *The Executive's Handbook on Trade and Business Associations* (New York: Quorum Books, 1991).

Mike Hudson, *Managing Without Profit* (London: Penguin Books, 1995).

Report of the CBI Conference on an Effective Structure for Business Representation (London: Confederation of British Industry, unpublished, 1994).

Case Studies

It is helpful to illustrate the points made in this chapter by briefly describing specific strategic planning exercises in trade associations where the information is publicly available.

Ian Deslandes, Director General of the **Building Employers Confederation**, speaking at a CBI conference in 1993, explained how the BEC had reacted to a serious deficit in 1990. A number of administrative changes had been made -

(a)   Staff had been cut from 237 to 124 and salaries frozen.

(b)   Regional activities had been concentrated in three centres instead of ten.

(c)   Office accommodation had been mothballed.

(d)   The monthly journal had been replaced by a shorter and more helpful document.

(e)   The committee system had been streamlined.

(f)   Cars were leased instead of bought.

(g)   Subscription collection had been centralised.

(h)   Income from commercial operations had doubled.

At the same conference, Colin Stanley, Director General of the **British Printing Industries Federation**, explained how his Association had reacted to the impact of the recession on his Federation -

(a)   Cutting staff numbers and freezing pay.

(b)   Dropping minority activities and concentrating on key strengths.

(c)   Investing heavily in marketing and information technology.

(d)   Encouraging members to understand that the Federation provided a competitive service and holding subscriptions down.

(e)   Providing services as locally as possible.

(f)   Researching customers, why they had joined and what they thought of the Federation. In this case, lobbying activities had scored very low in members' lists of priorities.

As a result of these various initiatives, non-subscription income had averaged 39% of total income over the previous five years compared with 19% ten years ago.

The *Annual Report* of the **Vehicle Builders and Repairers Association** for 1994 briefly sets out the results of a strategic review of that organisation. Set out below is an extract from the Chairman's Report.

"In 1994 the Association took the decision to stop being a reactive organisation and to start becoming a pro-active organisation. It therefore developed a new 5 year strategic plan for the Association.

For the first time the Association presented and launched a clear mission statement to the membership:

"To offer a professional, quality service and support to members, to develop their efficiency and profitability and to obtain better prices."

It also put into words the type of Association it intended to become:

"A pro-active, regulatory, forward-thinking, customer-orientated Association, which directs and leads the membership with significant influence with the industry key players."

It set out its objectives:

To ensure that membership of the VBRA was recognised as the sign of the professional crash repairer.

To develop membership criteria.

To develop membership profitability.

To develop relationships with the key industry players, and

To improve communications both internally and within the industry.

There have been times in the past when the Association has seemed unclear as to whom it should direct its lobbying and promotional efforts. Therefore for the first time it also defined its target markets in order of their priority. They were:

Insurance companies
Fleet managers
Accident Management companies
OEMs
Government
Suppliers
The Public

With this framework in place, and formally launched to the membership at the Association's highly successful 1994 conference in Harrogate, the Association was able to devote the second half of the year putting its new strategy and objectives into practice.

This produced a tremendous surge of activity during the second half of the year as new schemes and initiatives were put into place."

The **Electrical Contractors Association**, which represents some 2,000 companies involved in electrical installation work, has a planning system called Strategic Policy and Activity Review (SPAR). This is a development of its corporate plans of 1982 and 1987 and its Strategic Review and Activity Programme of June 1991. The 1994 Strategic Policy and Activity Review has six sections each of which has a brief strategy and then a number of activities are listed designed to achieve that strategy. The areas in the strategy are -

(a) **Commercial Preference/Promotion**
Support and further members' business interests by encouraging electrical installation owners and users and those influencing design standards and specifications to favour contractors qualified by membership of the Association. Develop a relevant market intelligence base.

(b) **People**
Endeavour to ensure that a stable, qualified workforce - management, staff and operatives - is available.

(c) **Commercial and Contractual Interests**
Endeavour to ensure that the conditions of contract and commercial practices under which members work are fair, reasonable and equitable.

(d) **Technical and Safety Issues**
Enhance the standard and safety of electrical installations and promote the standards, design and research relating to equipment, product and installation practices. Ensure that all technical considerations and proposals support the commercial development and performance efficiency of the industry in respect of costs.

(e) **External Relationships**
Represent the interests of the electrical installation industry as a whole at home and overseas.

(f) **Structure, Finance and Benefits**
Ensure that the Association has the structure, procedures and finance necessary to achieve its objectives and provide benefit services to members as required.

It is worth considering in more detail the activities listed in respect of Structure, Finance and Benefits as these are particularly relevant to other trade associations. Among the thirteen activities listed in the October 1994 Report were -

(a)   Consider widening membership to include related industry groups.

(b)   Review all guarantee schemes to ensure their commercial relevance.

(c)   Review the management and committee structure of the Association at all levels.

(d)   Encourage and seek such federation and confederation with other bodies as may be supportive of the Association's objectives and interests.

(e)   Ensure that the ECA is in a strong financial position to satisfy members' requirements and to improve individual benefit services.

(f)   Seek to acquire revenue from association activities such as inspection, training, and sale of publications.

(g)   Promote the interests and use of the ECA's affiliated companies' services.

The **Federation of Master Builders** published a comprehensive corporate strategy for 1994. This began with a ten point statement of the Federation's philosophy, the points ranging from "achieve a service superior to any industry trade body" to "assist members to develop quality management" to "provide members with the widest range of services at the most economic cost, consistent with quality". This is then followed with a four point mission statement and key objectives which are listed as being, in the short term, to retain the Federation's existing membership, urgently address efforts to recruit potential new members and to increase total membership by at least 5% per annum, and, in the medium term, to further strengthen the firm asset based financial structure of the Federation and to expand services to members which give "value for money".

A section on strategy and management covers eight areas, listing for each the objective and then how this will be measured. This merits reproduction in full.

"1. Lobbying

A two-fold thrust is needed:

-    To increase the influence of the Federation of Master Builders by improving the quality of its presentation to the UK Government, Parliament, European Commission, European Parliament, clients and consumers. To safeguard the long-term ability to compete requires a continuous process of contact both at ministerial and senior civil servant level.

- To press for the removal of unfair competition created by inequitable legislation imposed on small businesses which enables even smaller companies to gain unfair advantages and operate in the expanding underground or black economy.

Measurement

'Any fundamental changes achieved will be detected by an increase in the volume of references made to FMB from all targeted sources and a perception by members that they are not unduly disadvantaged by legislation.'

2. Service to Members

- To increase the range of quality services available to members.

- To improve the quality and content of the Federation's communications to its members.

- To reach those members who may not attend Branch meetings or social activities.

Measurement

'An indication of success will be an upward movement in the membership, better retention of existing members and by an increased percentage of total income from commercial activities.'

3. Membership Forum

- To sustain and strengthen the Branch and Regional structure especially by involving more members.

- To provide a wider range of services at regional level and to enhance existing business and social activities.

Measurement

'Impact will be seen by signs of increasing numbers of members in each region attending Branch Meetings, Regional Councils, Seminars and Social Functions. Plus recognition of growing unity between members and a broader conception of the local and national dimension of the Federation.'

4. Quality and Image

- Encouragement of excellence in building work by FMB members to enhance the image of the Federation and the Industry among the widest range of users of construction services. The promotion of excellence requires a profound overhaul to counter unfair and ill-informed observations, particularly from the consumer lobby.

Measurement

'Sustained favourable observations from the media, Government, Local Authorities, clients, consumers and growing support for FMB by current non-members will signal moves towards the objectives.'

5. Unity

- To pursue a culture of unity within the industry. This would give the Federation a stronger voice in the United Kingdom and Europe, thereby promoting its interests and views to a wider audience and it would instil collaboration among individual members on policy issues. It would also engender responsibility within the membership toward those users of the industry's services.

Measurement

'Benefits hinge upon the effectiveness of the Construction Industry Employers Council (CIEC) and notice taken by other organisations of FMB's views in other industry forums. Internally, signals of desirable momentum will come from FMB's ability to develop uniform policies based on consensus.'

6. Negotiating Ability

- To review the industrial relations machinery in the building industry and in particular strengthen the position of BATJIC. If desirable, support collaboration on an industry-wide basis.

- To ensure that FMB's views are considered during negotiations within Europe on industrial relations matters and especially the shaping of the agenda of any Social Charter.

Measurement

'Such difficult and complex aims will only be acknowledged by the securing of a competitive industrial action. But the retention of BATJIC is cardinal to the FMB sector.'

7. Training and Recruitment

- To maximise efforts with young people to persuade them to pursue a career in construction.

- To ensure an adequate supply both in quality and quantity of suitably trained operatives for the building industry by improving the scope and quality of training at all levels including management. The key element is the operation of a Statutory CITB and greater emphasis on Group Training embracing all users of construction skills.

Measurement

'Aspirations will be recognised by an early adequate supply of "New Entrants" to minimise skill shortages in the future. Evidence will also be needed of a perceivable improvement in productivity within industry to create and maintain a competitive edge.'

8. Health and Safety

- To promote high standards of health and safety on sites throughout FMB's membership and to upgrade liaison with the Health and Safety Executive to improve the industry's record.

Measurement

'If evidence of a reduction in accidents emerges and greater use of FMB advice on safety issues becomes apparent, added employer strength would exist to negotiate with insurers in the face of tough new legislation.'"

The chapter on the head office lists medium term priorities in respect of lobbying, service to members, the membership forum, quality and image, unity, negotiating ability, training and recruitment and health and safety. There is a similar set of priorities for the regions. Finally, on administration, objectives are set in respect of staffing, equipment and systems and quality assurance.

The **British Bankers Association** commissioned a review into its role and functioning by Professor Ian Morrison in late 1991. Professor Morrison reported in May 1992. The following paragraphs from the introduction to the report are fairly typical of similar studies into trade associations -

"Considerable common ground emerged in the course of these consultations undertaken by Professor Morrison as part of the review. There was impressive evidence of the banks' commitment to a strong association capable of promoting the interests of the entire banking community in the United Kingdom, and confidence in its executive. Equally, there was widespread recognition of the need for the BBA to be more active in identifying and handling issues affecting the banking industry, to upgrade the public relations and communications aspects of its role and to develop better mechanisms for reconciling the interests of its diverse membership.

The over thrust of the recommendations is clear. The banks' need for a strong trade association is greater than it has ever been if they are to contend with the daunting issues which now face them. Paradoxically, this need is all the greater now that the banks have abandoned most of their old collective practices and are pursuing increasingly distinctive corporate strategies.

In this environment, the BBA's decision-making processes must be streamlined and its officers and executive must be empowered to act with expedition in furtherance of agreed policy objectives. The balance of its activities must be broadly representative of the balance of interests and concerns of its entire membership. Individual banks, and groups of banks, must be more tolerant of the fact that their particular views and interest will not always hold sway. There must, on the other hand, be adequate checks and balances to ensure that the BBA does not lose the confidence of its members - a fate that can easily befall a trade association."

The conclusions of the review are set out below.

"The most important conclusions of this review were stated at the outset: the need for greater proactivity, better external relations and improved arrangements for reconciling members' varied interests. There is also a requirement for more streamlined decision-making, with further delegation of authority to the executive.

Differences between members arise along different fault lines, and every effort should be made to resolve them within the BBA, though allowing different views to be represented where necessary.

In defining the BBA's areas of interest, some involvement in competitive matters is inevitable, particularly when banks are under collective attack. More could be done to safeguard the United Kingdom's position as a financial centre.

The BBA's record in its representational work is one of winning many battles but losing several wars, often because of getting off to a poor start and lacking the natural support of the authorities. The banks' lack of accomplishment in lobby politics has been exposed, showing the need for greater attention to tactical detail in their representational work.

European issues will require greater attention in future.

Some element of self-regulation in the BBA's role seems essential, but subject to clear limits, the absence of sanctions, and first-rate consultation processes.

The provision of shared services is legitimate, though only if they arise naturally and at little extra cost from normal activities.

Various ways of enhancing the BBA's external relations activities are available. While the choice between them cannot be divorced from the personalities concerned, some elevation in this aspect of the key posts is essential, as is better orchestration of individual bank activity.

Better internal communications are vital if the BBA is not to lose the support of its membership, while members themselves must ensure that the BBA material they receive is correctly routed.

The present committee arrangements are not wholly satisfactory, and there is a strong case for fusing the General Council and the Executive Committee into a new Council. There should be intermediate bodies between the new Council and the standing committees but a President's Committee should be established to exercise the authority of the Council on a day-to-day basis.

The Retail Banking Group and most of the senior standing committees seem to have a legitimate role to play but there is scope for reducing the number of junior committees, some of which should be reconvened as advisory panels. The committee structure should be periodically reviewed in future but some "talking shop" activity may be unavoidable.

All the major constituencies need to be represented on the senior committee. Elsewhere, full clearing bank participation may be essential in some cases; but where it is not it would help if the clearers agreed to waive some of their present seats. Other banks must recognise that committee membership entails responsibilities as well as rights.

Two-year terms should remain the norm for committee chairmen but longer terms seem appropriate for the President and Vice-Presidents.

While generally praised, the executive has been criticised for lack of proactivity, poor external relations and a failure to handle certain major issues as well as it might have. A flatter organisation structure and better lines of communication might help, but mainly required is a clearer sense of the executive's true role. A new title and job description are required for the secretary-general.

It seems unlikely that the BBA could handle its increasing workload with fewer executive staff, but non-executive costs could be trimmed and there should eventually be substantial occupancy savings. An eventual merger with the BSA could generate further savings. Most important of all is the scope to cut the hidden costs of committee work.

Cost apportionment is contentious and must be kept in perspective. A limited move towards apportioning costs more directly to identified beneficiaries is desirable but the basic model should remain that of general purpose funding using a size-related formula

211

with a higher floor and a lower cap than at present. No changes should be made, however, until wider issues of role have been resolved. Meanwhile, other sources of revenue should be explored.

Relations with the other banking associations are not as good as they should be, partly reflecting inadequate awareness of what the BBA does and a failure to take proper account of foreign banks' needs. The coexistence of so many associations does compromise the BBA's effectiveness and it must work to build better bridges and enhance its own quality of service.

There is a case for changing the BBA's name and an even stronger case for single-status membership, as well as for retaining direct (ie non-federal) membership.

Committee participation should be broadly proportionate to size and interest but formal membership rights are less important than the quality of the contribution made. Nominees should be of appropriate seniority. There should be greater emphasis on identifying and serving special interest groups within the BBA.

Membership should remain voluntary but with greater efforts to convince non-members and waverers of the benefits of membership."

The **Association of British Insurers** produces for internal purposes an annual strategy statement. This begins by setting out the ABI's objectives which are to help members companies by -

(a) Representing their interests to government, regulatory and other bodies, particularly on public policy issues.

(b) Providing them with value-for-money technical services, in particular in respect of industry statistics, market and regulatory information and reducing the incidence of claims.

(c) Promoting insurance and insurance companies generally.

There is an ongoing five part strategy for achieving these objectives -

(a) Clear policy objectives and priorities being put to and agreed by the board so the Association can increasingly take the lead and set the agenda.

(b) Greater delegation to the secretariat which increasingly is taking responsibility for anticipating events, developing policy and exercising the representational function.

(c) An expanded programme of providing market and other information to members and more widely.

212

(d) A higher profile for the Association by enhancing relations with politician, civil servants, regulators, media and other opinion formers.

(e) Controlling costs by constantly appraising functions and the way that they are performed and maximising income.

The Association lists a number of success criteria -

(a) Policy priorities established by the Board annually are pursued vigorously and effectively.

(b) The performance of the Association is judged to be effective by members and by government and regulators, in absolute terms and in relation to the performance of other trade associations.

(c) The Association is successful in helping to set the agenda for the public policy debate and in securing satisfactory policy outcomes.

(d) The Association plays its part effectively in promoting a good public image for the Association.

(e) The membership of the Association covers over 90% and an increasing proportion of the company market.

(f) The finances of the Association are managed such that total subscription income falls year by year while the Association continues to run on a balanced budget basis.

(g) Top quality staff are employed, retained and developed.

(h) Other internal target established by the Board annually are achieved.

Key internal targets are set for the following year. For 1995 these included -

(a) As part of the overall delegation of authority for the Association's activities to the secretariat, the role and structure of ABI committees would be clarified.

(b) ABI's international work would be reviewed.

(c) The campaign to increase membership would be continued.

(d) More effective communication with members.

(e) Helping members participate more in public and Association policy issues.

(f) Improving the format of existing publications and introducing new ones.

(g) Developing closer relationships with the Labour Party and influencing opinion formers.

(h) Improving relationships with other market bodies and groupings of members outside the Association.

(i) Managing the finances of the Association with the objective of reducing average subscriptions year by year.

(j) Analyzing and co-ordinating various asset and loss registers.

Separately the Association identifies a number of key policy priorities. For 1995 these included the pension transfer and opt out issue, promoting the long term position of life insurance, the structure of the life insurance industry, contributing to the debate on genetic science, the image of insurance particularly on the life side, minimising the likely future incidence of insurance premium tax, promoting crime prevention and loss prevention, the cost and availability of insurance, promoting the role and status of the London company insurance market, environmental liability, employers' liability, long term care, corporate governance and the inter-relationship of private sector provision and state benefits.

CHAPTER 16

Analyzing the Effectiveness of Trade Associations

Measuring the effectiveness of commercial organisations can be done by using variables such as share price, profitability and return of capital. Companies can also analyze their performance in relation to their peers and unrelated companies through comparisons of key operating ratios and benchmarking. Such tools are not generally available to trade associations. Subjective criteria have to be used instead. Criteria for assessing the effectiveness of trade associations are now being developed.

THE NEED TO MEASURE PERFORMANCE

An organisation needs to be able to measure its performance. Companies within an industrial sector will often devote substantial resources to comparing their performance across a wide range of variables with that of their competitors. Those companies which are profit-seeking will also wish to compare their return on capital, profitability and, where appropriate, share price, against not only their competitors in a particular market but against all other companies.

By looking at key variables such as profitability and share price a company can assess whether it is doing well or badly against its competitors in the market in general. However, a comparison of such variables cannot help to explain why a company is doing well or badly. Examination of some key operating ratios can help here. Taking for example the building societies, which are all in broadly the same market, variables such as the cost/income ratio are a key indicator of profitability. It is obviously more helpful to a company to know where it is out of line with others rather than it is simply not competitive.

There are a variety of ways in which companies compare their performance with that of their peers. Such comparisons are not only done by companies themselves but also by, for example, stock market analysts, credit rating agencies and, from time to time, even government departments.

Often examination of published data, particularly for companies that operate across a wide range of markets, does not give sufficient information to enable performance to be measured in respect of a particular market. Some companies share information between themselves on a closed user group basis, perhaps run by a trade association or a specialist commercial company, so that they can compare their performance against that of their immediate competitors. Benchmarking is another tool that many companies find useful. Unlike broad financial variables such as profitability this looks at processes and requires a considerable input of resources from participants.

The Department of Trade and Industry has published *Benchmarking - the Challenge* as a practical guide to business improvement. This publication notes that most practitioners agree that benchmarking is "a systematic approach to business improvement where best practice is sought and implemented to improve a process beyond the benchmark performance".

It is noted that the benchmark performance can be based on other similar organisations, customer expectations, financial averages or a combination of the three.

The publication notes that the source of benchmark performance gives rise to four general types of benchmarking.

Competitor benchmarking is where the benchmark performance is set by leading suppliers of similar services or products. Improvement is achieved by adopting this approach. This type is best applied in three circumstances -

(a)   When organisations are regionally based and competition is local. Companies outside of the region will more readily work together.

(b)   In markets where organisations provide the same services but do not compete on a commercial basis, for example NHS Trusts, government departments, and universities.

(c)   When trade associations create a common interest and/or forum for debate.

Process benchmarking is where the benchmark performance is set by organisations undertaking comparable processes: for example sales order processing, recruitment or distribution. Improvement is achieved by implementing the best practices of these other organisations. This type is best applied in the following circumstances -

(a)   Where there are organisations who service similar customers or who have similar operating constraints, for example a theatre and a cinema, a building contractor and a heating contractor.

(b)   Where common customers set standards of performance across their supplier base, for example most automotive suppliers need to deliver "Just in Time".

Customer benchmarking is where the benchmark is customer expectations. Customers develop their own benchmarks of performance when selecting and judging suppliers. The improvement programme is aimed at meeting and exceeding customer expectation. This type is best applied in three circumstances -

(a)   When a company has many different customers.

(b)   Where customer demands are increasing and the industry/company is having difficulty meeting them.

(c)   When competition is increasing.

Financial benchmarking is where the benchmark is the financial performance of the leading organisations measured using standard accounting ratios. It is best used as a catalyst for action - most companies react quickly to poor financial results. This is often the first approach to benchmarking as it shows the relative performance of the whole company.

The DTI publication has a section What to Benchmark?. The table below reproduces a table from the publication showing typical benchmarks which support more general business goals.

Business Goal	Typical Benchmarks
To be lowest price producer	**Cost** - Materials cost per product - Labour costs per product - Overheads per unit of production - Cost of distribution channels - Procurement
To maintain or increase market share	**Product differentiators** - Customer service - Product/service functionality - Product development time
To maintain service at a reduced cost	**Resource utilisation** - Value added per employee - System efficiency - Effectiveness of automation
To maintain and increase customer loyalty	**Customer service** - Volumes of repeat business - Levels of customer complaint - Delivery performance - Complaints procedure
To be most innovative producer	**Innovation process** - Time to market - Number of patents per year - Investment in training
To generate cash	**Productivity** - Set up time - Direct to indirect labour costs - Efficiencies - Procurement - Stock levels - Supplier relationships

DIFFICULTIES IN MEASURING TRADE ASSOCIATION PERFORMANCE

The previous section has set out how companies can and do measure their performance against their peers. It is almost immediately apparent that these tools are not available to trade associations. The main difficulty is that to be effective a trade association needs to be the only association in its particular market sector. Therefore, by definition, it has no comparable institution within its sector against which it can benchmark or easily compare its performance.

However, trade associations should be able to benchmark against each other. By the end of 1995 serious consideration was being given to such benchmarking exercises - by associations themselves and by the government.

Trade associations are also non profit-seeking organisations and like other such organisations it follows that financial data cannot be used to measure performance. Profitability, for example, is primarily determined by an executive decision rather than by efficiency and there are no easily identifiable outputs against which costs can be measured.

Having made these points, it seems essential that there should be a system for measuring the effectiveness of trade associations. For the most part this must be a subjective exercise and suffers from all the disadvantages that any subjective exercise inherently involves. However, some financial data for trade associations generally can be of use in explaining, for example, why there are otherwise inexplicable wide variations in subscriptions levels between associations.

CRITERIA FOR ASSESSING THE EFFECTIVENESS OF TRADE ASSOCIATIONS

This section sets out suggested criteria by which trade associations can assess their effectiveness. It draws heavily on the analysis in this book. It needs to be recognised at the outset that trade associations differ considerably in their structure, financing and method of operation and this limits the effectiveness of comparative studies. These criteria are predominantly relevant to large associations representing major industrial sectors although the analysis can fairly easily be adapted for smaller associations.

Position in Market

To be effective a trade association should meet the following criteria -

(a)   It represents the whole of a significant industry sector with no rival associations.

(b) New companies coming into the sector should naturally wish to join the association and there should be no barriers to entry.

(c) Existing members should be broadly satisfied with the association with there being no discussion of breakaways or resignations.

(d) Where the boundaries of the sector are constantly changing the implications of this should be kept under constant review by the association with a view to expanding services or merging with other trade associations.

(e) Given that there are no rigid barriers between industries and markets and that therefore some overlap of trade associations is inevitable, a trade association should work with other trade associations in related areas where there are common interests. Where an industrial sector is part of an identifiable wider sector, for example the ice cream manufacturing sector is part of the food and drink sector, then the trade association should be an active participant in the appropriate federation.

Planning Process

An effective association should have -

(a) A mission statement which clearly sets out what the association is seeking to achieve.

(b) A long term strategy to which the governing body and secretariat are fully committed.

(c) A mechanism for reviewing the strategy on an annual basis and setting new targets and monitoring performance against these targets.

Management

An effective association should have -

(a) Represented on its governing body the chief executives of the major companies in the sector and in addition members representing a wide cross section of membership.

(b) A chairman who is a leading figure in the industry.

(c) A streamlined committee structure with leading industry experts participating.

Opportunities and Threats

(d)   A first class chief executive who has total delegated responsibility for running the organisation, developing policy and acting as the principal representative of the association.

(e)   A high class secretariat with strong trade association skills and the necessary expertise in particular professional disciplines and the industrial sector concerned.

(f)   Best practice in respect of training and personnel matters generally.

Finance

An effective association -

(a)   Has strong reserves sufficient to even out subscription income given inevitable fluctuations in expenditure. [Table 14.2 shows ratios of reserves to expenditure for the large associations ranging from zero to 300%. However, it needs to be recognised that the figures take no account of differences in accounting practices particularly in respect of the valuation of office premises which are likely to vary substantially from the book position, either favourably or unfavourably. An association should decide for itself what an appropriate reserve position is.]

(b)   Has a clear policy in respect of the subscription scale which is regarded by the members as being generally fair and equitable.

(c)   Takes every opportunity to sell services to members and non-members thereby generating additional income but without exposing the association to a downside risk should commercial activity fall below anticipated levels.

(d)   Has systems of budgeting and financial control appropriate to those for a commercial organisation of the same size.

The representative function

An effective association -

(a)   Gives responsibility for exercising the representative function to the secretariat with the chairman and other office holders being involved only to a limited extent and at a very high level.

220

(b)   Incorporates trade association skills and communication skills generally in the staff training programme.

(c)   Identifies the key politicians, officials and advisers relevant to the sector and maintains contact with them.

(d)   Effectively represents the interests of members to government, regulatory and other official bodies both in response to formal consultation exercises and informally as the need arises.

(e)   Is regarded as a credible representative body by the appropriate government department or agency.

(f)   Is accepted by the members as effectively representing them and that this function is performed well taking into account members' own representations.

Influencing the climate of opinion

An effective association -

(a)   Identifies academics who have a particular interest in the sector and maintains regular contact with them, using them on occasion for research projects.

(b)   Has an active media relations programme including responding quickly and efficiently to requests for information and maintaining contact with key journalists.

(c)   Maintains contact with relevant "think tanks" and ensures that they are supplied with the information they require.

(d)   Maintains contact with all MPs from all parties with an interest in the sector and provides them with a regular flow of information and responds efficiently to requests for information.

(e)   Identifies other opinion formers relevant to the sector and maintains close contact with them.

European representation

An effective trade association -

(a) Is an active member of the appropriate European association and has a major influence on the policy representations it makes.

(b) Maintains direct contact with the European Commission and the other institutions of the European Union.

(c) Influences developments at the European level through contact with the British government.

(d) Regularly monitors and keeps members informed of developments at the European level which might impact on its members.

Information to Members

An effective trade association -

(a) Provides members with timely high quality information on all matters in which the association is involved on representative work.

(b) Provides a flow of other relevant information to members.

(c) Is able to respond quickly to requests for information from members.

Statistics and Economic Analysis

An effective trade association -

(a) Ensures that there is an adequate provision of statistics about the information either through providing a statistical service itself or by co-operating with the relevant government agency or commercial body.

(b) Uses statistics and other information to provide a regular flow of information on the position of the industry in the national economy and in international markets.

GOVERNMENT POLICY, TRADE ASSOCIATIONS AND COMPETITIVENESS

The criteria covered in the previous section of the paper are concerned with the mainstream functions of trade associations, that is representing their members and providing information to them. The government however has recently made it clear that it expects trade associations to go substantially beyond this traditional role. Government policy was covered in Chapter 12 but a brief summary of this particular aspect is necessary here.

In his first trade association speech on 17 June 1993, the then President of the Board of Trade set out three minimum services that he thought all trade associations should be providing. Two, influencing government policy and the quality of public services and contributing to new government initiatives, would be accepted by most associations. The third services relates to competitiveness. The President said:

> "I am very strongly of the view that trade associations in this country ought to be playing a much bigger role in promoting the international competitiveness of their member companies, including UK subsidiaries where these are foreign owned. This goes considerably wider than the provision of legal services, economic data, and the basic lobbying role which at present remains the primary function of most associations."

The President said that only a minority of associations seem to regard the international competitiveness of the UK companies in their own sectors as a matter over which they have much influence or for which they have any responsibility. The President offered trade associations a challenge to let him have their proposals to create competitiveness clubs which would carry out benchmarking or a process important to their particular sector.

In his second speech on 3 February 1995, the President said that trade associations also had a major role to play in helping companies increase their exports.

The DTI's policy suggests a further checklist, covering the services analysed in Chapter 10. In respect of these services an association first has to consider whether it should be undertaking a particular function, and, if, so, how to assess its performance in undertaking the function.

Technical Services and Management Consultancy

A trade association can help individual members and therefore arguably the sector as a whole by providing technical services and management consultancy services. Some trade associations do this extensively, for example, the British Leather Confederation, but others do not do it at all. Such services can best be provided in a sector which is very specialised and where the companies either do not consider that they are competing strongly with each other or, if they do, they have more to gain by sharing some expertise and thereby expanding the total market. By contrast, in, say, the finance sector, a very large sector of companies competing fiercely with each other, there is less need for a trade association to provide such services because they are provided already by management consultancy and other firms, some of which are specialist to the sector, while others offer a service across the whole of industry and commerce. Effectiveness can be measured to some extent by the profitability of the service and member satisfaction.

Export Promotion

At first sight export promotion is a function which trade associations can sensibly take on. Their members collectively compete against other countries and shared resources can often be very valuable. Again, this is a service which is relevant to some sectors but not to others. In sectors where the industry is clearly "British" and where the participants are generally small then a trade association can assist in exporting, for example by providing information about foreign markets and by various export promotion campaigns including exhibitions and so on. The tourist industry obviously stands out as one where there is an important export element. The clothing industry is another where there is a separate body devoted to export promotion. The function, however, is less appropriate where a sector comprises large companies which compete extensively with each other in overseas markets as well as in domestic markets. This is particularly true when a sector has within it many foreign owned companies. Where export promotion is undertaken effectiveness can be measured by the growth of exports.

Standards

Many casual observers of trade associations believe that they should set an enforce standards for their members. Few associations, however, see this as one of their roles, and there has been a gradual pulling back from this function over the years. Many industries are very highly regulated and the function of the trade association is to represent the interests of members in ensuring that the regulatory framework is as favourable as possible for the members. This is the case in some financial services that are regulated under the Financial Services Act and also the utilities. In areas where there is no regulation the industry itself can play a role through the trade association in setting standards and operating codes of practice. This is done for example in the estate agency and motor repair trade. Effectiveness can be measured by testing adherence to standards through appropriate customer services and analyzing complaints.

Education and Training

The government expects education and training to be co-ordinated at the industry level. Some trade associations take on this function particularly those which traditionally have been involved with employment matters. For other associations the function does not sit happily with the rest of their activity. The appropriate industry body might be the professional body for staff within the industry if there is one or alternatively a dedicated training council which will have on it some representation of the trade association.

Technology

The government seems to want trade associations to take the lead in introducing new technology into their sectors. Again, this is something that might be appropriate in trade associations where the majority of members are very small. Trade associations also clearly have a role where there is a need for IT links between members or IT standards. The Association for Payment Clearing Services, APACS, stands out as a trade associations whose business is dominated by IT issues and indeed it goes further than what might be called a development role by actually operating the central clearing systems for the banks. In other sectors a trade association role beyond standards and links between firms is inappropriate. Information technology is a source of competitive advantage and companies that compete strongly with each other are generally not willing to share their expertise unless they all gain a very substantial advantage in relation to the cost.

Competitiveness

The Department of Trade and Industry wants trade associations to play a major role in promoting the international competitiveness of their members. The Department is looking to trade associations to commission studies on where the UK stands in the international market and how the UK industry can be made more competitive. This is a somewhat controversial area. Trade associations would generally argue that through all of the work they do they help promote the competitiveness of their members. This includes making representations to government and providing information and other services to members. It is possible to go further and through activities such as benchmarking and competitiveness clubs encourage companies to share information so that performance can be brought up to the standards of the best.

THE DTI MODEL TRADE ASSOCIATION

In February 1996 the DTI published *A best practice guide for The Model Trade Association*, setting out, in its view, the key characteristics that a modern, best practice trade association should display and the services it should provide. The introduction to the publication invites associations to consider whether they meet the criteria and whether the sector is represented as well as it needs to be. Much of the DTI paper is in with the section of this chapter of criteria for assessing the effectiveness of trade associations but there is a stronger emphasis on those covers covered in the previous section. The DTI paper is set out in full in the Appendix to this chapter.

225

THE AMERICAN EXAMPLE

It is helpful to conclude this chapter by briefly drawing on an American Society of Association Executives publication, *Assess Your Strengths and Weaknesses*, the purpose of which "is to aid association managers in taking a comprehensive but quick look at how their association is doing in ten general areas of management common to most associations."

Set out below are the self assessment criteria the publication suggests -

Self-assessment criteria: a summary rating chart

Purpose and Goals
  Mission statement clarity
  Mission consistent with member needs
  Effective annual plan
  Mission directs activities
  Mission re-evaluated as needed
  Staff focus on goals and objectives

Membership development
  Periodic needs assessment
  Membership development activity
  Membership retention activity
  Programs communicated to members

Governing body, officers and directors
  Governing body authority
  Election procedures
  Terms and duties of elected officers
  Governing body meetings
  Members informed about elected leaders
  Bylaws - reviewed and current
  Effectiveness of governing body

Organisational structure and documents
  Organisational structure qualities
  Documentation and communication
  Operating procedures
  Staff and volunteer responsibilities

Programs and services
    Plan for programs, services and activities
    Essential program elements
    Program implementation
    Evaluation of programs, services and activities
    Membership involvement in programs
    Fee and cost structure
    Modifications in programs

Association staff
    Organisation of staff
    Personnel system elements
    Staff development activities
    Productivity of staff
    Authority of the CEO

Financial management and control
    Budgeting process activities
    Accounting system elements
    Financial plan qualities
    Financial contingency plan
    Financial controls
    Annual financial review
    Procurement policies

Information management and automation
    Office automation plan
    Procurement of information technology
    Security of systems
    Maximum use of systems

Government affairs
    Planning for government relations
    Government relations program elements
    Program effectiveness

Communications
    Communications planning
    Communications implementation
    Assessment of internal and external publics
    Success in building support
    Levels of feedback

The American Society of Association Executives has developed a benchmarking programme for trade associations much of which would be applicable in the UK. A study involving 43 national associations sought to compile information for four key areas -

(a) What do association members want from their association in such broad categories as education, publications, meeting quality and so on?

(b) How do members of the average association rate these categories?

(c) How well does an association compare with others?

(d) In which areas are improvements needed?

Part of the survey was a series of telephone interviews with randomly selected lapsed association members. Five broad areas were identified as critical to member satisfaction for each group -

(a) Publications.

(b) Information services and training.

(c) Organisational member benefits.

(d) Trade association leadership.

(e) Benefits to members who are employees of member companies.

Survey questionnaires were sent to up to 2,000 randomly selected members of each trade association asking each respondent to evaluate its association on a 1 to 10 score in respect of eight variables -

(a) Relevance of information provided.

(b) Availability of learning opportunities.

(c) Variety of information vehicles to meet member needs.

(d) Availability of electronic means to communicate information.

(e) Trade shows.

(f) Conferences.

(g) Providing legislative information to members.

(h) Overall satisfaction with information services and training.

A mean score for the variables varied from 6.17 to 7.49. The spread between the highest and the lowest performer was between 1.7 points and 3.7 points. Each association has had a detailed report enabling it to compare its rating with those of the other associations.

BIBLIOGRAPHY AND FURTHER READING

Assess Your Strengths and Weaknesses (Washington DC: American Society of Association Executives, 1988).

Benchmarking - the Challenge (London: Department of Trade and Industry, 1995).

Robert MacDicken, Gauging Member Satisfaction, in *Association Management* (Washington DC: American Society of Association Executives, April 1995).

A best practice guide for The Model Trade Association (London: Department of Trade and Industry, 1996).

A Best Practice Guide for the Model Trade Association

Paper published by the Department of Trade and Industry, February 1996

INTRODUCTION

The Model Trade Association has been developed by DTI in consultation with a wide range of representative bodies in industry and commerce. It sets out the key characteristics that a modern best practice Trade Association should display and the services it should provide.

The Model has been prepared against a background in which the UK finds itself in a most highly competitive business environment. Government has a role to play in improving our competitiveness, but prime responsibility must lie with industry itself. Industry's representatives therefore also have a vital role to play in helping it to meet the challenges from increasing world-wide competition and in ensuring that its voice is heard and understood at all levels in the legislative process.

In this area, like so many others, we can learn from our competitors overseas. We have therefore included some examples of what foreign Trade Associations are doing to help their industries prosper. [These examples are not included in this appendix.]

Trade Association Executive Councils and their equivalents may wish to consider whether their Association meets the Model criteria and whether their sector is represented as well as it should be. DTI sector contacts are given at the back of this brochure for those wishing to discuss these issues further.

We accept that the circumstances of each sector of industry may vary, and that it may not be appropriate for some Trade Associations to perform the full range of services listed here. Nevertheless, members of such associations might question whether they are best served by continuing with their current arrangements.

KEY CHARACTERISTICS

- Represents the whole of a commercial or industrial sector and seeks to cover all products, services and processes.

- Members represent substantial proportion of sector (both in terms of output and numbers).

- Governing council includes representatives from the largest companies in the sector and a good cross-section of other members. Meets sufficiently regularly to direct action/strategy.

- Broadly-based membership with both large and small businesses and the key players.

- Enjoys active participation of a representative cross-section of its members. Is responsive to their views.

- Is properly resourced. Successful both in generating income from members' subscriptions and from sales of services to members, and to others.

- Is professional in its approach. Attracts and retains high calibre staff. Pulls in services of high level people from member companies for representation and policy development purposes when necessary.

- Has a business plan (annual/3 year) which sets out its mission, a clear strategy and priority areas. Developed in consultation with members. Monitors progress rigorously against it.

- Makes full use of information technology to minimize costs and improve quality of its services to members.

- Promotes co-operation within the sector, and between the sector, its customers and suppliers, to enhance international competitiveness.

- Forms appropriate links with other representative bodies, including the CBI, to ensure that services are supplied with the minimum of duplication, and in the most effective manner, to its members.

- Adopts best management practices in quality assurance, financial management and control, and training and development of staff.

- Prepared to work with non-members and co-operates with other associations in allied sectors on matters of joint concern.

SERVICES

Works effectively to represent the sector's interests at all levels of the legislative and regulatory process

Essential

- has an effective mechanism for consulting members and understanding their views

- monitors and anticipates the legislative and regulatory process; ensures that its views on matters which significantly affects its members are taken into account at the earliest opportunity

- is proactive in shaping policies and initiatives which will benefit the sector

- puts forward to Government well-researched, cogently argued cases, and is respected as a credible and authoritative advocate for its sector

- is able to form and present a view on issues where there may be conflicting interests among members

- represents the sector's interests effectively in Europe:

- liaises with counterparts in EU at both national and European level and takes joint action with them;

- understands the workings of the institutions of the EU including the Commission and Parliament.

Works proactively to improve the sector's competitiveness

Essential

- analyses the sector's competitiveness requirements

- takes action where necessary with the sector and others (including Government) to address weaknesses and build on strengths

- organises competitiveness improvement programmes, eg benchmarking clubs to spread best practices, supply chain initiatives

- supports international trade and investment

Desirable

- designs and implements support services

- monitors Government initiatives/support, eg Business Links, M90s and helps members take advantage of them

- adopts proactive approach to meeting other shortcomings identified by benchmarking activities

Supplies sound information and advice to members

- seeks out information relevant to members, eg market trends, intelligence on overseas competitors, parliamentary affairs, patents, standards, etc disseminates it on regular, say, weekly basis

- arranges briefings/conferences for members on key issues that affect them

- initiates and co-ordinates relevant action

- ensures provision of sound advice on legal, employment, health and safety, environmental issues relevant to its members, co-operating as appropriate with employer or other organisations to ensure effective delivery of these services

- ensures adequate statistical information on the sector from official or other sources; if necessary, collects and disseminates the information itself or commissions others to provide it

- disseminates information about Government science and technology policies and programmes to its members, eg Technology Foresight, Supernet

Desirable

- liaises with Central Statistical Office and other bodies to ensure high quality official statistics are available on the sector

Promotes good public relations and communications

Essential

- promotes a positive public image of the sector, its products and services

- acts as a focal point for public and media enquiries on the sector, and represents the sector to the media

Promotes exports and other market opportunities

Essential

- has an exports strategy in support of member companies, developed in consultation with them, taking account of investment decisions

- mounts promotional events, seminars, overseas missions, trade fairs, exhibitions, etc as part of an export strategy

- takes full advantage of export services from Government and other providers to add value for member companies

<u>Desirable</u>

- provides information on sources of supply from its members, eg buyer's guides, electronic databases and deals effectively with bespoke enquiries

- represents the sector to major customers

- liaises with Government Regional Supply Offices and other agencies on UK sources of supply/import substitution

Promotes training and education

<u>Essential</u>

- determines skills requirements for the sector, both short- and long-term

- works with relevant Industry Training Organisations and other employer organisations, professional institutions and training bodies to ensure identified training requirements are met

- promotes training standards and qualifications for the sector

Promotes standards and product/service quality

<u>Essential</u>

- identifies what standards the sector needs

- co-operates effectively on standards development, quality and conformity assessment procedures with appropriate bodies in the UK, EU and elsewhere

Promotes agreed standards and product service quality

<u>Desirable</u>

- proposes and polices standards or codes of behaviour for companies in the sector (may include customer guarantees)

- liaises with the Office of Fair Trading, where appropriate, over the preparation of codes of practice for safeguarding and promoting the interests of consumers in the UK, and disseminates these to its members

Promotes innovation and technology transfer

Desirable

- identifies technology needs of the sector

- co-ordinates and commissions pre-competitive research and technology work on behalf of the sector

- promotes technology transfer

- ensures appropriate technical advice is available to companies.

CHAPTER 17

The Evolution of Trade Associations

As a group trade associations are going through a period of significant structural change. The major outside pressures are the blurring of boundaries between markets and companies, the development of the single European market and government policy towards trade associations. Internal pressures stem from the effects of the early 1990s recession and a more hard headed attitude towards associations on the part of larger companies in particular. Trade associations are becoming more professional and businesslike with full time staff assuming a more proactive role. A rationalisation of trade associations is likely.

THE CHANGING ENVIRONMENT

Trade associations are at their most effective in an industry which can be clearly differentiated from other industries and which is dominated by specialist companies that operate in that industry and no other. Largely because of advances in technology the general trend is for a move away from this pattern of industrial activity. The building societies provide an excellent example of this. Fifteen years ago the building societies dominated the mortgage market and had a very significant share of the retail savings market. All building societies operated under the same legislation, the Building Societies Act, which applied to them and no one else. They were all limited to the same two basic functions of savings and mortgage lending and all operated with a mutual constitution. Clearly there was a need for a strong trade association. This existed in the shape of the Building Societies Association. Over the past ten years however, two of the largest societies have converted into or been taken over by banks and five others have announced that they are going to follow a similar route. Other institutions have come into the mortgage and savings markets and building societies have diversified quite widely into the retail financial markets. The Building Societies Association has adapted to this changing market partly by spawning a sister organisation, the Council of Mortgage Lenders. This blurring is evident through the financial services industry with banks, insurance companies, building societies and unit trust companies now increasingly operating well outside their traditional markets and with the borders between the markets being difficult to distinguish.

The second key factor has been the internationalisation of business. This can be well illustrated by the motor car industry. What precisely is the British motor car industry? If it is an industry of British owned companies then it is a very small industry with some of its activity being conducted outside the United Kingdom. If it the motor industry as it is carried on in the UK then it largely comprises Japanese, German and American companies. The consumer often now has no knowledge of where his car is built. A Ford might well be built in

Germany or Spain, while a Toyota or a Nissan might well be built in the United Kingdom. While, to a large extent, a trade association is able to represent members owned outside the UK, those members naturally have prime allegiances to their foreign shareholders and may have a difference perspective on, for example, government policy towards the industry. Most associations have coped with this issue fairly well simply by recognising that they represent everyone who operates in the UK and by warmly embracing foreign owned institutions even to the extent of some British associations having chairmen from foreign owned companies.

The third major factor affecting all associations is the Europeanisation of decision taking, a factor which is quite distinct from the internationalisation of business, notwithstanding much talk about the European single market. Europe is more important for most trade associations because of its impact on domestic legislation than it is because of its impact on competition. As Chapter 9 illustrated most British laws and regulations are now influenced by developments at the European level. European trade associations have been established to represent the industry at the European level. As the single market becomes more and more a reality, as it will over a period of many years, so increasingly decision taking will have to be centralised at the European level, and for some issues, for example bank supervision, internationally. The logic of a single European market must be single European trade associations for each sector but that position is still a long way away. However, over the years the balance of responsibility between national and European associations will become a major issue.

The final key issue for all associations is government policy as set out in Chapter 12. The government has made it clear that it wishes to see a smaller number of larger well resourced trade associations thereby supporting a trend which is desired by many leading companies. It remains to be seen how far the government will push its initiative. If it becomes more robust in talking to trade associations, that is being somewhat franker about the quality of their representative work and saying to some industries that it will only take account of their views if they are given by a single organisation, then this could lead to a quite radical restructuring of trade associations in some sectors at least. At the very least, the government initiative should have ensured that all trade associations should now be keeping under review the need to work more closely or merge with other associations in the same or related areas.

Paradoxically, there is one government initiative which may threaten some associations. The Business Links programme is designed to provide assistance to firms at the local level, and to some extent will compete with the services trade associations provide.

CHANGING ATTITUDES

As a result of the changing environment outlined in the previous section there has been a significant change of attitude towards trade associations on the part of major companies. It is fair to say that until perhaps ten years ago many trade associations were regarded as a sort of club which one joined and participated in. Few people would turn down the opportunity to become chairman of a large trade association. Many associations at this time were ineffective, being committee dominated and not sufficiently proactive in dealing with government. They were too reliant on industry practitioners who served for perhaps a short time and had little opportunity to develop the long term contacts and working relationships that are now so important in trade association work.

A good trade association, by securing a favourable operating environment for its members, can save its members millions of pounds. By contrast, a poor trade association will allow laws and regulations to come into effect which may be quite damaging to its members, perhaps not intentionally but accidentally through insufficient scrutiny being given to what the government has proposed. Leading companies have recognised the need to have an effective trade association run by full time professional staff, partly because they accept that this is the best way to achieve results but also because some have become increasingly concerned about the amount of time spent on industry matters by their own executives. The top people in an industry, whether it be senior management or specialists, will become involved in trade association work only if their time is used to good effect, and there is an expectation now that projects will be handled and issues managed with the same professionalism that applies in the larger companies.

There is an emphasis on value for money with trade associations being expected to scrutinise all activities so as to ensure that they are necessary and are being carried out in the most cost effective way. The old fashioned way of budgeting, that is of taking last year's figures and adding a few percent, will no longer do in a competitive environment where many companies are having to downsize. Less than competent staff are also tolerated less as they are in industry and commerce generally. A significant number of chief executives, even of the larger associations, have been retired early or in some cases dismissed, and other long serving executives have also been dispensed with.

RESTRUCTURING LARGER ASSOCIATIONS

The process of restructuring larger associations is a relatively simple one but often can take some years to implement. The first essential is top quality leadership. This requires leading people in the industry to become involved in the trade association, otherwise radical change is not feasible. The biggest members have to make clear that they want change and then if they do not get it they will leave the association, establishing their own body. If a period of rapid change is to occur then almost certainly the chairman or president of the association will have to be the chief executive of one of the leading companies. A top quality chief executive is essential to see through any restructuring. Company representatives, however good they might be, cannot manage trade associations as well as running their own companies. Recruiting the right chief executive is probably the most important single decision that any trade association can take. A poor chief executive can wreck a trade association while a good one can bring substantial benefits. Trade associations have recognised the need to pay the right salary for chief executives and have used head hunters to search the market. However, it remains the case that few people have the skill to manage a big trade association. The Civil Service, quangos and local authorities have proved a good source for many trade association chief executives but as associations have developed so there is increasing movement from one association to the other.

The chief executive, with the support of his or her officers, must be responsible for the strategy of the association, that is handling the key questions of what should the association be doing and how should it be doing it. When this exercise is conducted properly, rather than defensively, most associations see the need for restructuring. In some cases the right solution is a merger between two or more trade associations, but equally such mergers are very difficult to achieve largely for personality reasons. Timing is crucial in seeking to initiate merger proposals, a good time generally being the departure of a chief executive of one of the relevant associations. Some associations may see the need to widen their activities to cover, for example, more of the activities that their members are involved in thereby bringing them into competition with other trade associations. The resultant competition might lead to the emergence of a dominant association. Some associations, particularly smaller ones, may wish to merge or in other cases a federal structure might be the route forward.

In some sectors trade associations work together through arrangements which fall short of a federation. This can usefully be illustrated by reference to part of the construction industry. In 1993 the Specialist Engineering Contractors (SEC) Group was formed. This comprises the Electrical Contractors Association, the Electrical Contractors Association of Scotland, the Heating and Ventilating Contractors Association, the National Association of Lift Makers and the National Association of Plumbing Heating and Mechanical Services Contractors. The Group has a management board comprising members and directors of the constituent associations supported by their councils. The Associations continue to operate independently but combine within the SEC Group on matters of common policy representation. The SEC is in turn one of three constituents of the Constructors Liaison Group which was established in 1993. The other members of this are the National Specialist Contractors Council and the Building Structures Group. The Group describes itself as the reference and liaison centre for matters affecting the interests of trade associations whose members undertake the construction, finishing and services installation work of buildings and constructional projects. The Group itself has a management board comprising two representatives of each of its three trade association groups. The Constructors Liaison Group is in turn one of three groupings recognised by the government as a representative body for the construction industry. This sort of arrangement has the advantage of enabling individual associations to maintain their independence. On the other hand, it introduces further layers into the trade association structure.

Because of the difficulties of merging trade associations, normally it is possible to do little more than have a long term vision and to work gradually towards it hoping that the opportunity might arise for a significant restructuring. Restructuring is most likely to occur where the same companies are the largest members in more than one association. However, there are few such industries where this is the case although perhaps this may change in the future.

The DTI initiative on trade associations may accelerate the process of rationalisation of trade associations. It is relevant here to quote the President of BEAMA in his forward to the Association's annual report for 1994/95 -

> "Let me turn to.......the need to improve the strength of British trade associations. I agree with the then President of the Board of Trade that the UK trade association field is too fragmented, and that this prevents us from getting the best value for money in representation. BEAMA is a large federation in British terms, but is a fraction of the size of FIEE in France and ZVEI in Germany. In the UK we do not have a cross-engineering association group such as the highly successful Fabrimetal in Belgium. I am therefore pleased to find that there is a view within both METCOM and BEAMA that we should explore zealously and critically the possibility of a merger. Our two bodies are complementary in their activities, and together would have a reach across the whole of the electrical, power engineering, instruments, mechanical and metal sectors. If a merger is constitutionally and financially feasible, I know that all our members, and Industry generally, would be served well by the power and breadth of services which would be delivered. Such a merger could pave the way for further development depending on the wishes of other associations."

The President went on to say that the chief executives of METCOM and BEAMA had been asked to have preliminary discussions and that each association had appointed a working group to consider the matter.

Even if an association feels that it is currently correctly structured in terms of not needing to merge or make -any other radical changes then internal restructuring may well be required. Invariably this involves a sharp reduction in the number of committees, greater power being delegated to a smaller executive committee and significantly greater authority being given to the full time secretariat. Again, while the objectives and ultimate vision may be clear, achieving these sorts of changes is very difficult. It is not as if one is changing a company where the chief executive can give instructions which have to be carried through. In the case of a trade association there will always be resistance to change on the part of some members who feel that their interests will no longer be as well represented or who simply resent the fact that they are no longer as involved in the trade association as they once were.

Longer term, each trade association in the United Kingdom will have to consider carefully its role in relation to European and international associations. Given the internationalisation of business generally and the Europeanisation and internationalisation of some decision taking then it is logically to expect international and European trade bodies to gain in power at the expense of national bodies. However, the intrinsic difficulties of running international associations is such that national associations are likely to remain dominant for some years to come.

SPECIAL PROBLEMS OF SMALL ASSOCIATIONS

This book has concentrated predominantly on the larger trade associations although most of the analysis applies equally to small associations. Most trade associations in the United Kingdom are small, if not very small. The study of trade associations by Manchester Metropolitan University showed that 70% of associations have an annual income of under £450,000 a year. Most of these associations have a small staff, often poorly paid, and with inadequate facilities. Often the success of small associations will depend heavily on the commitment of the officers, bringing with it the conflict between being involved in trade association activities and running a company effectively. It has unfortunately been the case that chairmen of trade associations have all too often been people whose businesses have not been successfull.

At first sight, the climate for small trade associations might not seem favourable. The reality, however, is that small trade associations are being formed all of the time, generally because a group of specialist companies are dissatisfied with the service that they get from the established association. Also, of course, new industries develop which in turn require new trade associations. To some extent one can see a cycle with new associations being formed, growing, perhaps merging, perhaps joining a federation and then fragmenting. There is no stable state.

Provided that small associations operate in a fairly tightly defined market and perform their functions well there is no reason why they should not continue to exist and to be effective. Top quality management is all important, and obtaining the right staff to run such associations is an increasingly difficult task.

Where there are overlapping associations within a particular sector then merging is likely to be the best option. This may happen at the instigation of some members perhaps if they belong to both associations or when one or other of the associations has management problems.

Many small associations found that the ideal solution is to become part of a larger federation which enables them to tap in to top quality trade association services will retaining a reasonable element of independence with members having a clear sense of belonging. The association can effectively represent its members on those matters which are specific to its members while leaving the parent association to deal with matters relevant to the whole of the sector. The small association can also ensure that its members' views are given due weight in the parent association.

A number of large trade associations provide a complete management service to associations which are part of their membership. A good example is the Food and Drink Federation, itself a federation of 11 members. It also services 32 members out of its head office. These are all specialist associations such as, for example, the Rice Association, the Seasoning and Spice Association and the Pet Food Manufacturers Association. Each of these associations has an executive secretary with individual members of the secretariat servicing more than one committee. The division also services two European associations. A second example is the Paper Federation which services nine independent trade association all connected with the paper industry from its head office in Swindon. Taking a more specific example, the Catering Utensils Association was established because its members were dissatisfied with the service they were receiving from the Catering Equipment Manufacturers Association. The secretariat originally comprised one person. When the secretary retired the secretariat function was sold to the British Hardware and Housewares Association. The Catering Utensils Association therefore retained its independence but operates within the framework of a larger association.

A final option is to contract out the management of trade associations to a specialist company. There are as yet only a handful of such companies in the United Kingdom but they may well grow in size and importance if they are seen to be effective. Some trade associations might themselves be willing to take on such a role, not only for associations that are within their industrial sector but more widely. Management companies can offer a range of services from total management of the association through to handling only administrative matters such as finance and membership records. Such companies could also provide one off consultancy services.

CONCLUSION

The trade association sector in the United Kingdom is vitally important yet it is one that is much misunderstood and frequently badly organised. This is amply illustrated by the problems that many associations have encountered over the last few years. There is also a marked absence of professional support with few of the large management consultancies offering a specialist trade association service. Also perhaps surprisingly there are only a handful of management companies for smaller associations. The one professional body for trade association staff is small and caters largely for smaller associations. There is little literature available on trade associations and few training programmes are organised for trade association staff.

However, there are now significant developments in the trade association sector. The need to become effective is generally accepted but how this is to be achieved is often not clear, and there is much re-inventing the wheel. The DTI interest in trade associations has stimulated much thought and debate. In the long term it may prove to be a powerful catalyst not only for change but for the sharing of experience and co-operation between associations and the development of more effective consultancy and management services which are needed to implement change.